The Science of Strategic Con

Billions have been spent on land conservation, but too little attention has been paid to how cost-effective these investments have been. With budgets increasingly constrained, conservationists must learn new strategies and tools to fully harness their funds to protect critical resources. Messer and Allen are pioneers in making conservation priorities more strategic, cost-effective, scientific, and transparent. This book introduces powerful tools available for project selection, using real-life examples and a practical, step-by-step approach. Readers can readily apply these tools to their own work, accomplishing more with less by combining the benefits of structured decision-making and mathematical programming and understanding of market forces and human behavior. The authors highlight tools from conservation science, mathematics, land use planning, and behavioral economics, showing how they can be orchestrated to help protect key environmental resources. This is an invaluable volume for all students, professionals, and stakeholders associated with conservation programs.

KENT D. MESSER is the Unidel Howard Cosgrove Chair for the Environment at the University of Delaware, USA, and co-director of the USDA-funded national Center for Behavioral and Experimental Agri-Environmental Research (CBEAR). His work applies economics and behavioral science to solve problems at the nexus of environmental and agricultural challenges.

WILLIAM L. ALLEN III manages strategic conservation planning services, including green infrastructure plans, data-driven structured decision-making tools, and enterprise geospatial services, as part of The Conservation Fund. Allen previously served as Co-editor-in-Chief and Managing Editor of the *Journal of Conservation Planning* and was a cofounder of the Society for Conservation GIS.

The Science of Strategic Conservation

Protecting More with Less

KENT D. MESSER
University of Delaware

WILLIAM L. ALLEN III
The Conservation Fund

CAMBRIDGE
UNIVERSITY PRESS

CAMBRIDGE
UNIVERSITY PRESS

University Printing House, Cambridge CB2 8BS, United Kingdom

One Liberty Plaza, 20th Floor, New York, NY 10006, USA

477 Williamstown Road, Port Melbourne, VIC 3207, Australia

314–321, 3rd Floor, Plot 3, Splendor Forum, Jasola District Centre, New Delhi - 110025, India

79 Anson Road, #06–04/06, Singapore 079906

Cambridge University Press is part of the University of Cambridge.

It furthers the University's mission by disseminating knowledge in the pursuit of education, learning, and research at the highest international levels of excellence.

www.cambridge.org
Information on this title: www.cambridge.org/9781107191938
DOI: 10.1017/9781108123778

First published 2018

Printed in the United Kingdom by TJ International Ltd. Padstow Cornwall in March 2018.

A catalogue record for this publication is available from the British Library

ISBN 978-1-107-19193-8 Hardback
ISBN 978-1-316-64218-4 Paperback

Additional resources for this publication at www.cambridge.org/messerallen

Kent dedicates this book to his parents, Don and Bonnie; to his daughters, Madeline and Eleanor, and to his wife, Kate, with whom he joyously walks with through all of the seasons of their lives.

Will dedicates this book to his family, William IV, Jackson, and Tiffany, who endure his suboptimality in the pursuit of strategic conservation.

Contents

Online resource can be downloaded from
www.cambridge.org/messerallen

Foreword

Land. Here in the United States, we are blessed with an abundance of it. Forests, farms, ranches, wetlands, grasslands, deserts. Lakefront, riverfront, oceanfront. In the latter part of the nineteenth century, we began for the first time to think about the future of our magnificent legacy of land. So many acres of forest had been clear cut, so many acres of grassland plowed under. Cities rippling out into the surrounding countryside. For the first time, we could see the impact, feel the loss caused by the growth of our nation.

Fortunately, leaders stepped forward, especially Theodore Roosevelt, to identify and set aside for all time some of our most impressive natural assets. Roosevelt himself placed more than 230 million acres in public protection through establishing 150 national forests, 51 federal bird reserves, 4 national game preserves, 5 national parks, and 18 national monuments by enabling the 1906 American Antiquities Act. Our first national park, Yellowstone, was created in 1872, and since then, we have set aside hundreds of millions of acres into national and state parks, refuges, forests, and game lands and hundreds of thousands of acres into county and city parks and greenways.

Along with these protected acres, we now have an environmental movement that is strong and vibrant, with more than 10,000 organizations and more than 50,000 pieces of legislation and regulation on the federal, state, and local books. And yet, as our nation continues to grow, heading from 350 million people today to more than 600 million by the end of this century, open space is again under threat. Each year, we lose nearly 3 million acres of open space across the country to development. Cities are expanding – Atlanta is the fastest growing human settlement in history – and new energy development is sprawling across open space at an unprecedented rate.

If we are not careful, our children and grandchildren will not have the same access to open space that we have had. Nature will be like some foreign country that you get to visit only once in a while, rather than something that is nearby and accessible.

But protecting land in the future will be more complicated than it was in 1872 when Yellowstone National Park was created. Back then, you just drew lines on a map and passed legislation. Today, you need to integrate open space into housing, commercial development, energy and transportation infrastructure, and urban redevelopment. This is more complicated, and more expensive. The risk of doing things poorly, inefficiently, is high. The risk that you protect the wrong land, in the wrong way, so that neither conservation nor economic development is well served, can be paralyzing. The way we did things in the past now seems outdated, insufficient. There will never be enough money or political will to just buy up every acre. We need to be able to make decisions about species, recreation, water quality, climate change, and economic growth that we can be sure are the right decisions at the right time. What we need are new tools, new relationships, even a new language, that balance environmental and economic objectives, that include, rather than exclude, people from the end result.

This is a new way of thinking for the environmental movement. We have a half-century of success using the old ways, but going forward in the old ways will limit our ability to achieve conservation goals. In this book, Kent Messer and Will Allen, describe a new way of thinking. They explain how decision-making in the twenty-first century can balance environmental and economic objectives. They use real-life examples to show how we can identify and invest in the best possible solutions, how we can get more from each dollar we spend, and how we can engage communities in the critical decision-making process. They have analyzed the limitations of the conservation movement and come up with new ways of responding to conservation challenges, including the severe limitation on the amount of money available for conservation. They use the emerging field of behavioral science to show us how to protect more with less.

This book is a road map, a textbook, for how we should approach conservation in the future. I am proud of the authors for their ground-breaking work and pleased that we at The Conservation Fund now have the tools we need to conserve the very best of what remains of America's magnificent land legacy.

Larry Selzer
The Conservation Fund

Acknowledgments

One of the fundamental challenges that we faced in writing a book like this is how much do we discuss the conservation examples and research projects that we are most familiar with and how much do we discuss the important work that is being done by others that contributes to our understanding of the science of strategic conservation. We cannot say whether we were able to strike the right balance or not as we certainly worry that we over cited our own work and missed important contributions of others, but certainly this challenge was at the forefront of our minds during the writing process.

We want to acknowledge that the vast majority of the projects and research highlighted in this book were collaborations with some of the leading thinkers on these topics in the world. Undoubtedly, working with them influenced our thinking and we are deeply appreciative of the contributions of our colleagues. In addition to those already highlighted in the book, we acknowledge the following colleagues: Katie Allen, Ole Amundsen, Michael Arnold, Kendra Briechle, Andrew Birch, Caitlin Burke, Margarita Carey, Forest Clark, Frank Conkling, Jon Conrad, Joshua Duke, Steve Dundas, Jesse Elam, Rich Erdmann, Paul Ferraro, Whitney Flanagan, Jacob Fooks, Rick Hall, Leigh Ann Hammerbacher, Kris Hoellen, Peggy Horner, Zhivko Illeieff, Cindy Ivey, Tom Jacobs, Harry Kaiser, Peg Kohring, Hawkins Partners, Dan Hellerstein, Nate Higgins, Rob Johnston, Maik Kecinski, Dagny Leonard, Dick Ludington, Lori Lynch, Tom Magnuson, Gil Masters, Robin Murphy, Patrick Noonan, Len Ortolano, David Proper, Andrea Repinsky, Lesley Rigney, Mikki Sager, Bill Schulze, Michal Schwartz, Ann Simonelli, Justin Storck, Jordan Suter, Jazmin Varela, Christian Vossler, Steve Wallander, Shang Wu, Louise Yeung, and

Roberta Zwier. We are also deeply appreciative for all of the administrative and editing support provided by Natalie Karst and Maddi Valinski. Additionally, several University of Delaware students were involved in researching and testing the materials, especially Danny Bass, Sam Furio, Tara Israel, Melissa Langer, Kaitlynn Ritchie, and Emma Ruggiero. Ted Weber also reviewed the LSP exercises and provided much of the background research on green infrastructure and ecosystem services. Of course, this book would not have been possible without the financial support for the various projects and studies that are highlighted in this book. Financial support has come from the Center for Behavioral and Experimental Agri-Environmental Research (CBEAR), the National Science Foundation, USDA Economic Research Service, the US Fish and Wildlife Service, and the USDA National Institute for Food and Agriculture.

1   Strategic Conservation Matters

In July 2016, a Japanese company manufactured the last VCR, and there are probably a few holdouts who are grieving. Humans, for the most part, don't like change. Why, we wonder, does someone always have to go and muck up a perfectly familiar and predictable device, replacing it with some new form of technology that is going to cause confusion and may take a while to learn how to operate successfully? Eventually, we figure out how our newest smartphones work and realize we love their capabilities and have a hard time imagining living without them. But for many, it's an unnerving and grumpy process put off for as long as possible. Inertia in the face of new technologies is an ancient human trait. Imagine the early human who first realized that roasting food over a fire was a good thing. You can bet the rest of the group had their doubts.

Now consider the implications of our resistance to change and new technologies in the context of environmental conservation. Environmental problems such as water pollution or endangered species protection have been referred to as "wicked problems" (Kreuter et al., 2004; Redford, Adams, and Mace, 2013). They tend to be extremely complex, involving natural sciences, social sciences, and engineering, and the money needed to solve these problems is far from trivial. For instance, the annual budget for the Environmental Protection Agency (EPA) on water and air quality improvements has been around $4.9 billion (EPA, 2016). In European Union (EU) countries, the national expenditure for environmental protection in 2014 was around €297 billion, or US$324 billion (Eurostat, 2017). In the United States, the federal and state governments spent just more than $1.4 billion to protect endangered or threatened species under the Endangered Species Act in fiscal year 2014 (US Fish and Wildlife Services, 2014). Despite these apparently large expenditures, recent estimates suggest that the funds are still insufficient to meet important conservation objectives. For instance, McCarthy et al. (2012) estimate the need to spend up to $76.1 billion per year to protect endangered species around the world.

Since environmental issues broadly affect the public, the major source of funding has traditionally been public money collected from taxpayers, and the idea of raising and spending tax money is politically sensitive. In general, the more politically charged a problem is, the greater the anxiety associated with a new approach or technology possibly failing. Organizations such as the US Department of Agriculture (USDA) and National Park Service, which provide grants to environmental conservation organizations, face intense political and media scrutiny of decisions that are fraught with uncertainty even when using a known technology.

In fact, most of the government agencies and nongovernmental environmental organizations that allocate funds for conservation still rely on outdated and severely flawed methods of selecting projects. Research has shown that these approaches are as inferior and outdated as the VCR but are still used every day.

A key problem is that methods of selection commonly used in conservation efforts do not properly take the cost of the projects into account. Advances in applied mathematics and economics, such as linear programming, have led to the development of sophisticated systems that can analyze the costs and benefits of a suite of proposed projects and identify the set of selections that provides the total maximum conservation benefit for the lowest cost, and numerous studies have demonstrated that these algorithms could enable governmental and nonprofit agencies to provide the same or better outcomes as older methods while spending less money. Simply defined, strategic is a science-based planning process that evaluates multiple criteria to help identify the most important resources to conserve while accounting for the realities of budgets and other constraints. This is in contrast to relying solely on one criterion, such as environmental benefit, for selection.

Why have these conservation organizations so far failed to adopt these much-improved high-powered tools and technologies? They have good intentions, no doubt. They also follow emerging science in identifying new environmental threats and providing potential natural resource management solutions such as removing invasive plants. Certainly their leaders are not lazy and passionately care about the environment. As lifelong environmentalists who have worked closely with them, we know they are compassionate people who devote their personal and professional lives to addressing the wicked challenges facing the environment and work each day to accomplish great things. But they are not immune from inertia, risk-aversion, and political pressure.

These factors along with a lack of public pressure and limited budgets and staff resources all contribute to conservation organizations being "stuck" in the past when it comes to strategic conservation. There's no question that the mundane human tendency to avoid change plays a part. It is easier for individuals and organizations to continue to do what they already know how to do, even when it does not provide the best outcome and does not efficiently use taxpayer money. Skill sets also play a part. Most conservation professionals are not trained in economics or mathematics; they are trained as natural or physical scientists. In fact, many of them likely shunned economics courses because of a mistaken view that economics promotes business interests over environmental concerns, so they have not followed the development of economics and mathematical programming relative to conservation and have not imagined how these tools could enhance their work. Furthermore, computer programming and algorithms can seem complicated; it is easier to use a conservation selection mechanism you thoroughly understand and more difficult to explain a programming method to stakeholders who value a transparent, simple process.

The dirty little secret among those who fund such projects is that failing to adopt new scientifically proven techniques for allocating their funds is wasting literally billions of dollars and severely restricting what they are accomplishing with those funds. The question we address in this book is how to overcome those barriers. We highlight how conservation efforts have made mistakes and missed important opportunities, measure the magnitude of those errors, and provide, in essence, a quick start guide to superior technologies based on the science of strategic conservation.

A NUDGE (OR PERHAPS A SHOVE) IS NEEDED

We and other people who study conservation have long considered why conservation professionals have not actively sought cost-effective selection techniques to try and have called for greater collaboration between academics and conservationists (Prendergast et al., 1999; Armsworth et al., 2004; Allen et al., 2011; Messer and Allen, 2010; Banzhaf, 2010; Duke et al., 2013; Grand et al., 2017; Messer et al., 2016). Some writers had noted that, initially, there was a lack of awareness of the methods among conservationists (Ferraro and Pattanayak, 2006) and perhaps some misunderstandings about potential challenges associated with implementing them because they were perceived as too "prescriptive" (Prendergast et al., 1999). We and our colleagues have worked in the decades since to allay those concerns and demonstrate the value of adopting cost-effective selection methods.

A lack of public pressure plays a major role. Environmental crises such as contamination of the water supply with lead in Flint, Michigan, and increasing poaching of elephants in Africa attract media attention that stirs people living far from the affected area to demand action. People want to see these problems solved and understand that they won't be solved without spending money. However, many do not think much about where the money comes from (taxes they and others pay) or pay close attention to the processes by which their money is spent. So when a conservation program fails to meet its objectives, taxpayers rarely ask why the conservation organization failed to make the best possible use of their money. There is no public push for conservation agencies to upgrade their selection methods.

Many conservationists know that their current selection methods are inadequate and want to do better, but they report having little incentive or ability to make needed changes. Thus, public pressure – from the members of the public who care most about conservation – will be required to make effective conservation a higher priority.

While some in the conservation community may feel uncomfortable with our critique, we believe fundamentally that the best path forward includes honest assessments and critical analysis of the practices of the conservation community in the hopes of continually improving our efforts. Failure to openly discuss conservations challenges and failures will not improve conservation or get us closer to following the core principles of strategic conservation.

LEARN FROM BASEBALL HISTORY

As documented in the book *Moneyball: The Art of Winning an Unfair Game* and the subsequent movie starring Brad Pitt, the Oakland Athletics professional baseball team and general manager Billy Beane used new applied mathematics and statistical analytics (referred to as sabermetrics) and an evidence-based approach to assemble a winning team in the late 1990s and early 2000s, despite having a significantly smaller budget than other successful teams. They found that the collective wisdom of baseball insiders who relied on statistics such as runs batted in (RBIs), batting averages, and number of stolen bases to evaluate players did not produce winning teams. So instead, the Athletics' management used statistical analyses to identify factors that did affect a team's ability to win, such as players' on-base percentages and slugging percentages, and sought players who excelled in those areas and could be acquired at a lower cost. The approach was unconventional and was initially dismissed by baseball 'experts'. But after the Athletics repeatedly made the playoffs despite a payroll about one-third the size of the New York Yankees' $125 million payroll, the approach spread widely, first in baseball and eventually in numerous sports as teams hired sabermetric experts.

We believe a similar transformation is needed in conservation. Agencies and organizations that fund and initiate environmental projects can make better use of the public and private funds they administer and significantly improve their "batting averages" in terms of how well they protect and remediate the environment with their efforts by hiring people who specialize in strategic conservation tools and principles.

THE NEXT GENERATION OF ENVIRONMENTAL PROBLEMS

Current conservation efforts are often less about saving large, irreplaceable landscapes or even protecting charismatic endangered species. Instead, large sums are being spent to reduce carbon emissions, improve water quality through better nutrient management, conserve open space and farmland, and protect green infrastructure, such as forested headwaters, that provide drinking water and flood protection. In the vast majority of cases, the projects under consideration for funding are not unique; many of them, if not all of them, can deliver the desired benefit to some degree. Some projects provide a greater benefit than others, but the cost of acquiring them also varies. These types of projects are the next generation of conservation, and they are uniquely suited to strategic conservation approaches.

HOW TO USE THIS BOOK

This book seeks to both introduce readers to the principles of strategic conservation and educate the reader to the level where they could apply these techniques and decision support tools in their own work. In writing this book, we assumed that the reader has general knowledge of environmental and natural resources issues, but not specific skills in economics, geographic information systems (GIS), mathematics, or planning. The book is designed to be read in full by conservation practitioners and program administrators. Likewise, the book is designed to be a textbook for upper-level undergraduate or Master's level classes in environmental planning, conservation biology, or environmental economics. The book, especially the first four chapters are also well designed for lower-level undergraduate courses such as those in environmental studies, environmental and resource economics, planning, and sustainable development. The last two chapters are hands-on activities that help put into practice the techniques of strategic conservation, as they provide a free introduction the readers to the online tools related to the optimization and the Logic Scoring of Preference methods. For the reader who wants to understand things at a deeper level, Appendix A describes the mathematical foundations of the Logic Scoring of Preference method, while the Jozo Dujmović book entitled *Soft Computing Evaluation Logic: The LSP Decision Method and Its Applications* (Dujmović, 2018) provides an in depth examination of its many complexities and applications. For readers who want to understand the underpinnings of optimization, we encourage people to read Kent's coauthored book, entitled *Mathematical Programming for Agricultural, Environmental and Resource Economics* (Kaiser and Messer, 2011) and an online Appendix B is provided with this book as it is a user manual of the Optimization Decision Support Tool. Finally, to learn more about the various case studies and conservation projects highlighted in this book we encourage readers to check out the references provided in the text.

OUR BACKGROUNDS IN STRATEGIC CONSERVATION

It may seem a bit odd and perhaps overly vain to include a description of our backgrounds as part of the first chapter. However, we felt that by telling our stories, as lifelong environmentalists who had dedicated our professional careers to solving these wicked problems, we could help provide some insights into the challenges that conservation efforts in general face. We can also explain where these principles and tools for strategic conservation have come from and what problems they were designed to address. If you find this background information to be a bit too much self-reflection, then we encourage you to jump to the serendipitous convergence section later in this chapter where we describe our initial collaborations in optimization.

We have worked on conservation issues within nongovernmental agencies, governmental agencies, and academia. We love spending time outside with our families and are passionate about environmental protection. However, we have to admit that we are also nerds. We grew up marveling at state-of-the-art computers such as the Commodore 64, and our summer camps included not only hiking and camping but also computer programming. While many of our geeky contemporaries took their love of computers and programming into creating the businesses of Silicon Valley, we sought to combine our passion for computers with our love for the outdoors. So while we saw millions of people stand in line for the next iPhone so they could more quickly play Candy Crush, we stood amazed as the science of strategic conservation continually evolved and the rush from the environmental community for these new tools and technologies was more like a whisper.

Background of Kent Messer

In 1992, Kent Messer attended the United Nations Earth Summit in Rio de Janeiro, Brazil, as a student reporter. That global summit was attended by leaders of more than 150 countries and by several thousand nongovernmental organizations (NGOs) and laid the groundwork for the Climate Change Convention, the Kyoto Protocol, and the Paris Accord. The issues negotiated were (and are) complex scientifically and politically. As a sophomore in college, Kent had previously experienced environmental conservation mostly as slogans on T-shirts and posters. It became clear to him at the Earth Summit that conservation work would require teams of experts in various disciplines, including science, behavior, sociology, and economics; no one person could bring all of the expertise needed even for relatively small-scale problems.

Kent was earning his bachelor's degree at Grinnell College in Iowa in the anthropology department, studying human behavior in general and the nexus of agricultural and environmental concerns in particular. To understand how farmers made decisions about moving to sustainable practices, he supplemented his anthropology courses with time spent riding tractors and combines during the fall harvest and sitting around dinner tables talking with farm families about the risks and financial challenges they faced. He also spent a summer in the Talamanca Mountains on the Caribbean side of Costa Rica, where poor farmers were actively clearing the rainforest to plant rice and beans in the hope of securing a better future for their families. Once again, the behaviors observed were more complex than he expected. Some farmers in Iowa, for example, were early adopters of no-till agriculture to prevent soil erosion and integrated pest management, while others stuck with traditional methods and at times over-applied fertilizers, thus polluting streams and aquifers. In Costa Rica, some poor farmers retained the rainforests on their property despite the financial sacrifice it meant for their livelihoods. These experiences convinced Kent that the only way he could have a positive influence on the environment was to understand the economic forces that drive both positive and negative behaviors by governments, organizations, and individuals.

Fresh out of college and armed with a better understanding of human behavior, Kent responded to a three-line newspaper advertisement for the job of executive director of Bluff Lake Nature Center, a newly established environmental education program in Denver, Colorado. The fledgling organization's four-person board of directors had secured nine months' salary and hoped to find someone crazy enough to take the job. At 23, Kent embraced the challenge and began developing environmental education programs for low-income residents of a handful of inner-city communities who had lived next to Bluff Lake for generations and never visited it because it was sequestered behind barbed wire fences as part of the old Stapleton International Airport's "crash zone."

Given its outdoor location, its young (and cheap) staff, and its reliance on volunteers, Bluff Lake Nature Center (like the Oakland Athletics) could deliver high-quality educational programs to schoolchildren for a low cost. Kent quickly learned, however, that governmental and philanthropic funders were not very concerned about cost-effectiveness. As he struggled to write grants to fund Bluff Lake's educational programs, he noticed that the funding agencies, such as Denver's renowned Scientific and Cultural Facilities District, which spends more than $50 million per year of taxpayer funds, seemed not to care that Bluff Lake's educational programs delivered a similar-quality educational experience at much lower cost to what was delivered at the large and fancy Denver Museum of Nature and Science down the street. Instead of receiving extra points by grant reviewers for Bluff Lake's cost-effectiveness, the museum's proposals, prepared by a large team of professional staff members committed to grant writing and fund-raising, were frequently funded at high levels, and Bluff Lake would get a trickle of the remaining funds.

Kent's story is not one of sour grapes over failed grant proposals. In fact, as executive director, he raised sufficient funds for his own salary and for salaries for two additional staff members and put the organization on a solid financial path; Bluff Lake Nature Center and its environmental education programs were still thriving at the time of writing, 25 years after its founding. Instead, it highlights the fact that reviews of grant proposals rarely consider the cost of the successful outcomes of the applicants. Thus, if the Denver Museum of Nature and Science submitted a well-polished grant proposal that delivered an exceptional educational program to 1,000 students for $45,000, that was considered superior to a solid grant proposal that delivered a very high-quality educational program to 1,000 students for $15,000. Sure, the educational programs at the Denver Museum of Nature and Science were likely better. But the differences weren't that great and certainly not worth three times more money per kid. Thus, if the goal was truly to educate kids about the environment, why weren't the funders more concerned about getting a good "bang for their buck" when it came to limited funding?

Kent also became aware that this problem was not limited to a handful of foundations focused on education; it was widespread. Another example was the Great Outdoors Colorado, which has spent approximately $1 billion of funds raised through the Colorado Lottery on environmental and recreational projects in Colorado since it was created in 1992. Again, another large environmental funding agency was dedicated to doing great things but not formally incorporating methods that ensured that these important projects were achieved in a cost-effective manner.

Thus, these experiences influenced Kent's thinking as he went to graduate school, first to receive a master's degree in resource policy and behavior in the School for Natural Resources and Environment at the University of Michigan and then to receive a PhD in resource economics in the Dyson School of Applied Economics and Management at Cornell University. At Cornell, Kent was fascinated by the idea that mathematics and economics could be used to help conservation become more cost-effective. Members of the Cornell faculty, such as Jon Conrad and Harry Kaiser, were developing the theoretical underpinnings for optimization approaches that could help land conservation managers get more "bang for their buck" from the limited funds available for conservation.

Kent's experience with conservation and fund-raising efforts at Bluff Lake in Colorado had given him an intuitive understanding that many funding decisions in the world of conservation were flawed and went against the effort to protect the environment rather than support it. Therefore, Kent wanted to learn these techniques and see whether they could be made into user-friendly software applications that would allow conservation professionals to quickly compare all possible combinations of potential conservation projects and make the best possible choice. In particular, he wanted to build tools that facilitated the expertise of conservation professionals and their tremendous understandings of the local landscape and ecology. Therefore, he considered it best if the tools would complement – instead of substitute – for the conservation group's traditional project evaluation criteria. With these tools, the conservation agency could select the set of projects that guaranteed the maximum possible conservation benefit given their limited budget.

Kent also wanted to develop these decision-support tools to integrate with GIS and be flexible to accommodate a variety of constraints, not just budget constraints. For example, the tools should be able to accommodate acreage goals or recognize that the staff capacity to acquire land in a given time period is limited. Thus, he was interested in developing tools that conservation organizations and agencies could use when they faced situations in which they had a much larger pool of potential projects than they could afford to acquire.

As a professor and eventually the Unidel Howard Cosgrove Chair for the Environment in the Department of Applied Economics and Statistics at the University of Delaware, Kent has subsequently published more than 70 related academic and popular articles on topics that include forest preservation, protection of water quality, agricultural land preservation, and the US military's efforts to meet its obligations under the Endangered Species Act while actively using its bases for training to ensure military readiness. His efforts to advance the use of sophisticated new technologies for selecting projects to fund or pursue have been extended in recent years to personally addressing his economist and conservation colleagues whenever the opportunity arises, including speaking at the *LTA National Land Conservation Conference* and at the National Conservation Training Center. Kent served as editor of the Agricultural and Resource Economics Review and associate editor for the American Journal of Agricultural Economics. He also has been an investigator of research proposals worth over $46 million from numerous sources including National Science Foundation, the Environmental Protection Agency, the National Oceanic and Atmospheric Association, and the US Department of Agriculture

In 2014, Kent was selected to be the codirector of the USDA-funded national Center for Behavioral and Experimental Agri-Environmental Research (CBEAR). As a recognized USDA Center for Excellence, CBEAR seeks to implement innovative ideas that can improve the effectiveness of the governments' conservation program and to carefully measure the true outcomes of those efforts.

Background of William L. Allen, III

Ironically, Will was the one who thought he wanted to become an economist when he was in high school and selected economics as his likely major when filling out college applications. He grew up in the Washington, DC, metropolitan area where there was constant talk of economics in the context of balancing the government's budget and stimulating economic growth while also feeding the military-industrial complex of the 1980s. It seemed like every family Will knew had at least one member working at the Pentagon or as a bureaucrat involved in federal policy or finance. Will found that politics seemed to get in the way of a logical, rational approach to spending within means and balancing budgets, and he was determined to help change that!

In high school, Will was enamored with the idea of economics as a means of imposing efficiency on government and formulating cost-effective policy solutions. But his notion of efficiency was largely abstract and general, associated only with monetary and fiscal policies. He loved nature and treasured his experiences with conserved landscapes such as the Arizona desert and the California coast but never thought about linking economics and nature in a tangible professional sense.

While at Stanford during his freshman year, Will started exploring the environmental movement. That fall, 1989, the Berlin Wall fell and suddenly policies and financial investments designed to counter the Eastern bloc could be redeployed for good of a different kind. Will started thinking about using economics for protection of the environment – save the planet and save some cash at the same time! This newfound interest in the environment led to coursework in environmental engineering, statistics, and a class on oceans in the geology department.

Between his sophomore and junior years, Will interned in Washington, DC, at Economists Incorporated, a consulting firm cofounded by Stanford faculty member Bruce M. Owen. It seemed like a perfect opportunity to merge his interests in economics and the environment. But, as is often the case with internships and early career experiences, he mostly learned what he didn't want to do. His exposure to economics was limited to antitrust issues in the US steel industry and deregulation of Puerto Rico's phone service (the Ma Bell break up came late to the island), which matched the expertise of the firm's principals but did not align with his interests. Now what?

At the time, there was no "environmental" major at Stanford. The Department of Economics had no apparent environmental focus. He was not interested in the biological angle – it seemed too detached from environmental policy (perhaps ironic given Paul Ehrlich's (1968) work on the population growth and links between economics and human development policy). Perhaps counterintuitively, Will chose urban studies as a major. It provided an opportunity to "specialize" in environmental planning and design (other specializations included architecture and community organizing), allowing him to assemble a curriculum that integrated environmental and land use planning into the policy realities of built environments. This was his introduction to city and regional planning as a profession.

During his junior year, Will enrolled in Stanford's Washington, DC, residency program where he took courses in economic regulation and federal environmental policy and had a full-time internship at the World Wildlife Fund working on an initiative called the National Commission on the Environment (1993). This was an incredible experience with opportunities to interact with three former Environmental Protection Agency (EPA) administrators, Alice Rivlin (who has been, among other things, director of the Office of Management and Budget and vice-chair of the Federal Reserve), and many others.

Will thought the National Commission on the Environment's recommendations were first rate; many were way ahead of their time in using "nudge" tactics, Pigouvian taxes, and other tools to support policies that could reduce "externalities" that plagued many well-intentioned environmental regulations at the time. Ultimately, though, adoption of these rational, cost-effective environmental policies came down to politics. Ironically, the election of Bill Clinton to the White House actually dampened prospects of adopting many of the policies outlined in the report. Many of the leading commission members had served under Republican administrations, so they were in a much better position to influence policy had George H. W. Bush been reelected. So for the most part, implementation of the recommendations mostly languished during the Clinton years.

Coming back to Stanford for his senior year, Will had to finish his urban studies degree and decide what to do next. The primary project in the required applied earth science class involved the development of a general plan for the City of Pacifica, California (on the coast near San Francisco International airport). Will learned all about land use planning – what to do and mostly what not to do when developing land in environmentally challenging areas. Pacifica was (and is) notorious for losing structures due to landslides and coastal bluffs eroding into the ocean. The professors, Irwin Remson and George Mader, took students on great field trips throughout northern California, showing creeping earthquake faults that were tearing up streets and sidewalks and stopping for lunch on the former foundation of a house that slid into the Pacific Ocean.

Noticing Will's interest in environmental planning and sustainable development, Professor Mader suggested that Will should apply to city and regional planning schools. After some research and ruling out management consulting and investment banking, which seemed to be the only on-campus jobs offered by recruiters in the early 1990s, Will applied to graduate programs at University of Virginia and University of North Carolina – Chapel Hill. His application essays? How can the planning profession best support sustainable development and environmental protection efficiently and cost-effectively using a mix of regulations and incentives?

Will ultimately chose UNC, and his faculty advisor, David Brower, recommended a class in GIS. Will had an affinity for maps – his father had worked at the National Geographic Society – but had always thought of maps as art and still had nightmares about coloring slope maps and using dot-matrix printers for suitability maps in his class on applied earth science at Stanford. As it turned out, taking the GIS class was a revelation for Will. Computer cartography allowed him to make maps using unlimited layers of information without hand-drawing anything! He had learned about suitability-analysis mapping, pioneered by Ian McHarg in his book *Design with Nature* (1969), but GIS was many steps beyond gray-scale transparency sheets. These emerging GIS and remote-sensing technologies were producing sophisticated map information that could be used to identify land that was the most sensitive environmentally and to identify areas where development would be most suitable or would at least have the smallest environmental impact. That class and an additional hands-on GIS class taught in the Department of City and Regional Planning became the foundation for Will's first employment during graduate school.

In 1993, Will had lunch with Patrick F. Noonan, founder and president of The Conservation Fund (the Fund) and former president of The Nature Conservancy. Pat had a degree in both city and regional planning and business administration. Pat founded the Fund in 1985 with a unique dual charter with the Internal Revenue Service to focus on both environmental protection and economic development. Pat described how the Fund worked with public agency partners to acquire and protect high-priority land for conservation while being cost-effective and efficient, thus saving millions of dollars because the land would be acquired at discounted prices. Will mentioned his GIS studies and interest in assisting agencies in identifying the most important parcels for conservation, allowing them to better achieve their missions. He felt that the planning profession needed to do a better job taking advantage of these new tools to cost-effectively protect important conservation lands. Pat said something to the effect of "Oh, so you are learning GIS? We need somebody to do GIS. Go meet with our office in Chapel Hill and see if they have a project for you to work on." An office in Chapel Hill!

Will went to work full-time for the Fund after graduation. He continued to work on GIS and planning services in eastern North

Carolina but also expanded his portfolio to other parts of the country, including supporting establishment of the Midewin National Tall-grass Prairie near Joliet, Illinois. He learned about a project under way in the Fund's south Florida office called the Loxahatchee River Green-way. At the invitation of Fund colleagues Beth Dowdle and former fellow UNC–Chapel Hill graduate student Matt Sexton, Will flew to Palm Beach County, Florida, to learn about this cutting-edge project involving both acquiring land for conservation and strategic conser-vation planning.

The John D. and Catherine T. MacArthur Foundation had sig-nificant land holdings in northern Palm Beach and southern Martin Counties within the Loxahatchee River watershed, which is part of the Everglades ecosystem and a source of drinking water and, at the time, was Florida's only Wild and Scenic River. Due to urban sprawl and agricultural development, increased fragmentation of the water-shed was likely without a strategic conservation plan for restoration and preservation of the Loxahatchee River. The key to the strategy was to identify the suitability of the MacArthur Foundation holdings for development and conservation. Particularly suitable conservation land that prevented habitat fragmentation and protected fresh water supplies could be sold to the South Florida Water Management Dis-trict, and land more suitable for development could be sold to generate revenue that would support the mission work of the foundation.

The Fund, with the support of the MacArthur Foundation, con-vened more than a dozen resource agencies and nonprofits involved in various resource management issues related to the Loxahatchee River. Through GIS-based modeling, the group identified important core natural areas that best supported watershed protection and areas best suited as greenway corridor connections for recreational trails and habitat connectivity (Diamond and Noonan, 1996). The planning process was completed in the mid-1990s and by 2004, most of the core areas and potential greenway linkages had been acquired and protected. The GIS methodology developed for the project served as a foundation for future collaborative work with nonprofit Thousand

Friends of Florida and the University of Florida's GeoPlan Center to create the Florida Ecological Greenways Network.

Will decided this was the model that the Fund should use for its strategic conservation planning services. The key obstacle to scaling this model across the country was an inability to share GIS data and tools with local stakeholder groups interested in planning and implementation of conservation solutions. Virtually all of the professional GIS analyses at the time were done on UNIX hardware, and the software available for personal computers had limited capabilities. Will saw two potential approaches to tackling the problem. The first involved development of a GIS for a strategic conservation planning course that was co-developed with University of Florida's GeoPlan Center. Starting in 1998, Will and Paul Zwick taught the class at the US Fish and Wildlife Service's National Conservation Training Center in Shepherdstown, West Virginia. The second strategy involved partnering with Frank Conkling, the MacArthur Foundation staffer who developed the GIS modeling for the Loxahatchee project.

Will collaborated with Conkling to develop customized GIS applications that provided decision-support capabilities for land-use planners and other resource managers. The Loxahatchee River work had been completed using Esri's ArcInfo software platform, and at the time, Esri provided a set of developer tools called MapObjects that allowed for development of free-standing, lightweight GIS applications that provided mapping functionality on personal computers without an ArcInfo license. The first pilot GIS application was developed for the Midewin National Tallgrass Prairie and was called the Midewin Prairie Explorer. A key feature of the tool was the ability to explore land use planning and conservation scenarios and to assemble packages of data and text that could be submitted to the USDA Forest Service as comments for their land and resource management plan process.

The next project it was used for was in the Catoctin Mountains in Maryland. Maryland's Department of Natural Resources (MD DNR) had identified the mountainous areas of Frederick County as a top conservation priority in western Maryland. Catoctin Mountain Park was a National Park Service property that was famous as the home of the presidential retreat known as Camp David. The Fund worked collaboratively with MD DNR and the Catoctin Land Trust to develop the Catoctin Mountain Explorer application. Both groups used the tool to identify potential conservation acquisition opportunities.

SERENDIPITOUS CONVERGENCE

At Cornell, a graduate student was in search of a dissertation topic. Kent was working on applying optimization methods to conservation projects as part of his doctoral dissertation in applied economics. His research sought to apply cost-effective conservation techniques to an ongoing land-acquisition initiative in the Catoctin Mountains in central Maryland. In 2001, Maryland established the "GreenPrint" program with a budget of $35 million. Administered by MD DNR, the program established a source of land conservation funding to protect the state's most important ecological land. In particular, the state sought to protect a network of large contiguous blocks of resource land, "hubs," linked by "corridors" that would form a "green infrastructure" network. Estimates were approximately three-quarters of the desired network lacked formal protection and was subject to development. MD DNR selected the Catoctin Mountain region as an area of special attention because of its ecological, historical, and political importance. The mountains are situated in central Maryland and are an extension of the Blue Ridge geological feature of the Appalachians. A significant portion was already protected by a variety of local, state, and federal agencies, and Kent's PhD study had focused on the northern section of the mountain range, which was primarily in Frederick County.

The results of Kent's study were profound. As shown in Messer (2006), Kent found that GreenPrint could achieve a significantly greater aggregate conservation value if it used the cost-effective conservation technique of Binary Linear Programming (BLP) (see

Chapter 8 for details) rather than its traditional benefit-targeting (BT) approach, which simply ranked the projects from highest to lowest in terms of conservation value and then purchased as many as possible until the budget was exhausted. For three budget scenarios – $1 million, $2.5 million, and $5 million – being considered by GreenPrint for this area, use of BLP would have achieved aggregate conservation values that were 4.9, 3.6, and 2.0 times greater, respectively, than would be achieved by BT (Table 1.1). Additionally, use of BLP achieved higher scores for each of the biophysical attributes the GreenPrint program had identified as important. For example, with a $2.5 million budget, BLP preserved 1.6 times as many acres of green infrastructure and the aggregate ecological score was 4.2 times higher.

Another way of measuring the benefits of the approach was to evaluate savings that cost-effective conservation could deliver. One way to calculate the savings was to determine how much money would be required for BT to achieve BLP's aggregate conservation value. For the three budgets used in the study, BT would have required an additional $3.1 million, $3.7 million, and $3.9 million respectively. With a $2.5 million budget, for example, BLP achieved an aggregate conservation value of 283.5; the cost for BT to obtain that value was $6.177 million (147 percent higher). In other words, BLP could have achieved the same level of conservation benefit as BT while spending $0.9 to $3.5 million less. Those are large numbers, and the research also showed that the greatest efficiencies were achieved in the low-budget scenarios. This was particularly important since conservation efforts frequently do not have enough financial resources to fund all of the valuable projects available.

Given these results in the first case study, Kent and Will immediately understood that the results were not unique to forest protection in Maryland. They could be readily replicated in a variety of settings, including watershed protection, endangered species conservation, and farmland preservation. In all of those instances, BLP techniques could secure substantial benefits that would otherwise be lost. Kent and Will soon collaborated with colleagues on additional projects that demonstrated the value of cost-effective conservation

Table 1.1 *Portfolios of funded projects generated for the GreenPrint program*

	Benefit Targeting		Binary Linear Programming			
	Value	Percentage of Total	Value	Percentage of Total	Times Greater	Percentage Increase
$1 million budget						
Number of parcels	7	3.8	45	24.2	6.4	542.9
Conservation value	34.7	5.0	171.5	24.7	**4.9**	394.2
Cost	$999,700	6.9	$998,970	6.9	1.0	−0.1
Acres protected	1,178	11.4	1,932	18.8	1.6	64.0
Ecological score	629	3.9	3,928	24.6	6.2	524.5
$2.5 million budget						
Parcels	17	9.1	74	39.8	4.4	335.3
Conservation value	79.8	11.5	283.5	40.8	**3.6**	255.3
Cost	$2,497,320	17.2	$2,498,170	17.2	1.0	0.0
Acres protected	2,112	20.5	3,333	32.4	**1.6**	57.8
Ecological score	1,524	9.5	6,469	40.4	**4.2**	324.5
$5 million budget						
Parcels	49	26.3	111	59.7	2.3	126.5
Conservation value	212.8	30.6	419	60.3	**2.0**	96.9
Cost	$4,999,000	34.4	$4,995,740	34.4	1.0	−0.1
Acres protected	3,754	34.7	5,070	49.3	1.4	41.9
Ecological score	4,440	27.8	9,615	60.1	2.2	116.6

in projects involving agricultural preservation and green infrastructure in Kent County, Delaware and Baltimore County, Maryland. This book was borne from the initial revelations of the Catoctin study and refined over more than a decade of working together to apply strategic conservation throughout the United States. The results of these studies and knowledge we have gained through these collaborations form the core of this book. We focus on identifying cost-effective project-selection methods that target specific lands, carefully incorporate both benefits and costs, and seek to maximize conservation outcomes that are important to the public.

2   A $100 Bottle of Wine and a Hammer: Core Principles of Strategic Conservation

In an unusual experiment (Messer and Borchers, 2015), Kent and his colleague Allison Borchers of the USDA Forest Service presented individuals attending conservation and environmental conferences with bottles of wine and asked them a simple question. Which did they prefer – one bottle of a French Bordeaux wine that costs $100 or four bottles of a French Bordeaux that each cost $25? The total cost was the same but quality of the wines was not (see Tables 2.1 and 2.2). The differences in the wines were demonstrated using Robert Parker's Wine Advocate ratings of 0 to 100 for each type of wine. The ratings showed that all of the wines were high in quality with the $25 bottles' ratings ranging from 83 (B, Good) to 88 (B+, Very Good) and the $100 bottle rating at 94 (A, Outstanding).

More than 200 conservation professionals from more than 75 organizations were asked this question. What did they choose? They overwhelmingly – approximately 70 percent – opted for four bottles of $25 wine. Not surprising perhaps. After all, the wines all scored at least a Good rating, and the opportunity to receive four times as much good wine seems like a great deal, especially since most of us likely consider a $25 bottle of wine expensive.

WHAT DOES WINE BUYING TEACH US ABOUT CONSERVATION?

Kent's experiment was designed to demonstrate the value of strategic conservation. Among those 200 or so individuals involved in conservation and environmental quality professionally, nearly three-quarters chose to acquire their wine resources strategically – they purchased multiple excellent-quality wines rather than a single

23

Table 2.1 *Wine choices*

Name of Wine	Year	Wine Advocate Rating
One bottle of Bordeaux costing $100		
Château Brane-Cantenac Margaux	2005	94 (A)
Four bottles of Boudreaux costing $25 each		
Château Ampélia	2005	88 (B+)
Château Côte de Baleau	2006	83 (B)
Château Les Trois Croix Fronsac	2006	87 (B+)
Château Villars Fronsac	2005	87 (B+)

outstanding-quality wine, extending the quantity of wine-drinking benefit of their overall purchase.

Ironically, when choosing to acquire or preserve natural resources for their organizations (either directly or by providing funding), no such strategy is applied. Most federal and state agencies use rank-based methods referred to as benefit targeting (BT) to evaluate and select conservation projects. Had they applied this approach to their wine choices, the clear winner would have been the $100 bottle of Château Brane-Cantenac, which had the highest score at 94 (Outstanding according to the Wine Advocate Rating System) and could be purchased with the available budget. BT measures the benefits of the

Table 2.2 *Wine Advocate Rating System*

Score	Grade	Description
98–100	A+	Extraordinary
94–97	A	Outstanding
90–93	A−	Excellent
86–89	B+	Very Good
80–85	B	Good
70–79	C	Below Average
50–69	D	Avoid

options available (wine to drink), ranks them from highest to lowest, and selects the top-ranked projects until the budget is exhausted. The system implicitly ignores the relative costs of the options available and thus provides no information about whether a project's benefits are "a good deal" for the price.

The question, for wine enthusiasts and conservationists, is whether the $100 bottle of wine was truly the best deal. In both cases, the benefits can be difficult to measure and compare. But if the goal is to do as much of something as possible, whether to drink good wine or to protect a forest, the rank-based, benefit-targeting choice has a limited effect; one exceptional resource is acquired but four very good resources are lost. Convert a bottle of wine to 80 acres of at-risk forest, and the rank-based approach saved 80 acres but lost 320.

The experiment shows why it is important for conservation organizations and funders to carefully consider how they choose projects on the much larger scale of millions of taxpayer dollars in an effort to conserve resources that will otherwise be destroyed. Because most conservation programs worldwide currently follow a BT approach, they wind up buying that $100 bottle of wine, which acts as a budget sponge, absorbing most of the funds, and in the process losing out on acquiring a much larger stock of very good wines – and forests. Consumers are generally very concerned about getting high quality at a relatively good price so they can make the most of their budgets. Strategic conservation is motivated by our belief that conservation organizations and funders should be more like consumers and actively seek out good deals – sets of projects that deliver the greatest value given the funds available. There is never enough money to do everything a conservation group wants to do. With strategic conservation, the groups can make the best possible use of the funds available and prudently spend public dollars to conserve and reclaim the environment. Sometimes, that $100 bottle of exceptionally fine wine will be the best choice; however, we want to come to that conclusion after a strategic analysis that considers multiple factors – quality, cost, and competitors. Strategic conservation can help identify those times as well. A bit later in this book, we will discuss the implications when these wines are threatened with extinction...by a hammer!

THE DANGERS OF A BUDGET SPONGE

In 2016, the US National Park Service marked its hundredth anniversary, celebrating a century of protecting some of the most beautiful landscapes and historical treasures in the nation. On its anniversary, the Park Service maintained more than 84 million acres with parks in all 50 states and several territories. Yellowstone, the Grand Canyon, and Yosemite are household names, and the parks literally range from A (Arcadia in Maine) to Z (Zion in Utah). The parks hosted more than 330 million visitors in 2016, which broke 2015's record by 23.7 million (7 percent).

In his PBS documentary on the US national park system, Ken Burns called it "America's Greatest Idea." The goal from its inception was to protect the environment for the enjoyment of the public instead of exploiting such areas for their abundant natural resources or allowing them to be privately owned and solely benefit the rich. In the past 100 years, the idea of public national parks has expanded dramatically both in the United States and throughout the world. In the United States, federal government agencies have expanded the system by establishing 129 national monuments and more than 700 national wilderness areas that collectively preserve approximately 107,000 million acres, and cities, counties, and states have protected millions of more acres of parkland. Internationally, the number of protected areas was estimated at 161,000 and the United Nations Educational, Scientific, and Cultural Organization's World Heritage Center had identified more than 1,000 environmentally or culturally important sites.

When the National Park Service protected "priceless" irreplaceable treasures such as the Rocky Mountains in Colorado, the Grand Canyon, and the Great Smoky Mountains, there was no competitive process in which multiple similar tracts of land vied for protection. And as one of the country's earliest conservation organizations, the

National Park Service poured the mold into which future selection processes would be crafted. The legacy of treating each conservation project as an irreplaceable and "priceless" opportunity is reflected in marketing materials by conservation organizations such as The Nature Conservancy, which used to describe part of its objectives as saving "Earth's Last Great Places." As a result, the cost of available projects was not incorporated into conservation selection despite conservation's evolution into a highly competitive setting with multiple projects or organizations seeking funding from a relatively limited budget. An omission that mattered little in the early days of the National Park Service now makes little sense since even the Park Service's conservation efforts are often addressing problems such as climate change and poor water quality – a ton of carbon emitted into the atmosphere does essentially the same damage regardless of whether it comes from South Dakota or India. Likewise, conservation funders typically must choose from numerous somewhat-similar tracts of wetlands or agricultural fields because they cannot fund all of the available properties. Consequently, the next generation of environmental protection must leave behind a century-old approach and adopt strategic conservation.

To understand the gravity of the situation, consider how the National Park Service made its conservation selections in 2012. The 34 projects on the national priority list collectively offered nearly 93,000 acres that cost approximately $110 million, far more than the $25 million budget available that year (Messer and Borchers, 2015). The Park Service ranked the projects from highest to lowest based on the quality of the benefits they would provide and selected the highest-ranking projects until the budget was exhausted. As a result, two projects in Florida were funded: 43,000 acres in Big Cypress National Preserve at a cost of $5.5 million and 477 acres in Everglades National Park at a cost of $25 million.

Had the National Park Service taken cost into account when ranking the projects, it could have instead allocated the $25 million to 28,607 acres of high-quality landscapes in other states instead of protecting less than 500 acres in the Everglades. The same amount of public taxpayer money would have protected 67 percent more acres and benefited a greater number of states (and taxpayers). That difference is the key advantage of applying the core principles of strategic conservation – the ability to balance costs and benefits and identify net benefits from the funds invested.

Now, a skeptic may wonder whether those 477 acres of Everglades were truly outstanding and perhaps represented a once-in-a-lifetime type of opportunity that exceeded the value of the other 28,607 acres in other locations throughout the country. This is a question we cannot answer definitively, as the National Park Service did not provide that type of comparison in its publicly available data. However, the pattern of buying the best regardless of price is observed in many conservation efforts and there is little evidence to suggest that it didn't happen in this case. However, even if this was an exceptional political case, it still would be worthwhile for the National Park Service to be clear about how and why it made this potentially costly choice.

THE MAGNITUDE OF COST-INEFFECTIVENESS

Since the National Park Service was established more than 100 years ago, tremendous resources have been invested in protecting and maintaining parks, wilderness, endangered species, farm land, open space, and a variety of other lands that provide ecosystem services. Much of the money has come from public (taxpayer) sources. For example, in the United States, USDA allocated $29.3 billion for various environmental programs between 2014 and 2018. Approximately $9 billion went to USDA's Conservation Reserve Program (CRP), which pays owners to retire agricultural land temporarily. CRP enrolled 25 million acres in 2016 and was estimated paying landowners more than $1.8 billion (Congressional Budget Office, 2016). Between 1989 and 2004, federal, state, and local agencies in the United States spent more than $11 billion for the protection and recovery of endangered species (Langpap and Kerkvilet, 2010).

Since 1980, states, cities, and counties spent about $3.89 billion to permanently protect 2.58 million acres of agricultural land (American Farmland Trust, 2015) through the agricultural conservation easement program and many more acres in parks and environmental activities. Conservation groups spend about $3.2 billion annually (Lerner et al., 2007), and the more than 1,500 private land trusts in the United States have protected more than 37 million acres (Aldrich and Wyerman, 2006).

The EU planned to spend €35.4 billion on agri-environmental programs between 2007 and 2013 (European Union Directorate-General for Agriculture and Rural Development, 2009), and large-scale conservation programs in Australia have spent billions of dollars to preserve millions of acres (Gole et al., 2005; Stoneham et al., 2003). A number of environmental initiatives are ongoing in developing countries. For instance, the Sloping Land Conversion Program in China has spent an estimated $48 billion to preserve land and to establish forests on former wastelands and agricultural areas (Xu et al., 2010).

Many environmentalists seem to equate the problems experienced when designing conservation programs for governmental and large NGOs as relatively insignificant – "typos" that are inevitable, questioning whether these "small details" really make a big difference, and the unfortunate answer appears to be a resounding "yes." Study after study has shown that cost-ineffectiveness has real environmental costs. Consider a couple of examples.

- In a project related to the protection of endangered species, Ando and coauthors (1998) demonstrated that savings could have amounted to as much as 75 percent if costs had been systematically accounted for in process.
- Polasky and coauthors (2001) found that correctly accounting for land costs could have increased the cost-effectiveness of protecting terrestrial vertebrates in Oregon by 10 times.

- We looked at agricultural preservation in Delaware and showed that cost-effective selection could have preserved the same number of acres and achieved the same level of aggregate environmental benefit using $21 million less, a savings of nearly 20 percent (Messer and Allen, 2010).

THE PROBLEM OF CONSERVATION BUDGETS AND WHO PROVIDES THE MONEY

Environmental conservation and preservation efforts depend on funds being spent in a fiscally prudent manner, and it is well established in the conservation literature that conservation efforts by public and private organizations rarely meet the most basic standards for efficiency (Babcock et al., 1997; Ferraro, 2003; Ribaudo, 1986; Duke et al., 2014). BT, the most common selection method used in conservation programs, is not cost-effective. In fact, it is not even close. The BT approach generally considers a variety of projects for funding, ranks the available projects according to their environmental benefits from highest to lowest, and then selects the project with the highest rank, working down the list until the budget is exhausted. This approach is widely used by governmental organizations and large NGOs and has been applied to efforts to establish and expand national parks (Babcock et al., 1997; Wu et al., 2001), protect fish and wildlife (Wu, 2004; Wiest et al., 2014), preserve forests (Fooks and Messer, 2012), conserve agricultural land (Messer et al., 2016a), and prevent nonpoint pollution (Fooks and Messer, 2013).

In economic terms, a fundamental problem facing conservation is the fact that their budgets are too constrained. In a truly "economically efficient" process, all potential conservation projects for which the social benefit exceeds the social cost will be funded. In other words, there is a compelling need to protect the ecosystem services provided by land and conservation activities in locations where the benefits of conservation exceed the costs. However, this does not mean that every piece of land should be conserved; certainly some land should be allocated for provision of a variety of goods and services provided to humans, including food and fiber production, housing, industries, and infrastructure.

From a societal perspective, then, large conservation budgets are a good thing since they allow for funding of all of the projects needed to effectively provide benefits to society (Babcock et al., 1997; Arnold et al., 2013). In fact, if the budget is large enough, selecting projects is not a problem because no trade-offs are required as a sufficient amount of funds are available to protect all of the lands where social benefits exceed social costs. Thus, the first efficiency problem in conservation is that the budgets are too small. And combining small budgets with poor selection methods makes a bad problem worse. Optimization and cost-effective selection methods are most important when budgets are too small because they help the organization purchase the best bang for its limited bucks.

By definition, any selection process that is not cost-effective ultimately sacrifices some of the achievable benefits that could otherwise be obtained for society. Conservation projects are primarily funded by three groups: governmental agencies funded by taxes, NGOs such as land trusts funded by governmental programs and private donations, and individual actions and donations. As discussed previously, by far the largest actor in terms of dollars spend is governmental agencies – local, state, and federal entities that spend tax dollars to achieve conservation objectives directly or by funding NGOs. The programs funded vary in scale from small local projects to national and international programs with large budgets that request applications for funding for projects by NGOs, which vary from local land trusts to large international organizations such as World Wildlife Fund. These programs require the most strategic planning since they use public money to achieve public objectives. If the selection processes of these large government-sponsored programs can be improved, then, like a line of dominos, the positive benefits will flow down the line of conservation organizations and their activities.

NGOs sometimes obtain funding from government sources such as the US Land and Water Conservation Fund, USDA Forest

Legacy Program, and the US Department of Defense's Readiness and Environmental Protection Integration (REPI). They also obtain funds (and property) from private foundations and individuals. Projects selected for funding by NGOs depend on the environmental benefits they provide and on the organizations' historical goals, political connections, and other considerations. While we believe that it is wise for all environmental conservation groups to follow the methods of strategic conservation proposed here, we recognize that private foundations and individuals have unique motives and preferences and should not necessarily be held to the same standards of accountability as government agencies in terms of maximizing the public benefit of funds invested.

Land trusts and other similar NGOs primarily address local problems and typically select from a relatively small number of projects. Those organizations frequently take advantage of their knowledge of the region and work with local contacts to identify high-quality projects with willing sellers. Such groups often buy (and at times serve as long-term caretakers for) properties that are identified for a particular project or goal (ad hoc) and acquire properties through private donations. Consequently, their responsibility, ultimately, is to track the cost of the long-term care of those lands. Their challenge is to know whether new acquisitions that arise from an ad hoc process are truly cost-effective and whether the acquisitions fit into a broader strategic vision for protecting the environment in that area.

Large environmental NGOs with national and international scopes, such as The Nature Conservancy, the Trust for Public Land, Conservation International, and World Wildlife Fund, can at times develop large enough pools of money to consider a large number of varied conservation projects. However, their local chapters and offices operate more like local land trusts, pursuing more-limited sets of projects in an ad hoc process and at times funneling those projects to the national organization for funding. These large NGOs would certainly benefit from adopting more-strategic approaches to funding conservation projects, but with a base of private donors, they also must consider a variety of political and other considerations when spending their funds.

THE CORE PRINCIPLES OF STRATEGIC CONSERVATION

Traditionally, conservation officials have prioritized projects offered using maps and other rating systems in an effort to identify the projects or parcels of land that would provide the greatest ecological value or public value in terms of resources and acquired those projects until their funds were exhausted. From an economics perspective, however, strategic conservation is important because, even in a capitalist free-market economy, markets are well known to "fail" especially in the context of the environment. In a conservation context, traditional markets underprovide public goods such as environmental preservation and ecosystem services. Both government agencies and NGOs such as The Conservation Fund (Will's organization), The Nature Conservancy, World Wildlife Fund, Conservation International, and thousands of land trusts worldwide work locally and regionally, and few follow the core principles of strategic conservation and thus fail to be as effective as they could (or should) be.

Strategic conservation is a science-based planning process that evaluates multiple criteria to help identify the most important resources to conserve while accounting for the realities of budgets and other constraints. It can be applied to any environmental concern, including habitat protection for endangered species, erosion control, and preservation of farm land, forests, and open space at risk of development. The specific criteria needed vary somewhat with the location and aims of the organization but generally will include the environmental benefits and the cost to acquire or fund the project. In recent years, a number of methods such as Binary Linear Programming and Goal Programming have been developed that provide algorithms capable of comparing all possible sets of projects to identify the best deal overall.

We have defined eight core principles of strategic conservation.

Core Principle 1: Set Aspirational Goals and Establish Measurable Objectives

The goals, naturally, are the desired end results or state – such as significantly improve water quality of a particular watershed in 10 years. Measurable objectives could include providing a monetary incentive to farmers to reduce their annual use of fertilizers and pesticides by 20 percent. Even better would be to install high-frequency environmental sensors in the watershed and directly measure the change in nitrogen and phosphorus levels in the river and look for reductions, since after all it is the quality of the water (output) that you want to measure, not just the inputs (such as the amount of fertilizers applied). Such metrics allow one not only to track progress toward the goal but also to quantify the benefits of the project. Cost-effective conservation tools can then compare those benefits to the cost required to obtain them.

Core Principle 2: Use the Best Available Science, Data, and Tools

Many recent advances in the disciplines that underpin strategic conservation – including environmental planning, environmental and resource economics, land suitability analyses, GIS, decision theory, multicriteria decision analyses, behavioral economics, structured decision-making, landscape ecology, conservation biology, geospatial analysis, and operations research – have enhanced the ability to make decisions, and "big data" and massive computer processing capabilities have made a wide variety of new information sources available for solving strategic conservation problems. The most cost-effective conservation efforts will make use of those sophisticated new tools.

Core Principle 3: Consider Both the Benefits and the Costs

Every year, significant resources are devoted by conservation organizations to mapping and measuring ecological benefits offered by areas targeted for acquisition while the cost of those acquisitions is entirely ignored during the selection process. This occurs despite the fact that measuring the cost is relatively straightforward in most cases because the real estate markets are private. Organizations and agencies can search these markets for information about the cost of the land or an easement, the transaction, and legal fees. Likewise, costs associated with monitoring and stewardship can be readily discovered. By including these costs as a factor when strategically evaluating and comparing a pool of potential projects, conservation groups can significantly improve the efficiency of their funding use.

Core Principle 4: Recognize Opportunity Costs and Trade-offs

One should understand what might be given up when using a particular selection strategy. The wine example illustrates the trade-offs associated with pursuing a highest-rated option that costs significantly more than other options that deliver high quality at a lower price. Even conservation projects that offer unique and irreplaceable benefits still involve opportunity costs. Conservation organizations should carefully evaluate whether substitute projects are available that deliver more total environmental benefits at a much lower cost.

Core Principle 5: Acknowledge Limited Resources

As with any endeavor, the available time, money, and human capital are limited. While an economist would define an "economically efficient solution" as one that invests in all of the conservation projects for which the social benefits exceed the social cost, the unfortunate reality is that limited budgets for conservation generally preclude that solution. Strategic conservation acknowledges and embraces those constraints, using them in the selection process to ensure the best possible conservation outcomes on the ground. Ultimately, with constraints come opportunities to protect what is truly valued on landscapes and in communities.

Core Principle 6: Embrace Complexity but Strive for Simplicity

Identifying strategic conservation priorities can involve complex modeling and interpretation of resources on the landscape and human needs and preferences for protection of those resources. Sometimes the benefits provided by these resources are difficult to measure, but we can establish easy-to-understand proxies for their value using scientifically valid methods that allow us to make "pretty good" estimates of the likely conservation benefits. The algorithms developed to measure these benefits can be applied to the comparison of dozens to hundreds of potential sets of choices and thus provides an opportunity to both embrace complexity and solve selection problems using decision support tools that rely on scientific information and processes and do the heavy lifting in terms of calculations. Science-based decision-support tools allow conservation professionals to make solid, well-informed decisions.

Core Principle 7: Take Advantage of the Idiosyncrasies of Human Decision-Making

Humans can be incredibly rational at times, carefully calculating various benefits, costs, and risks associated with a choice. At other times, they behave irrationally, making choices that are actually detrimental to their own good. Behavioral economists refer to this as "bounded rationality." At times, the idiosyncrasies (irrationality) of human decision-making can provide important information for conservation professionals because programs can be designed to better account for people's preferences. For instance, people will traditionally accept less money today rather than more money in the future. This phenomena, known as "hyperbolic discounting," can be important when designing conservation programs. For instance, programs may get greater voluntary involvement if they offer landowners a large lump sum of money today instead of small payments over time. In fact, it may be possible that the government can get even more conservation by offering an initial lump sum of money that is less than the total of the small payments over time. These types of opportunities should be pursued when available and ethically permissible.

Core Principle 8: Innovate and Select the Right Tool to Get the Best Bang for the Buck

The next generation of conservation efforts will likely require conservation organizations and agencies to be innovative and seek ways to stretch their available funds farther. They can ensure that benefits are being accurately calculated by taking advantage of tools such as land suitability analysis, structured decision-making, and the Logic Scoring of Preference (LSP) method. They can achieve cost-effective conservation by taking advantage of the best tools available – conservation markets, behavioral nudges, and selection techniques such as linear programming, goal programming, and hybrid optimization.

We believe that adoption of these core principles of strategic conservation can transform conservation efforts in the United States and throughout the world, thus better improving drinking water, protecting endangered species, securing magnificent landscapes, and adapting to a changing climate. In terms of practical implementation, the sheer computing power of mathematical programming will allow conservation organizations and agencies to compare tens to hundreds of potential combinations of projects using multiple criteria – their costs and benefits at a minimum but also additional criteria such as geographic or demographic distributions of funds and weighting of various factors – to identify the one optimal set that best meets all of the conservation goals and priorities given the amount of funding available.

3   From Great Ideas to Costly Habits

Today, BT is the most common selection method used by government agencies and large nonprofit organizations, and cost is either ignored or not included in a way that follows the core principles of strategic conservation. Numerous studies (e.g., Ando et al., 1998; Azzaino et al., 2002; Messer, 2006; Naidoo et al., 2006; Polasky et al., 2001; Wilson et al., 2006; Wu et al., 2001; Duke et al., 2013; Babcock et al., 1996) have found that conservation efforts in a variety of contexts would have achieved significantly better results if they had used strategic conservation approaches instead of BT, and we are aware of no study that has demonstrated that focusing solely on the benefits of a project and ignoring its cost is the most effective way to maximize the overall conservation benefit of a program. In fact, Newburn et al. (2005) pointed out that only 13 percent of the papers published in *Conservation Biology, Biological Conservation*, and *Landscape and Urban Planning* between 1999 and 2003 referred at all to the economic cost of conserving habitat as a component of selection.

The failure of conservation and environmental organizations to adopt strategic conservation methods is ironic given the large body of scientific evidence that they are superior to methods that ignore costs. Environmental work is, by nature, a scientific endeavor, and these organizations routinely look to the most recent scientific studies for guidance when conserving species, managing agricultural land, or remediating pollution. Furthermore, they often promote their work as adhering to the best science available. But when they step away from measuring the physical characteristics of the environment and internally decide how to allocate financial resources, scientific evidence does not play a role even though their decisions now involve choosing a few high-quality projects from a large number of projects that are close substitutes in terms of environmental benefit but vary substantially in cost. Whether acquiring land for conservation or buying some fine Bordeaux wine, they often get much less than they could. Numerous studies have shown that even minimal conditions for efficiency are rarely met (Ribaudo, 1986; Ferraro, 2003; Messer and Allen, 2010), and Babcock et al. (1997) pointed out two decades ago that conservation organizations could achieve significant efficiency gains through a greater provision of benefits, reduced costs, or both by incorporating benefit/cost efficiencies in their selection methods.

Environmental economists also have long advocated for the monetization of benefits (put in terms of willingness to pay estimates), especially since the cost of the land is ultimately measured in dollars (Duke et al., 2013). One reason these benefits should be measured in dollar terms is that traditional conservation benefit measures such as the Environmental Benefits Index used by CRP often do not do a good job capturing the value of the ecosystem services provided as measured by the people paying for the programs (the public) (Smith, 2006).

HOW CONSERVATION PROGRAMS ARRIVED AT THIS STRATEGY

How did conservation arrive at this sorry state of affairs? As we discuss in greater detail later in this book, an important principle of strategic conservation is development of scientifically sound benefit criteria that can be combined with accurate cost estimates to identify cost-effective conservation projects. One of the earliest advocates for measuring the benefits of parcels of land and incorporating those benefits as a criterion when evaluating public decision-making was Frederick Law Olmsted, a well-known landscape architect and leading figure in the national park movement. In 1853, Olmsted traveled through Texas on horseback for five months, and his travels influenced his professional practice of designing parks. In a subsequent talk before the Prospect Park Scientific Association, Olmsted recalled his trip and how each day he studied the landscape in search of the optimal camping spot (Olmsted, 1868; Szczygiel and Hewitt, 2000). He developed his observations into six benefit criteria that, he asserted, pioneers later should use to select areas for settlements:

1 Near good, clean water for drinking and bathing.
2 Near good pasture for their cattle.
3 Fire wood at a convenient distance.
4 Seclusion for greater safety from ruffians.
5 Like to have game near at hand.
6 We made it a point to secure as much beauty as possible from our tent door.

Olmsted further suggested that development of this type of benefit criteria would be helpful in evaluating lands proposed for public parks. Olmsted had a great impact on the park movement and the use of benefit criteria illustrates the appeal, focus, and application of a strategic selection procedure in the early years of park planning as a direct forerunner to BT approaches used today.

Federal and State Mandates for Measuring Benefits

Another factor in the rise of benefit criteria was the desire to develop a transparent selection process that could ensure the trust of stakeholders and the public and prevent corruption. Many state agencies and conservation organizations adopted benefit criteria to show that their land-acquisition decisions were based on objective merit rather than political motives. Interest in using benefit criteria to strengthen public support and confidence can be found in the land trust community's recent efforts to address greater public scrutiny of their use of conservation easements. Many trusts measure their compliance with public-benefit requirements for federal tax deductions by paying stronger attention to their use of benefit criteria in the decision-making process and the value that provides in terms of conservation (Amundsen, 2004). The land conservation community has been subjected in recent years to public investigations and stinging criticism asserting that the programs were used in the past to pass taxpayer money to wealthy landowners in the name of conservation for easements on parcels that actually provided little environmental benefit.

Some states have used benefit criteria to balance the regional or social equity of their distributions of funds to rural and urban areas in an effort to increase the credibility of state land-acquisition programs with public and state legislative bodies (Fooks and Messer, 2013). State (and federal) conservation managers need effective decision-support tools so they can separate worthy projects that provide numerous resource benefits from projects that provide little benefit. Furthermore, the significant federal funds provided to state agencies frequently come with benefit-criteria approaches attached. States increase their chances of competing successfully for those federal funds with utilizing similar benefit criteria.

In general, use of benefit criteria has largely fulfilled the mission of maintaining the public's trust, preventing open corruption, targeting high-quality parcels, and improving conservation managers' ability to evaluate projects and meet their federal mandates. However, more questions are being asked on the inefficiency of these benefit-criteria approaches, and there is keen interest in alternatives that can measure both costs and benefits to efficiently achieve conservation objectives using public funds.

Case Study: The Problems of Too Much Political Influence in Project Selection

A primary challenge facing conservation programs is the opportunity via politics for powerful individuals to profit in the name of the being good environmental stewards. An example of this occurred recently, in Kent's home state of Delaware.

Delaware has long been home to one of the most successful and cost-effective agricultural preservation programs in the United States. Since its inception in 1996, 20 percent of available farm land in Delaware's most populated county has been protected through the state's voluntary Delaware Agricultural Lands Preservation

Foundation (DALPF) (Cherry, 2016b). The process of selection traditionally involved deals in which farm owners voluntarily sold their development rights at a discounted rate in exchange for being allowed to continue to live and farm the land for a profit. Through this system of discounting and competitive bidding, the DALPF program was able to purchase development rights for an average of $2,159 per acre (Messer, 2014). Individuals administering in the program proudly boasted that Delaware had protected more agricultural land *per capita* than any other state (keep in mind, Delaware is the second smallest state in the country).

However, DALPF's history of cost-effective conservation came under direct attack several years ago when politicians sought to direct the program's public funds to pay to protect land owned by two politically powerful farmers, one who was the public service commissioner and the other who was the former president of the Farm Bureau in the county. Instead of seeking the traditional discount from them, the politicians tried to quietly arrange to purchase their development rights for approximately 233 acres at an appraised value of $6.3 million, which equated to an average cost of approximately $27,000 per acre, more than 10 times the traditional cost to conserve agricultural land in the state. (Cherry, 2016b)

At the center of the controversy was the County Executive, who had a history of questionable political actions, including being indicted on charges of racketeering, mail fraud, and wire fraud. During the investigation of the land deal, a string of 120 emails between the County Executive and the landowners showed actions that were against the conservation program's policies.

A number of farmers expressed concern, noting that if the deal went through, "the future of farm land preservation in New Castle County and the state [would be] at risk" (Cherry, 2016a). In particular, people were worried that this taxpayer-funded deal would reduce political support for the program. In September 2016, the effort to obtain development rights from these landowners was finally abandoned.

Obviously, many Delaware residents were relieved that a bad deal had been avoided, but the political damage to the once model program was significant. The DALPF program has received no state funding in the preceding five years because the public was no longer confident that its funds would be spent in a fair, effective, and efficient manner. Fortunately, this story has a positive ending. In 2017, the program was able to again obtain some limited funding and was able to make selections based on agricultural quality and a market-based selection system – not a forced selection through political pressure. The outcome? Three preserved farms and the cost was as low as just around $2000 per acre! (Wilson, 2017; Cherry, 2017)

Use of Benefit Measurements in Prioritizing Project Selection

Once the concept of benefit criteria had been developed, the next question was how to use that information to inform selection processes, and at that point, the conservation community made a catastrophic and costly error. What developed throughout the conservation community was BT, a selection process that focused almost entirely on the benefits of a project and largely ignored the project's cost. It seems that the hope, in those days, was that additional money could be raised or would become available in the future, allowing additional projects on the list to be accepted later.

Programs that aim to conserve farm land have a long history of using rank-based selection methods to evaluate applications by farmers to sell development rights. For instance, at the federal level, the USDA Natural Resources Conservation Service (NRCS) started proposing the use of a rank-based approach in 1981 with a criteria system for evaluating parcels for overall agricultural quality and site-based factors in Orange County, New York. Shortly thereafter, NRCS launched a 12-county, 6-state pilot study of what would become known as the Land Evaluation and Site Assessment (LESA) model (Pease and Coughlin, 1996). Based on the evaluation of both land attributes such as soil quality and other factors linked to the ability of the parcel to support farming (such as zoning or distance to a grain elevator or other market), NRCS aimed to obtain a more-comprehensive understanding of each parcel's relative worth, but it did not include the proposed cost of acquiring a projects' development rights in the rating system. Use of the LESA ranking system by state and county offices of NRCS subsequently influenced programs run by states and counties, which adopted LESA-type criteria as a strategy by which to stretch their budgets by submitting projects they were unable to fund to federal agencies without having to conduct a new analysis. In Maryland, Baltimore County's original agricultural preservation program used a LESA ranking system, and the optimization decision-support system we later developed for them used many of the criteria from the original LESA model.

You can see the roots of this tendency to ignore cost in Olmsted's original calculation of an area's potential as a good settlement. What mattered most, according to his criteria, was benefits: clean water for drinking and bathing, pasture for cattle, firewood, safety, and beauty. In his time, of course, there were no significant land costs to consider. The elements of economic cost for Olmsted were the distances required to reach the sites, and those costs were implicitly incorporated as a measure of the benefits, an approach we discuss in greater detail shortly. The conservation selection processes built on these foundations failed to recognize that public decision-makers had a duty to seek the best investments for taxpayer money, which requires careful evaluation relative costs and benefits.

Wine Problem Revisited (with a Hammer)

There is another significant player in how conservation funding approaches evolved. As previously mentioned, a key question in evaluating a resource has been whether it was considered irreplaceable. In a report to the US Army's Compatible Use Program (Allen and Messer, 2009), we used the following story to illustrate the challenges that arise when something viewed as irreplaceable faces imminent destruction.

> Imagine you are the curator of a museum in California built near the San Andreas fault. While you are working late at night by

yourself, an earthquake begins. Your museum contains many rare, valuable, and fragile pieces of art but does not have insurance against earthquake damage. As the earthquake begins, you must decide which museum pieces you will attempt to save given your limited time. Would your board of directors and public patrons prefer that you save the one exceptionally famous painting located on the fifth floor or the dozens of rare vases and historical treasures located in rooms on the first floor near the museum entrance?

If the rare vases and historic treasures on the first floor are reasonable substitutes for the famous painting upstairs, ignoring the relative costs and saving the painting lead to a highly inefficient outcome. However, if the painting is the Mona Lisa, saving it and nothing else could be the best choice in this difficult situation.

Conservation professionals routinely face the same difficult choice: which piece of habitat or farm land should we save, knowing that the others could be irreparably destroyed? In other words, should conservation efforts focus solely on the benefits of the projects (the quality of the art treasures) and ignore the costs of preserving them (time and effort needed rush the treasures out of the building)?

To answer that question, let's go back to the bottles of wine, and this time, we are bringing a hammer!

Recall that 70 percent of the conservation professionals who participated in the experiment chose four bottles of $25 Bordeaux wine over one $100 bottle. We wanted to see what would happen if the resources – our bottles of wine – were at imminent risk of being destroyed. So for some of the groups of conservation professionals, we added a twist to the setup. When displaying the bottles of wine and providing information about their ages, Wine Advocate ratings, and prices, Kent held up a hammer and informed them that any wines that were not selected would be smashed with the hammer. He

FIGURE 3.1 Broken bottle of wine.

assured them that his threat was serious and that the bottles would be destroyed immediately after the experiment – plus, they could come out and watch him destroy the bottles (Figure 3.1)!

As individuals involved in conservation of some pretty great places ourselves, we were not particularly surprised by the results: when faced with the threat that an exceptional wine could be destroyed, many more participants (47 percent compared to 30 percent in the other experiment) chose to preserve the $100 Bordeaux, a 58 percent increase! The experiment provided clear evidence that threat of destruction increased the chance that the one highly rated, expensive bottle of wine would be protected, leading to the destruction of multiple slightly lower quality wines (Messer and Borchers, 2015).

The results of this experiment poignantly illustrate how an emotional and/or moral sense of responsibility for a resource that could be destroyed affects people's decision-making, causing them to lose sight of the fact that a $100 bottle of wine is not truly unique or irreplaceable. Certainly, wine and environmental resources such as open space differ in many respects. But when potential destruction of a single bottle of nice wine can shift people's priorities, imagine how conservationists might respond to potentially giving up an expensive 477-acre swath of something like the Everglades for even 4,770 acres of valuable but less iconic marsh lands. Conservation efforts often involve situations in which a resource is threatened with imminent destruction so adoption of some of the core principles of strategic conservation is understandably met with some resistance. However, we should continue to focus on the overall picture of total protection and be less focused on a specific parcel of land, especially when spending taxpayer money.

WHY CONSERVATION ORGANIZATIONS REMAIN "STUCK" ON BENEFIT TARGETING (BT)

After emphasizing the value of strategic conservation approaches at conferences and meetings for more than a decade, we were disappointed with the results. Audience members, all involved in conservation and environmental work in some capacity, had nodded their heads in agreement during the presentations and complimented our work afterward but had rarely adopted strategic conservation. And the mathematics behind the tools discussed in this book have been available for nearly two decades. Why had they failed to catch on despite the enormous benefits they provide? This was a perplexing question and likely had a complicated answer.

Certainly part of the lack of change is associated with human and bureaucratic inertia. For people in general and organizations in particular, it is just easier to keep doing what they have always done. Lack of familiarity can also breed contempt, or at least suspicion. How could they unequivocally determine whether the new tools were easy to learn and could deliver better results? Would their constituents understand the tools and resulting selection processes? Would they face public criticism if they advocated for change?

Another impediment was the language that environmental economists use to write about their ideas. The mathematical models underlying strategic conservation are standard fare for economists, but fail to convey accessible information to most conservationists whose expertise is in the biological and physical sciences rather than in math or economics. Of course, it is important to mathematically test the models, but that work has already been done. Now, the challenge is to convey the models' proven success to the people whose programs and efforts will directly benefit from them.

Another barrier is challenges associated with putting a price on the environment. Some ecologists find it difficult or even reject the idea outright. Odling-Smee (2005), for example, noted beliefs that efforts to monetize the environment and nature violated "ethical and spiritual dimensions of conservation." Others have found that economic and mathematical approaches fail to capture fully the complex relationships between nature and human behavior (Arponen et al., 2010; Gowdy et al., 2010), a longstanding critique of many economic approaches, including measurements of ecosystem services and benefit–cost analyses.

Some realities of conservationists' own economies may be involved as well. Funds and staffing for many conservation groups and programs in the United States were cut after the economic crisis in 2008, leading to bare-bones staffs and budgets. Those agencies and programs have had to concentrate on survival and have not been able to develop or adopt new approaches and technologies.

IDENTIFYING THE KEY FACTORS BEHIND FAILURE TO ADOPT STRATEGIC CONSERVATION

Despite an already long list of contributors, we were not convinced that we had the whole story so we conducted additional research to better understand the views and preferences of conservation professionals. In one of the studies, which was conducted in the Mid-Atlantic United States (Messer et al., 2016a), we found that agricultural preservationists there overwhelmingly favored cost-effective selection processes. A second study to see if those results would be

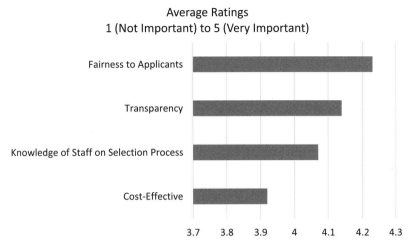

FIGURE 3.2 Conservation professionals' priorities in the selection process. From Messer et al. (2016a).

replicated used an international sample of conservation professionals in agricultural preservation context and found that 91 percent of the respondents believed that cost-effective conservation was a good idea (Grand et al., 2017). But…none of the participants in either of the studies viewed cost-effectiveness as their primary goal. Instead, participants in the Mid-Atlantic US study rated the fairness and transparency of the process as most important and cost-effectiveness and ease of administration as relatively unimportant. Likewise, for the international conservationists, as shown in Figure 3.2, those respondents also rated fairness to applicants (an average score of 4.2 out of 5.0) and transparency (an average score of 4.1 and described in the survey as the ease of explaining the process to various interest groups) as the most important criteria. The cost-effectiveness of the process ranked lowest (average score of 3.9 out of 5.0).

In this research, when we explored the issue of fairness further, we found that one challenge to adoption of cost-effective techniques such as BLP was a perception that those approaches were not as fair as their current selection techniques. Simpler cost-effective techniques such as Benefit-Cost Targeting (also referred to as Cost-Effectiveness Analysis, discussed in greater detail in Chapter 8) were also viewed less favorably than their current selection processes. These responses indicated that concerns about perceived fairness were an important barrier. Though the vast majority of the participants in the surveys indicated that cost-effectiveness was a virtue in conservation programs, they did not consider it to be nearly as important as other program criteria and worried that only low-cost projects would be selected.

Participants in the surveys had similar views regarding the transparency of various selection methods. Their ratings indicated that, on average, they viewed BLP as 33 percent less transparent and Cost-Effectiveness Analysis as 16 percent less transparent than their current selection methods.

Clearly, both fairness and transparency were significant concerns. We also presented several questions designed to evaluate the degree of difficulty of challenges they faced when adopting cost-effective conservation. We were surprised to find that the biggest obstacle to adopting cost-effective conservation was the lack of an incentive since program administrators tended to view it as a low priority. Their lack of previous experience with the programming and selection tools was rated as the least challenging of the obstacles presented.

Fortunately, there was some encouraging news, as shown in Figure 3.3. The conservation professionals who responded to the surveys expressed greater willingness to adopt cost-effective techniques if they had easy access to the optimization software and to training. Among the agricultural preservationists, willingness to adopt jumped 10 percent when they were offered access to the software and another 16 percent when they were offered both the software and training. Thus, making the software and training readily available, combined with an increased sense of urgency within the programs, could potentially accelerate adoption of cost-effective conservation by those groups.

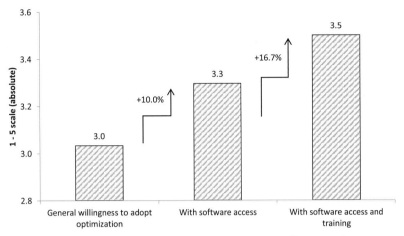

FIGURE 3.3 Increased willingness to adopt cost-effective techniques among conservation professionals. From Messer et al. (2016a).

SETTING A HIGHER STANDARD FOR CONSERVATION

If we are finally to realize our goal of making cost-effective strategic conservation a reality, we must develop practical tools and a culture and expectations within conservation organizations that prioritizes efficient use of funds and a willingness to try new approaches. To be honest, such a change is likely to be the most difficult obstacle to overcome and could require public pressure from taxpayers, the media, and policymakers to allocate those millions of public dollars as effectively as possible. We constantly encourage government agencies and nonprofit organizations to embrace a "test-learn-adapt" model that carefully evaluates the effects of changes to a program and that encourages *and rewards* individuals in an organization who are willing to try new things and learn from the successes and the failures of those efforts (Ferraro et al., 2017). As we discuss later, this type of evidence-based policy is critical when following the core principles of strategic conservation.

4 Avoiding Budget Sponges and Other Lessons from Conservation Failures

Environmental scientists spend considerable time and effort measuring changes to the environment and often find that human actions are the primary cause of environmental problems. Likewise, environmental economists study various elements of conservation, such as payment programs and markets in their efforts to clearly identify the source of a problem and propose potential solutions. We argue throughout this book that one thing humans are currently doing that hurts the environment is not carefully designing their conservation programs and we propose cost-effective conservation strategies as a solution to the many problems that have plagued conservation efforts so far. We next consider some of those problems in greater detail.

SELECTING BUDGET SPONGES BY IGNORING COSTS

As previously discussed, BT has some intuitive appeal to conservationists since it insures that projects with the greatest environmental benefits are funded. However, its Achilles Heel is that it ignores costs and thus it violates the third core principle of strategic conservation: *Consider both the benefits and the costs.* Therefore, BT frequently selects large "budget sponges" such as 477 acres of the Everglades that absorb a disproportionally high percentage of the funds available, requiring the program to reject more than 28,000 acres of other high-quality projects located throughout the country. As you will recall, the National Park Service in 2012 evaluated 34 projects for funding under a $25 million budget using a strictly rank-based BT process and ignoring project costs (Messer and Borchers, 2015). As a result, the Park Service funded two projects in Florida: 43,000 acres in Big Cypress National Preserve at a cost of $5.5 million and 477 acres in Everglades National Park at a cost of $25 million. Had cost been considered, the Park Service could have funded 28,607 acres of high-quality landscapes in other states instead of less than 500 acres in the Everglades. Strategic conservation approaches would have allowed Park Service officials to balance costs and benefits and provide a greater aggregate benefit from the funds available.

SQUANDERING FUNDS BECAUSE OF ASYMMETRIC INFORMATION AND ADVERSE SELECTION

We are likely all familiar with the uncomfortable feeling of being presented with a large bill by an auto mechanic or a dentist to fix something that has yet to become a problem. It is reasonable (and common) to wonder whether your car's transmission actually needs to be replaced or if the mechanic only sees an opportunity to make some extra money. If that tooth doesn't hurt yet, does it actually need an expensive crown? Economists have identified these types of instances as situations where there is "asymmetric information" – situations in which one side of the transactions knows much more about the situation than another. Few of us know much about car mechanics and therefore have a hard time evaluating whether or not one's transmission is going to have serious problems in the near future.

Conservation organizations face a similar problem. Landowners have private information about their preferences for conservation and generally know more about the cost of providing ecosystem services on their land.

Case Study: Lancaster Agriculture Preservation Program
In Pennsylvania, Lancaster County has been the largest receiver in farmland preservation dollars from the State from 2005 through 2014. For instance, in 2014, Lancaster County received $2,852,565, saving 744 farms, and totaling 64,313 acres (LancasterOnline, 2017). While this may seem like a universally positive result as Lancaster County and its farmland are certainly some of the most beautiful farmland in the state and in the nation, the question needs to be asked about whether these taxpayer funds (estimated at $133 million) were really needed to keep Lancaster County's beautiful farms.

As some readers may know, Lancaster County has the largest Amish settlement in the world. The Amish population, also known as the "Plain People," are known for their simple living and agricultural lifestyle. Thus, their personal and religious preferences make it more likely for them to keep the land as agricultural use even if there were no government programs paying them to preserve their farmland. When the conservation goal is to preserve as much farmland as possible, one needs to ask the question whether it might be wiser to spend limited taxpayer funds on the land that was under development threat that was owned by people who were relatively indifferent to keeping the land in agriculture. From an economics perspective, one worries that the State of Pennsylvania ended up "paying the Amish to be Amish" as ultimately these expenditures have an opportunity cost, that is the acres that could have been preserved in other places under development threat elsewhere in Pennsylvania.

Individuals managing government conservation efforts rarely know the true intentions of landowners, such as whether they want to develop their land. Many people have deep connections to the land they live on and value managing it to support a wide variety of wildlife and habitats. They are willing to privately finance conservation and do not need government support. However, when a program offers to pay them for those efforts, they are unlikely to say no. Consequently, asymmetric information leads to an incentive problem called "adverse selection" in which publicly funded programs pay people to do what they would have done anyway or pay them more than is required to obtain their participation.

Adverse selection is common in conservation programs. As pointed out by Kent and his colleagues Michael Arnold and Josh Duke, adverse selection is particularly problematic in situations in which the goal is simply to acquire the most land at the lowest cost – programs that use cost targeting or reverse auctions that do not account for the benefits and development risk of the project (Arnold et al., 2013). In those cases, the landowners who are most likely to enroll in the conservation program at a low price are those who were most likely to be inclined toward conservation in the first place.

Adverse selection is difficult to avoid unless an organization can find a way to identify landowners who are willing to make private contributions to the environment without the program (Arnold et al., 2013; Wu and Babcock, 1996), and the effects of adverse selection can be significant. For instance, Kirwan and coauthors (2005) evaluated CRP and estimated that 10–40 percent of the program's payments went to landowners at prices that were higher than the cost to the landowner of providing the services. Given the program's average annual expenditures of nearly $2 billion per year, upward of $0.8 billion per year was transferred from taxpayers to the landowners without any improvement in environmental outcomes.

Surprisingly, the remarkably large squandering of funds by CRP so far has not caused significant concern in the conservation community. Some may argue that conserving those areas helps ensure that the ecosystem services they provide are more likely to be preserved in perpetuity rather than only as long as the landowner is interested. Certainly, there is often the possibility that the properties would be developed in the future and lose their conservation value without the program. However, in that case, the degree of development threat should be accounted for when choosing how to spend limited conservation funds, and that would require additional information about the landowners' future intents (or about the intent of the landowners' heirs) – certainly a challenging undertaking, but not impossible. This is the challenge presented by "additionality" since the goal is for public money to go toward securing additional environmental benefits, not just paying for benefits already provided (or, in some cases, paying multiple times for the same benefits).

IGNORING THRESHOLDS AND SPATIAL DYNAMICS

In environmental contexts, there can be situations in which sufficiently large changes make returning an environment to a more natural state impossible or impossibly expensive. Examples of these types of thresholds in the natural world include lakes switching from a clear to algae-filled states, aquifers of fossilized water drained or irrevocably contaminated (Li et al., 2014), salinized soils from salt water intrusion in irrigation or storm surges, and the extinction of a species. These thresholds are serious complications that most conservation programs have generally ignored.

An emerging literature in environmental economics seeks to address the importance of these thresholds and spatial dynamics (e.g., Parkhurst et al., 2002; Parkhurst and Shogren, 2007; Banerjee et al., 2012, 2014; Fooks et al., 2016; Duke et al., 2015; Drechsler et al., 2010). While those studies demonstrate the important role of clustering conservation activities to achieve thresholds, most conservation programs (and, frankly, academic studies) ignore on-the-ground realities such as recognizing that the combined conservation benefit provided by two adjacent parcels is likely greater than the combined benefit provided by two identical parcels that are father apart.[1]

Strategic conservation acknowledges that, in many cases, there is a minimum level of conservation that needs to occur (Wu et al., 2000; Wu and Skelton-Groth, 2002; Wu, 2004) – a minimum amount of land or habitat needed to sustain an endangered species, retain a viable agricultural industry (Lynch, 2006), manage growth (Stoms et al., 2009), or preserve a scenic vista. Unless that threshold is achieved, the conservation effort is wasted. The optimal selection is often made more complex by possible spatial synergies. Suppose the

---

[1] The desire for continuous land protection may be appreciated at a profound level by humans. For example, Kent recalls the time he took his daughter to the Philadelphia Zoo. In part of the jaguar display, there was a small machine that allowed visitors to donate a dollar to protect jaguar habitat in Central America. The machine displayed a blurry map of the habitat that would be protected by the dollar donation (essentially a GIS map enlarged to the point where a $1 donation would be meaningful). Kent proposed purchasing one of the squares on the edge of the display, but his five-year-old daughter corrected him, suggesting that it would be wiser to conserve land for jaguars that was next to other protected areas (though those $1 protected lands would be unlikely to encompass the entire area needed by the jaguars). Needless to say, Kent adjusted his purchase to accommodate the agglomeration inclinations of his precocious and wise daughter.

selection is completed under the assumption of spatial independence while the actual process depends on synergies created by spatial interdependence, it is likely that the selections will suffer from systematic bias (Duke et al., 2015). In such a case, the cost-effectiveness of the selection results will be harmed.

Success Profile: Delaware Wild Lands and the Rationale for Noncontiguous Land Preservation

The previous discussion enumerated benefits associated with preserving contiguous land parcels. However, it is important to note that strategic conservation at times calls for preservation of parcels that are not contiguous. One such case is migratory birds, which do not need an uninterrupted corridor of protected land. Rather, they need a series of safe stop-overs during their migrations. Sometimes these protected areas only need to be protected for a certain time of the year (Jayachandra, 2017).

Additionally, there are times where protection of lands that are not contiguous can be advantageous when preserving areas from commercial development. For example, in the 1960s, Delaware Wild Lands successfully used *noncontiguous land preservation* to protect the shoreline of the Delaware River Basin from the development of a large oil refinery by Shell Oil. The leaders of Delaware Wild Lands recognized that the small nonprofit was unlikely to preserve the entire Delaware coastline but also recognized that a refinery required a relatively large amount of continuous land on the shoreline. They intentionally acquired a patchwork of small parcels that they then refused to sell to Shell Oil and successfully stopped development of the refinery. Their efforts subsequently led to passage of Delaware's Coastal Zone Act, which protected the Delaware coast line for more than 50 years. According to Delaware Wild Land's current executive director, Kate Hackett (Figure 4.1) "strategic conservation helped protect an internationally renowned migratory bird sanctuary. Delaware Wild Lands's efforts proved that being cost effective . . . and smart . . . can make an important environmental impact for generations."

FIGURE 4.1 Kate Hackett, Executive Director, Delaware Wild Lands. Photograph by Courtney Jacobs.

THE PBJ PROBLEM: NULLIFYING BENEFITS BY SPREADING FUNDS TOO FAR

A common problem with conservation programs is that they often get caught up in political processes that seek to spread out their allocations of funds to various jurisdictions rather than seeking to maximize the aggregate environmental outcome. For instance, CRP traditionally has stipulated that no more than 25 percent of a county's crop land can be part of the program (Sullivan et al., 2004). Think about making a sandwich with a teaspoon of peanut butter and a teaspoon of jelly. To cover the entire piece of bread, both will have to be spread thin – so thin that they do not contribute to the sandwich's flavor in any meaningful way. Conservation programs have the same problem. Spreading their resources over numerous regions or groups could potentially generate widespread political support for a program but simultaneously dilute the outcome of the program so much that

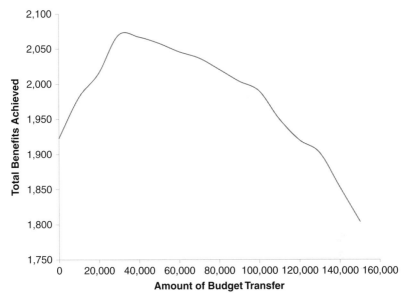

FIGURE 4.2 Total benefits achieved given the amount of budget transfer between counties.

the funds ultimately are wasted. Adding these types of jurisdictional constraints will, by definition, fail to improve the cost-effectiveness of a program by restricting the set of feasible solutions (Kaiser and Messer, 2011).

Consider Pennsylvania's Dirt and Gravel Roads Program, which seeks to reduce nonpoint-source water pollution by improving the quality of rural roads. It first allocates the available money to counties and then tries to identify the best projects within each county. As described in Fooks and Messer (2013), sometimes the allocations of funds are so thin that individual counties cannot fund even one project. As shown in Figure 4.2, just a small amount of flexibility in terms of budget transfer between counties to better target cost-effective projects could significantly improve the total benefit achieved. Requiring this transfer ultimately also becomes ineffective since a required transfer exceeding $40,000 begins to decrease the overall benefits achieved. Therefore, programs should be flexible enough to allow the targeting of best opportunities over political jurisdictions.

CONSERVATION SUPPLY AND DEMAND

Ecosystem services are rarely included in traditional markets for goods and services. You cannot buy them on Amazon or bid for them on eBay. Economists have long noted that a major failure of markets is the under-provision of public goods, such as ecosystems services (Gardner, 1977). As will be discussed later, economists often believe that the best thing to do is measure things, even things as complex as ecosystem services, in monetary terms (Duke et al., 2014). However, most conservation efforts have yet to incorporate the measurement of the public's willingness to pay for these ecosystem services as a measurement of conservation benefit. Instead, conservation programs have generally targeted goals such as air quality, biodiversity preservation, scenic vista quality, and habitat provision, and then develop measurements of benefits that can arise from a particular project (or set of projects). These various benefits can then be weighted by the priorities of the organization. For example, when considering conservation projects near the presidential retreat of Camp David in the Catoctin Mountains, the State of Maryland's Department of Natural Resources assigned the following weights for the available projects (Messer, 2006):

Acres of green infrastructure	2
Percentage of green infrastructure	1
Ecological score	3
Protected land within one mile	1
Percentage gain in protected area	1

These weights imply that for this program, the ecological score (which consisted of 16 criteria) was three times more important than having the land being within one mile of other protected land.

Likewise, the total number of acres was twice as important as the percentage of the land of the parcel that was within the designated green infrastructure hub and core areas.

One of the advantages of using weights is that they can be updated. For instance, the Wetland Reserve Program and CRP periodically update the weights used to target lands (Cattaneo et al., 2006). While weights make intuitive sense, they also are challenging to identify correctly, especially if one considers not only an individual's choice but also the preferences for others (Hajkowicz et al., 2009; Messer and Allen, 2010; Fooks et al., 2017).

Case Study: The Devil Was in the Details – the Failure of Transfer of Development Rights Programs

For environmentalists, the idea of real estate developers paying for conservation seems like a dream too good to pass up. So when the proponents of transfer of development rights (TDR) programs started talking with conservation professionals in the 1980s and 1990s and showing them some promising results from a couple of places, there was a rush for local governments to establish their own TDR programs in the hope of a "magical money tree" for conservation. However, a couple of decades later the evidence is clear – these magical trees bore little to no fruit. Why? Like most things related to conservation project selection, the devil was in the details.

The basic concept of a TDR program seems so inviting. You limit the number of units that developers can build in urban areas (the receiving area) and allow developers to purchase the right to have denser development in the receiving areas by having them pay for conservation efforts in more ecologically sensitive locations (the sending areas). In an ideal TDR program, the developers would buy these development rights directly from willing sellers; the only thing the government needed to do was establish the rules of the market and perhaps certify the trades.

Despite the minimal financial burden and the ecological benefits provided, TDR programs were never successful. In Kent's previous research (Messer, 2007), he identified the TDR programs that had been established in the United States. Yet less than 33 percent of these program had ever preserved more than 300 acres. In fact, when he looked deeper into the TDR programs that did report having preserved a substantial number of acres, he found that several were not TDR programs at all, they were really just programs that had the government purchasing the development rights. The funds for the conservation activity had not come from private developers; they were provided by the government to create a "bank" of TDR credits with the hope that developers would later come along and purchases these credits. However, in many cases these private buyers never emerged. Therefore, these programs were effectively a traditional Purchase of Development Rights program that relied upon government money and not a TDR.

One example of this is in Sarasota, Florida, where the TDR program reports having preserved 8,200 acres. However, inspection of this program shows that Sarasota County had actually purchased 99.5 percent of this total (Pruetz and Standridge, 2008). Similarly, in the Seattle area, King County, Washington, set up a TDR program and reportedly conserved more than 91,000 acres in the sending zones. However, the vast majority of these acres were purchased by the county, not private developers (Messer, 2007).

Why did these TDR programs fail? Simple economics. There was not enough demand to meet the potential supply. In other words, plenty of people in the sending areas were willing to sell their development rights – for the right price. The problem was that there was not enough demand in the sending areas to create situations where the price that developers would pay was higher than the price that suppliers were willing to receive. In most cases, the zoning regulations were not strict enough on developers, and thus developers found alternative ways of meeting their development objectives. These alternative ways, such as requesting zoning variances or developing in areas outside of the receiving area, ended up being cheaper and more profitable than buying the development rights through a TDR program (Messer, 2007). For instance, in Birmingham Township, Pennsylvania, developers ended up buying up the two core receiving areas and then used their political ties to get these areas rezoned to permit development. Not surprisingly, the TDR program in Birmingham was subsequently discontinued (Pruetz and Standridge, 2008).

BENEFITS THAT ARE POORLY DEFINED, MEASURED, OR SCALED

Conservation has suffered from numerous pitfalls related to how benefits were identified and/or measured. Olmsted's recommendations for selecting a campsite, for example, included both a benefit (a supply of firewood) and a cost of obtaining that benefit (firewood located at a convenient distance). Considering a reduction in the cost of obtaining a benefit (in Olmsted's case, the time cost of travel) as a "benefit" can lead to a variety of suboptimal choices (Hajkowicz et al., 2009; Duke et al., 2013). Therefore, for a selection process to be strategic, it must measure the benefits directly (for Olmstead, adequate firewood being available) and then account for the costs (travel time) as a constraint on the optimization problem, as will be described later in Chapter 5.

One also must be careful when evaluating projects and measuring their conservation benefits to not confuse scales. Both benefits and costs can be measured per project, parcel, or acre. As we showed in our 2010 article (Messer and Allen, 2010), the selection process will mistakenly target small parcel at the expensive of higher-quality, larger parcels (Table 4.1) unless the scales of the relevant conservation benefits and costs match. Table 4.1 illustrates the dangers of having some environmental benefits being measured on a per-parcel level. In this hypothetical example, consider four parcels with per-parcel benefit scores and an acquisition budget of $300,000. Parcels A, B, and C each have a relatively low parcel benefit score (40, 50, and 60 out of a possible 100) and are relatively small. In contrast, Parcel D is a 100 acres and has a benefit score of 100 out of a possible 100. If the goal of the acquisitions is to maximize conservation benefits, then without scaling the benefits by the size of the parcel, then you would end up selecting the three small, low-quality parcels at a total cost

Table 4.1 *Importance of scaling benefits by parcel size*

	Parcel Benefit Score	Acres	Scaled Benefit Score (Parcel Benefit Score × Acres)	Acquisition Cost
Parcel A	40	30	1,200	$120,000
Parcel B	50	25	1,250	$100,000
Parcel C	60	20	1,200	$80,000
Total (3 Parcels)	**150**	**75**	**3,650**	**$300,000**
Parcel D	100	100	10,000	$300,000
Total (1 Parcel)	**100**	**100**	**10,000**	**$300,000**

of $300,000, since the total benefit score from these parcels adds to 150 (which is higher than the 100 score from Parcel D). However, this result is clearly problematic from a real-world perspective. Scaling the benefit score by the size of each of the parcels (multiplying the parcel's benefit score by its number of acres) solves this problem. By doing this scaling, the solution of selecting Parcel D is clear as it has a higher total score of 10,000 instead of 3,650 from Parcels A, B, and C, and it still is affordable given the available budget.

INADEQUATELY MEASURING AND APPLYING COSTS

Measuring all of the costs of conservation, including the parcel acquisition, the transaction expenses, the ongoing costs of monitoring and enforcement of environmental protection and the cost of stewardship costs should be straightforward as generally these costs can be measured through existing markets.[2] However, Ando et al. (1998) noted that these costs generally were not appropriately included in targeting decisions.

---

[2] For a more complete list of costs associated with conservation, see Wilson et al. (2009) and Naidoo et al. (2006).

One challenge to strategic conservation is that few conservation efforts collect information on costs *before deciding* which projects to pursue even though they nearly always collect some information on the conservation benefit. Therefore, a tenet of strategic conservation is that the entire cost of a project (for acquisition and subsequent stewardship) should be measured *before selecting* projects to fund.

INTERDEPENDENT SYSTEMS ADDRESSED IN ISOLATION

The numerous conservation programs in the United States target different areas of concern and consequently have unique sets of objectives and rules. Some desire to preserve forests, others to protect water quality, and others to protect endangered species. Since each program works in isolation, it can ignore the fact that ecosystem services are often jointly produced. Protecting a forest is likely to benefit water quality, which can, in turn, better support species diversity. If the selection processes of those various programs could be integrated, aggregated environmental benefits could be better achieved.

As an example, consider the case of agricultural land preservation in Maryland. As detailed in Messer et al. (2016), officials in Baltimore County had two primary sources for funding agricultural land preservation: state funds and county funds. Each year, they received a pool of potential sellers and county officials made their funding decisions for both funding pools sequentially. However, if they made their decisions simultaneously for these pools of funding they could have protected 5.7 percent more conservation benefits and 4.4 percent more acres. In a three-year period, these increases in benefits would have cost the county approximately $1.2 to $1.7 million to achieve. Again, this was an opportunity to use strategic conservation to protect more with less.

INABILITY TO ACCOUNT FOR RISK OF DEVELOPMENT

Conservation efforts are frequently made in a context that includes uncertainty over the future. In some cases, private landowners choose to act to conserve their properties and protect them from development, providing environmental benefits to the public for "free" (Fooks et al., 2015). In other cases, the provision of ecosystems is seriously endangered by landowners' desire to profit from development. Thus, conservation organizations are interested in targeting the lands that are most vulnerable to development. Unfortunately, academic studies have not yet reached a consensus on how to most effectively do that. For instance, some research, such as Messer (2006), has sought to predict development threat through parcel characteristics, such as its soil quality and proximity to highways and urban areas. If these attributes can be successfully measured, they can then be used to weight the conservation benefits of potential lands. Similarly, Newburn et al. (2005) and Costello and Polasky (2004) developed selection processes that sought to account for development risks.

SMALL FLAWS CAN CAUSE BIG PROBLEMS

In this chapter, we have presented the nature of the critical problem facing the conservation community: (1) selection processes that squander natural and financial resources, severely limiting what can be accomplished with the substantial but also inadequate funds available and, thus, abusing the public's trust and (2) failing to adopt powerful new tools that offer the ability to select projects for funding and implementation by weighing each candidate project's relative benefits and costs and potentially consider additional factors as well. We have examined how the flawed system currently in place developed and identified barriers to replacing it. And throughout our discussion, we have emphasized the significant magnitude – millions to billions of wasted public dollars (translating into large losses for the environment) – and forgone opportunities that are the consequences of clinging to an outdated and ineffective approach for funding conservation.

Now, we turn our attention to the science and mechanics of establishing and practicing strategic conservation by adopting powerful mathematical programming tools and honing processes for identifying and quantifying costs, benefits, and outcomes.

5 Moving from Mission to Vision to Criteria

Imagine someone walking into your office and asking you to prepare a conservation plan for your community. Where would you start? We have thought about this issue quite a bit over the years since this happens to us all the time! And our initial reaction to such requests is to find out what exactly they want to conserve. "Conservation" can be applied to everything from historical structures and artifacts to hundreds or thousands of acres of land or to a way of life associated with farming or forestry. Through creation of the National Park Service, conservation initially was applied mostly to scenic landscapes such as Yosemite and Yellowstone. In the mid-1900s, the focus shifted to natural ecosystems such as wildlife habitats, watersheds, and forests. That focus on the environment has expanded in the last 30 years first to efforts to preserve farm and natural landscapes from development and then to global environmental issues associated with climate change. Increasingly, a significant motivation of many conservationists is ensuring that various communities around the world are resilient – that they can withstand natural disasters such as floods and extreme weather and adapt to the consequences of sea level rise and climate change.

So when a group decides to "make the community resilient to flooding" or "protect drinking water from pollution," what steps will that require? What resources are available to be preserved? Which groups should be involved? On the ground, what will the goals be? How much will it cost to achieve them? How will success be measured? These are core questions that strategic conservation is designed to answer. The process of establishing an optimal decision-support process for project selection is an exercise in clearly defining the overall goal and objectives and in gathering the data needed to make good decisions. In other words, to do good conservation work, you should go through the same analysis required to prepare an optimization model even if you do not use one. So why not also reap the efficiency benefits associated with using optimization? The core principles of strategic conservation allow us (and you) to hone in quickly on the community's most important goals and then to achieve them by identifying the best projects available under a constrained budget.

ESTABLISHING A VISION, GOALS, AND MEASURABLE OBJECTIVES

In the early stages of planning a conservation project, we rely on the first principle of strategic conservation: *Set aspirational goals and establish measurable objectives.* Over the past 30 years, leaders of businesses and nonprofit organizations have been asked to define the vision of their organizations – to identify the organization's primary mission. This same process can be applied to conservation projects. Articulating an aspirational vision, goals and measurable objectives helps the group to define exactly what it is trying to accomplish, who or what the beneficiaries will be, and benchmarks or metrics that will determine whether the project succeeds. An example of an aspirational vision is "Preserve rural communities and small farms in Georgia from urban sprawl." In this case, the beneficiaries are humans rather than ecosystems, plants, animals, or landscapes. Another example: "Reduce pollution in Chesapeake Bay to preserve commercial and recreational fishing." In this case, the vision addresses benefits for both the environment and humans.

Perhaps "vision" seems like little more than a buzzword. In fact, whether you are a member of a nonprofit organization, a Fortune 500 company, or a conservation project, the vision is the organizing principle and primary marketing tool. Articulating that vision is an important process that captures the project's overall goals in a single concise, compelling statement that should guide implementation and sway the various organizations and individuals you want to support it.

Once you know what you want to accomplish, the next step is to identify a set of basic goals and concrete objectives for accomplishing each goal. Goal-setting provides a clear, relevant basis for developing a strategic conservation plan and, later, for decision-making and evaluation (Kaiser et al., 1995). Project goals can also be aspirational. They typically are expressed as statements of intent that will drive identification of highly specific measurable objectives.

Our collaborative GIS-modeling project with the Upper Neuse Clean Water Initiative (described in greater detail later) illustrates the process of establishing goals and objectives. The overall conservation vision was to *"protect drinking water supplies through land protection"* (as one of many ways to protect the watershed's resources). The goals of the GIS project were identified by project stakeholders:

- Protect water sources and conveyances.
- Conserve upland areas.
- Promote water infiltration and retention.
- Avoid development of vulnerable areas.

Each of these goals had associated measurable objectives that had available GIS mapping resources that could help visualize where conservation actions could take place to achieve these goals, which falls in line with our second core principle of strategic conservation: *Use the best available science, data, and tools.* For the goal of protecting water conveyances, one objective was the land's proximity to streams, an area known often as the riparian zone. Another objective was to protect intact watersheds, where the level of fragmentation can be easily measured.

Why spend so much time on vision, goals, and objectives? Strategic conservation can establish an environmental legacy for future generations in the most efficient and cost-effective manner possible. Furthermore, it allows decision-makers to effectively address one of the most difficult problems they face – synthesizing and distilling large amounts of information – thus giving them the ability to find elegant solutions to complex problems and address the real needs of communities for productive livable spaces and for clean air, clean water, wildlife habitat, and climate resilience and adaptation.

USING THE CONCEPT OF GREEN INFRASTRUCTURE

A useful construct for conservation planning is the concept of green infrastructure. The term surfaced in the early 1990s as a way of thinking about the interdependent nature of natural resources and the value they provide to society equitable to "gray infrastructure" such as highways, power lines, and dams.[1] It officially entered the mainstream via President Bill Clinton's Council on Sustainable Development in 1999 and has since evolved into a recognized approach to planning.

Various definitions of green infrastructure have evolved along with the concept (Allen, 2012), but Benedict and McMahon's (2006, p. 1) definition best describes the process as we view it: "a strategically planned and managed *network* of natural lands, working landscapes, and other open spaces that conserves ecosystem values and functions and provides associated benefits to human populations." Tables 5.1 and 5.2 provide examples of the types of attributes, functions, and benefits associated with green infrastructure.

In our view, "strategically planned and managed" means that the planning process should identify the best locations for green infrastructure and then plan the associated gray infrastructure around the green infrastructure network. Gray infrastructure connects communities and improves the efficiency and effectiveness of the economy and have been viewed for centuries as basic building blocks of society that must be planned and maintained as investments in a community's future. As environmental conservationists, we view green infrastructure as providing equal value to communities and are

---

[1] Will was an early adopter of the idea of green infrastructure through incorporating it into the Albemarle-Pamlico Bioregional Greenway Plan in 1995.

Table 5.1 *Natural ecosystem values and functions of green infrastructure*

Attributes	Examples of Places	Examples of Functions
Ecological communities	Parks, preserves, and reserves	Protect and restore native plants and animals
Fish and wildlife resources	Wildlife refuges, game reserves, wildlife corridors, streams, lakes	Provide habitat for wildlife, support migration
Watersheds and water resources	Riparian lands, wetlands, groundwater recharge	Protect and restore water quality, aquatic habitat

Source: Adapted from M. A. Benedict and E. T. McMahon, *Green Infrastructure: Linking Landscapes and Communities* (Washington, DC: Island Press, 2006). Used with permission.

"must haves" that require the same amount of effort in planning and design.

As the concept of green infrastructure evolved into a structured planning process, it incorporated our second core principle of strategic conservation: *Use the best available science, data, and tools.* It comprehensively addresses all the elements of natural systems thanks to advances in numerous fields, including landscape ecology and environmental planning, and the work of many experts such as Frederick Law Olmsted, Warren Manning, and Eugene Odum. GIS layers and mapping, in particular, have allowed conservation planners to accurately identify the various types of resources provided in a region, identify their interactions and interdependencies, and translate that information into functional visual and spatial representations.

Viewing all natural resources as networks of different landscapes, ecosystems, and environmental functions means that resource and land planning professionals, elected and appointed officials, and interested members of the public can come together and ultimately

Table 5.2 *Associated benefits to human populations*

Attributes	Examples of Places	Examples of Functions Provided
Recreation and health resources	Parks, greenways, trails	Encourage exercise, connect with nature, disease vector prevention
Cultural resources	Historic/interpretive sites, outdoor classrooms	Preserve link to natural and cultural heritage
Growth pattern and community character	Greenbelts, scenic vistas, viewsheds, greenways	Guide patterns of growth, foster community
Water resources	Wetlands, floodplains	Protect water quality and quantity, manage stormwater
Working lands with economic values	Farms, orchards, ranches, managed forests	Protect working lands as a business, maintain rural character

Source: Adapted from M. A. Benedict and E. T. McMahon, *Green Infrastructure: Linking Landscapes and Communities* (Washington, DC: Island Press, 2006). Used with permission.

agree on a vision and set of conservation priorities for their community, region, or state to guide future investments. The power of this collaborative process lies in its scientific rigor and transparency for all the parties involved, providing for planning that unifies rather than divides.

Using the concept of green infrastructure to develop a conservation plan involves four basic steps – goal-setting, analysis, synthesis, and implementation (McDonald et al., 2005). Responsibility for the process typically falls to leadership forums or advisory committees. Those groups can take various forms per the project scope and budget, but they generally are composed of representatives of the stakeholders associated with the project. A diversity of perspectives,

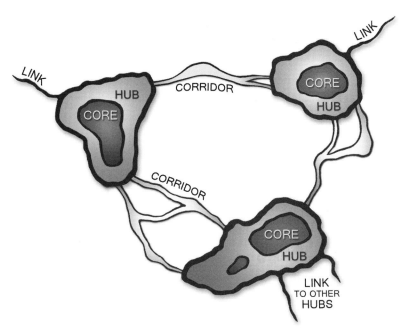

FIGURE 5.1 Green infrastructure network components.

backgrounds, and skills provides the strongest foundation for developing sound, effective goals and objectives.

The concept of the green infrastructure network is based on well-established principles of landscape ecology (Forman and Godron, 1986) and conservation biology (Ehrlich and Mooney, 1983). Figure 5.1 depicts the basic components of such networks, which operate at the ecosystem scale, providing essential wildlife habitat and linking broader natural functions and processes. In the network, corridors of natural areas link core areas that provide high-quality habitat for native plants and animals (Weber et al., 2006), and hubs represent cohesive regions encompassing one or more core areas with adjacent land in undeveloped land uses. Corridors are functionally connected, linear features that link cores and hubs together and allow animals, plants, and people to move from one hub or core to another.

Suitable wildlife corridors can be identified using a variety of scientific approaches (Lindenmayer and Nix, 1993), and several modeling tools have been developed as well (Corridor Design, 2013).

In recent years, we have focused on using functional connectivity approaches, which describe the degree to which landscapes facilitate or impede the movement of organisms and processes. The links between habitats and areas are identified using techniques pioneered by David Theobald and John Norman at Colorado State University and are incorporated into automated GIS models (Theobald et al., 2012).

The functional connectivity analysis examines the ability of a representative organism to move through the landscape. With those data, we generate "movement suitability surfaces" for forests, wetlands, and other types of landscapes that are based on existing pathways of natural vegetation and, in many cases, areas that need be restored when the landscape has been heavily modified by humans. Movement suitability is based in part on a layer that represents the resistance to movement as a "cost," which is calculated by identifying (1) impassable barriers such as interstate highways and open water, (2) the least favorable habitat areas (e.g., roads and developments), and (3) the most favorable habitat areas for each organism. The result is the pathway/corridor that connects two core areas with the fewest obstacles.

Cores and corridors are organized and mapped based on landscape types. The four types of landscapes commonly considered in conservation studies in the United States are (1) *woodlands and forests*; (2) *prairies, grasslands, and savannas*; (3) *wetlands and marsh lands*; and (4) *freshwater aquatic systems* such as rivers and lakes. Other types of landscapes can be used as well based on an area's specific geography and available data sets. These landscapes determine which resource attributes or features should be included in the conservation plan and connected through a green infrastructure network (Benedict and McMahon, 2006).

Interconnected networks of habitats are resilient and adaptable to climate change because they both support essential habitat and provide corridors for migration of plants, animals, and humans in response to changing conditions. They improve the ability of ecosystems to resist dramatic changes in habitats and to recover from extreme weather events and changes in temperature and precipitation that can increase incidences of flooding, wildfires, and pest outbreaks. They also allow species to shift their ranges and transition into new areas when their current environments no longer sustain them (Millar et al., 2007; Galatowitsch et al., 2009). Scientists studying the effect of climate change on the environment generally agree that these types of well-defined spatial networks will be essential to efforts to conserve functioning ecosystems. In formulating a conservation plan, the green infrastructure approach provides a spatial framework to help identify elements of the landscapes that are most valuable now and in the future as the climate changes (Lerner and Allen, 2012).

Success Profile: Ted Weber

Ted Weber is the strategic conservation planning science manager for The Conservation Fund (Figure 5.2). There, he collaborates with managers from other organizations to ensure that projects supported by the Fund use the best scientific approaches and data available and a strategic conservation approach. He relies on GIS mapping and the concept of green infrastructure since spatial relationships are a critical part of planning the Fund's projects. At the most basic level, they need to know where things are before they can protect them, and GIS techniques are much faster, more effective, and more accurate than the old approach of manually drawing lines on maps.

Ted feels green infrastructure planning avoids the pitfalls associated with reactive, opportunistic approaches that waste money and are not selected through more analytical methods. Green infrastructure planning can identify and address many issues, including establishing criteria by which to rate various sites and facilitating connectivity for species and ecosystems. It can identify sensitive areas to set aside during development planning, and it allows us to determine the allocation of conservation dollars that will have the greatest benefit. GIS is a valuable tool for conservation just as green infrastructure is a valuable set of strategies. Together, they are a very powerful combination when it comes to strategic land conservation.

Ted Weber sees the next frontier in strategic conservation as involving refining practical techniques to value ecosystem services, automated collection of GIS data using drones, faster processing software, and deployment of micro-camera and micro-sensor arrays to collect data on species, populations, and ecosystems at a fine scale over large areas.

FIGURE 5.2 Ted Weber.

GREEN INFRASTRUCTURE AS A FRAMEWORK

Having set out the fundamental concepts behind the concept of green infrastructure, we next provide examples of the various types of conservation efforts where green infrastructure has been used as a framework to design conservation projects and help choose investments. In this discussion we include short case studies to illustrate how these concepts can be implemented in a real world context.

Protecting Resource Networks

The Greater Baltimore Wilderness Coalition is a voluntary alliance of public agencies, NGOs, professional associations, and conservation organizations that envisions creating a protected green infrastructure network in populous central Maryland stretching from Chesapeake Bay to the Piedmont by investing in improvements on every scale, from individual sites to entire landscapes. The goal of this ambitious project, known as the Baltimore Wilderness Regional Green Infrastructure Vision, is to provide cost-effective protection on a regional scale for valuable transportation, energy, and water-treatment structures and shield homes and businesses from adverse impacts such as flooding with a priority placed on underserved and vulnerable populations. Simultaneously, the green infrastructure network developed to protect human needs will sustain natural ecosystems and support clean air and water.

In this process, the Greater Baltimore Wilderness Coalition is using GIS mapping, sensor data, and other spatial tools to identify the most important watershed areas to include in the green infrastructure network and strategies to implement given existing development plans and environmental regulations, policies, and programs. The criteria developed by the coalition for areas that should be protected include state-designated ecological significance, watershed conditions, natural resource features (such as wetlands, forests, and steep slopes), and community and equity considerations (such as population densities, demographics, and household incomes).

Restoring Ecosystems and Habitats

Restoration has historically been aimed at mostly relatively small sites rather than large regions. In some cases, these sites abut planned green infrastructure but were excluded from the original network because they did not meet the threshold for selection. Such sites sometimes host important microhabitats that can enhance the overall ecosystem and plant and animal species. In restoration efforts, GIS mapping is often used to document areas in which presettlement habitats have persisted. Former woodlands and grass lands, for example, may currently be used for other purposes, such as agriculture or

urban greenbelts, but retain soils that can support their original vegetation covers. Former wetlands may retain the hydric soil characteristics needed to restore them to their original function and potentially
reconnect isolated patches of wetlands into a network. And undeveloped areas near streams and rivers can be used to restore floodplains
to recreate functional aquatic systems and mitigate the impacts of
flooding for developed areas.

Our work with Chicago Wilderness is a good example of green
infrastructure planning used as a framework for efforts to restore natural resources by identifying sites to add to an existing network. The
products served as the overarching green infrastructure vision for the
region and provided a visual representation of the Chicago Wilderness
Biodiversity Recovery Plan (Conservation Fund, 2012).

We derived GIS data sets that represented the core areas and
corridors for the four primary types of landscapes mentioned earlier
(woodlands and forests; prairies, grasslands, and savannas; wetlands
and marsh lands; freshwater aquatic systems), potential restoration
sites not already part of the network, and composite layers that combined the scientifically mapped ecological network with inventories
of protected and managed lands. In the models, the functional connections were corridors linking the various types of landscapes to each
other. The data inputs included sites designated as state and local natural areas, known habitats for endangered species, areas designated by
the Audubon Society as important bird areas, and habitat patches that
met a minimum size threshold. The goal of the mapping project was
to identify sites that could contribute to restoring large blocks of habitat using undeveloped areas of grasslands and wetlands that could be
restored to their original functions.

GREEN INFRASTRUCTURE PLANNING AT WORK

As was the case back in 2005 when we wrote our first peer-
reviewed article on green infrastructure planning, best practices for
environmental conservation and restoration involve coordinated

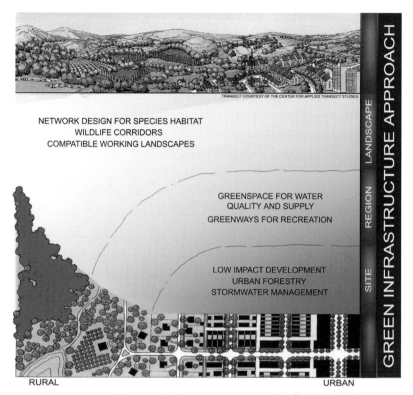

FIGURE 5.3 The green infrastructure approach at multiple scales.

planning and implementation across three spatial scales: landscape, region, and site (McDonald et al., 2005). Figure 5.3 (Allen, 2012; Firehock, 2015) illustrates the role of each scale in a green infrastructure network. On the broadest scale, landscapes, the green infrastructure network maintains ecological functions and processes that contribute to clean air and water, habitat for plants and animals, wildlife migration corridors, and compatible working landscapes. At the regional level, the infrastructure network supports human communities by providing specific ecosystem services and potentially also providing recreation areas and connections. At the site level, the green infrastructure enhances communities by employing environmentally sensitive design techniques, making use of urban forestry, and providing stormwater-management systems that reduce the environmental impact of human settlements.

There are numerous ways to develop multiscale strategic conservation projects that protect more with less using the green infrastructure approach. The following examples share a common thread: a vision of a solution to a complex problem and clearly articulated objectives that can be accomplished using the most effective scientific methods, data, and tools available.

Designing a Network of Species Habitat

When gray infrastructure such as roads, utility lines, energy facilities, and pipelines is developed in the United States, the agencies responsible for overseeing those projects assess their impacts on federally listed threatened and endangered species and require that those impacts be either avoided or minimized. If the impacts cannot be adequately avoided or minimized, the US Fish and Wildlife Service (FWS), which administers the Endangered Species Act, requires compensatory habitat to mitigate the unavoidable impacts. Maps of the existing green infrastructure network facilitate the process of identifying suitable areas to use as mitigation, which consists of preservation and/or restoration.

We contributed GIS mapping products for a large a multispecies habitat conservation plan (HCP) being drafted by the FWS and NiSource Inc. (now part of TransCanada), which operated a network of 15,500 linear miles of natural gas pipelines covering more than 6.4 million acres across 14 states. At the time, NiSource delivered nearly a trillion cubic feet of gas annually to nearly four million customers, and its pipeline network extended from the Gulf of Mexico to New York and from the Atlantic coast to the Great Lakes. We collaborated with NiSource, FWS, and the natural resource agencies in those 14 states to design a decision-support framework that was based on geographic ecosystems to identify the best mitigation sites for the endangered and threatened species affected by the pipeline.

Traditionally, FWS had addressed such impacts through a permitting process outlined in Section 7 of the Endangered Species Act in which permits typically were anchored to the impacts of an individual construction or maintenance project and required mitigation to occur on-site or in close proximity to the project. Unfortunately, this approach led generally to small-scale isolated mitigation projects that failed to provide the maximum possible benefit for the impacted species and for the project developer. In compliance with federal law, NiSource had conducted numerous biological consultations regarding federally listed species that could be affected by routine pipeline construction, operations, and maintenance each year. This permit-by-permit, year-by-year approach was costly and time-consuming for the company and FWS and failed to best protect the impacted species.

Compensatory mitigation projects can deliver the greatest "bang for the buck" when they take advantage of economies of scale associated with pooling the impacts of multiple projects together, and the planning process is most cost-effective when the mitigation sites are selected using a transparent, defensible decision-making process. Therefore, NiSource and FWS set out to develop a multispecies HCP that, once completed, would allow NiSource to forgo multiple individual permits and to operate instead under a single, consolidated 50-year permit covering numerous federally listed species. The plan would establish measures NiSource could take to avoid, minimize, and/or mitigate potential impacts, and NiSource would fund the mitigation projects needed to satisfy the compensatory mitigation requirements for the covered species for 50 years.

Success Profile: John Shafer
John Shafer (Figure 5.4) served as manager of sustainable natural resource practices for NiSource, Inc. (Columbia Gas Transmission and Columbia Gulf Pipeline) and developed sustainable environmental strategies for the company's energy business units. While at NiSource, he was project manager for the company's HCP, which

FIGURE 5.4 John Shafer.

led to NiSource receiving a 50-year permit. To date, it is the largest HCP ever filed, approved, and implemented in the United States.

The problem most energy companies and developers have is that they do not have the personnel or expertise to optimize their selection of mitigation proposals. They usually choose the first mitigation proposal available that is likely to be approved rather than identifying the best available mitigation parcel or proposal. Green infrastructure planning, done properly, eliminates disconnected mitigation parcels and programs and helps energy companies and developers get the "biggest bang for their buck." It not only allows them to do the best conservation for the money applied but also builds long-term sustainable relationships with permitting agencies and local communities.

Shafer has found that one solution to this problem is to partner with a business that locates available mitigation proposals, projects, or parcels to assist in the process of sifting through the proposals to determine the best one available. In the past two decades, energy companies have become more aware that it makes good business sense to acquire properties that satisfy required compensatory mitigation *and* provide some quality public relations and even enhanced relationships with the states in which the impacts occur.

Green infrastructure planning allowed NiSource and FWS to identify the most effective mitigation sites and determine which of those sites would also advance the communities' planning objectives. The subsequent decision-support framework consisted of four elements.

1 Identify the type and amount of mitigation needed through a transparent process that clearly defines the mitigation requirements and is based on the best available science and stakeholder reviews.
2 Design and map green infrastructure to provide a strategically planned, interconnected ecological network that delivers multiple ecosystem benefits based on the latest peer-reviewed scientific studies.
3 Establish selection criteria for the mitigation project that could be applied in a logically consistent manner and were consistent with regulatory requirements.
4 Evaluate the projects and select the ones that provide the greatest benefit at the lowest cost.

A key element of the first step, defining the mitigation needed, involved a series of focus group meetings by staff members and species experts from the state natural resource agencies, staff members from conservation nonprofits, and FWS personnel, which were convened at pivotal points in the project. The first set of focus group meetings introduced the state agency staff members to the concept of green infrastructure, obtained specific information on criteria and thresholds for designing the network, and solicited feedback on an initial set of potential mitigation opportunities. The second set of focus group meetings obtained feedback on selection criteria for mitigation projects and refined the list of potential mitigation opportunities for HCP species. We solicited feedback from the state agencies, NiSource, and FWS on the draft design protocol for the green infrastructure network.

When designing the ecological network, we chose selection criteria that would help evaluate the extent to which a potential mitigation project met the endangered species' habitat mitigation requirements in terms of the habitat's quality, location, and likely protection in perpetuity.

Preserving Compatible Working Landscapes

A growing part of conservation work worldwide is preservation of working landscapes on which functioning commercial farms and forests are managed for both production and provision of ecosystem services. These areas are economically productive but also provide significant value to green infrastructure networks by remaining undeveloped. Protection of working farms and forests follows the same principles of network design as protection of natural areas, but there is a greater focus on soil capabilities, particularly when considering farm land. Thanks to USDA's Natural Resources Conservation Service, many programs that protect farm land have established LESA (land evaluation site assessment) systems.

Green Spaces for Water Quality and Supply

One of the most effective ways to protect drinking water sources is to protect the land around them. Forests, wetlands, and open fields absorb rain and runoff, giving water time to filter gradually through the soil, trapping sediment and pollutants before they flow into streams and lakes, and recharging aquifers. These green spaces also benefit local communities by creating parks and open spaces and protecting natural functions such as flood protection and pollination of crops.

The Upper Neuse Clean Water Initiative in North Carolina used a green infrastructure approach when developing its recent conservation strategy, demonstrating the value of land conservation as a key investment to protect drinking water supplies. The resulting plan identified the most important areas to conserve to ensure water quality downstream and set an ambitious but feasible goal of preserving 30,000 acres over the next 30 years in a voluntary market-driven system. The initiative is coordinated by the Conservation Trust for North Carolina, and its members – Ellerbe Creek Watershed Association, Eno River Association, Tar River Land Conservancy, The Conservation Fund, Triangle Greenways Council, Triangle Land Conservancy, and representatives of local governments and state agencies – are collaborating with willing landowners to protect areas critical to the water supply.

The initiative's planning process produced a GIS-based watershed protection model that used the best available scientific information and geographic data to map the most important areas for conservation. A technical advisory team convened multiple meetings to evaluate potential mapping criteria and ultimately selected 12 GIS data layers best representing the initiative's goals and objectives. Project staff members collected and organized the best available GIS data so that new GIS layers could be derived in a consistent format.

Greenways for Recreation

As our work on an open space plan for Nashville, Tennessee, illustrates, incorporating recreational greenways into a green infrastructure vision can make communities more competitive economically and more viable ecologically and can preserve and enhance the quality of life they offer. As described in the plan, "Open spaces affect every citizen in some way, from walkers, gardeners, historians, birders, cyclists, hikers, hunters, athletes, dog-walkers, or outdoor enthusiasts to new parents, retirees, business owners, real estate developers, and other private landowners" (Conservation Fund, 2011, p. 2).

The Nashville Open Space Plan (Conservation Fund, 2011) identified four major objectives: connect wildlife and water networks, support urban and rural farming, preserve historic and iconic resources, and connect people to green infrastructure through greenway corridors of undeveloped land preserved for recreational use and/or environmental protection. "Nashville should expedite development of an interconnected network of parks and greenways to promote active, healthy lifestyles, link residents to community open spaces, and provide alternatives to motor vehicle transportation" (p. 22). The plan prioritized recreational connections that would link residents to areas identified in the ecological green infrastructure network.

When the plan was prepared, Nashville had 76 miles of existing greenways (completed or under construction). Thanks to the city's commitment to implement the plan, Nashville increased the area dedicated to parks by more than 25 percent and built 39 miles of greenway trails, a 50 percent increase that exceeded the original goal of adding 25 miles in five years. Other improvements included protection of a prized 12-acre site on the west bank of the Cumberland River for a park and greenway and a new pedestrian/bike bridge over railroad tracks to connect a downtown neighborhood with the newly constructed Music City Center convention space and the riverfront (Allen, 2016).

Urban Forestry

Urban forests provide much more than tree-lined attractive streets; they also contribute to improved air and water quality, store carbon, and reduce the amount of energy consumed for cooling buildings. In recent years, many tools have been developed to assist conservationists in measuring urban forest canopies and setting goals for tree canopies (Schwab, 2009). Nashville's open space plan also focused on developing urban forests, establishing a goal of doubling the downtown area's tree canopy, creating new pocket parks and landscaped gateways, and transitioning suitable impervious surfaces (e.g., asphalt or concrete) to pervious surfaces and/or natural plantings (Conservation Fund, 2011). The Greater Baltimore Wilderness Coalition also identified tree canopy enhancement and restoration in dense urban areas as a key strategy to reduce stormwater runoff, ameliorate the effects of urban heat islands, and improve air quality (American Planning Association, 2016b).

Low-Impact Development

Green infrastructure planning is ideally suited to making urban areas and critical gray infrastructure (hospitals and emergency management facilities, transportation corridors, power plants and transmission facilities, and wastewater treatment plants) more resilient to the effects of climate change and limiting their negative impacts on the environment (American Planning Association, 2016a). The Greater Baltimore Wilderness Coalition employed a green infrastructure planning approach in its efforts to reduce the threats posed by extreme weather events by mapping areas of the region that fell within the storm-surge and sea-level-rise influence areas and the 100-year and 500-year floodplains. They used those maps to model areas at risk of flooding and identify critical community infrastructure in those areas. The coalition also emphasized preserving, building, and restoring coastal defenses that provide buffers against flooding, storm surges, and rising sea levels. Data sets from the State of Maryland's Coastal Resiliency Assessment were used to identify the location of those resources, and the coalition prioritized areas of forest, marsh, and other natural ecosystems that could be restored (American Planning Association, 2016b; Nature Conservancy, 2016).

Stormwater Management

The Center for Neighborhood Technology and American Rivers are national nonprofit organizations that promote sustainable communities and protect water resources. One of their approaches for making communities more resilient from flooding and extreme weather events is establishing a green infrastructure network consisting of decentralized stormwater-management structures such as green roofs, urban forests, rain gardens, and permeable pavements that can capture and absorb rain where it falls, thereby reducing stormwater runoff and improving the health of surrounding waterways (Center for Neighborhood Technology and American Rivers, 2010). While these strategies reduce stormwater runoff, some also provide ecosystem services such as reductions in energy use provided by shade trees, improvements in air quality through carbon sequestration, and reductions in the effects of urban heat islands. This green infrastructure network also provides public education through its aesthetic appeal.

In addressing stormwater concerns, the Greater Baltimore Wilderness Coalition chose to retrofit developed areas as a strategy to reduce the amount of impervious surface. In the planning process, the coalition identified a menu of best management practices for restoring the landscape's ability to absorb and transport water that included bioretention basins, infiltration basins and trenches that absorb water and transfer it to underground aquifers, dry and wet ponds, constructed wetlands, grass swales, porous pavement, surface and subsurface sand filters, and vegetated filter strips (American Planning Association, 2016b). The coalition targeted areas with a large amount of impervious land cover and no stormwater-management practices in place. The sites were then ranked by their ability to capture stormwater according to EPA measures, potential pollution loading in the watershed from impervious surfaces and agricultural land, and the area of impervious surface that drained to the site.

Success Profile: Erik Meyers

Erik Meyers is vice president for climate and water sustainability at The Conservation Fund (Figure 5.5). His work focuses on policy and program leadership through service on the boards of several nonprofit organizations and as part of coalitions and working groups. In addition, Meyers is involved in planning and implementing projects that demonstrate adaptive management and integrated responses to

FIGURE 5.5 Erik Meyers. Photograph by Whitney Flanagan, The Conservation Fund.

climate change and water challenges. In other words, his work makes human communities more resilient to changes beyond their control. When Mother Nature strikes and the environment is damaged by disasters such as floods, what characteristics in the environment can blunt the damage caused and allow the environment to bounce back afterward?

Meyers's resiliency projects focus on mitigation and adaptation in urban and rural areas. As part of Blackwater National Wildlife Refuge's salt marsh and climate resiliency project in Maryland, he participated in strategically selecting prime salt marsh habitat for birds that could be elevated, researched cutting-edge environmental designs to successfully inundate higher-elevation marshes, and mapped the locations of invasive salt marsh plants and mammals in identified marsh migration corridors around the refuge so they could be removed. These solutions addressed the impacts of an accelerated rate of sea level rise on the eastern coast of the United States related to climate change and the resulting losses of marsh lands. In urban areas, resiliency projects are focused on integrated water management systems for metropolitan areas to address current and future challenges related to water resources threated by development, environmental restoration needs, and climate change. In those cases, watershed concerns are being addressed with site- and region-specific green infrastructure projects to increase available water supplies and ecological benefits, reduce flooding and sewer overflows, and advance environmental equity.

Meyers has found that building resiliency to changing climates and more-extreme weather events requires doing a little bit of everything on the menu.

THE STRATEGIC VALUE OF ECOSYSTEM SERVICES

Only recently has it become possible to quantify and reliably estimate the contributions that green infrastructure makes to human well-being and measure the positive ecosystem services nature provides at no cost to us (Conservation Fund, 2014). We have reviewed the literature on ecosystem services and have developed a list of 24 services that, at least conceptually, can be discretely calculated (Conservation Fund, 2014). These services, which are described in Table 5.3, fall into one of the three primary categories shown in the table: (1) regulation and support services (e.g., regulating water flows or loss of carbon into the atmosphere), (2) provisioning services (e.g., production of food or soil), and (3) human cultural services (e.g., recreation, property values). The regulation and support services consist of processes that ameliorate hazards (such as floods), influence climate change (such as carbon storage), and support biological organisms (such as pollination).

Conserving Strategically by Taking Advantage of Nature

Ecosystem services are an extremely important part of the calculation of benefits and costs associated with strategic conservation projects. Risks associated with flooding and storm events are a good example. More-frequent and more-intense storm events due to climate change are expected to result in greater amounts of stormwater and higher

Table 5.3 *Ecosystem service valuations that support green infrastructure*

Ecosystem Service	Description
REGULATING & SUPPORTING	
Hazard Amelioration	
Water flow regulation/flood control	Maintain water flow stability and protect areas against flooding (e.g., from storms)
Water purification	Maintain water quality sufficient for human consumption, recreational uses like swimming and fishing, and aquatic life
Erosion control and sediment retention	Maintain soil and slope stability, and retain soil and sediment on site
Groundwater recharge	Maintain natural rates of groundwater recharge and aquifer replenishment
Air purification	Remove particulates and other pollutants from the air
Climate	
Microclimate moderation	Lower ambient and surface air temperature through shading
Regulation of water temperature	Moderate water temperature in streams
Carbon storage	Sequester carbon in vegetation and soils, thereby reducing atmospheric CO_2 and global climate change
Biological	
Native flora and fauna	Maintain species diversity and biomass
Pollination	Provide pollinators for crops and other vegetation important to humans
Pest and disease control	Provide biota that consume pests and control diseases
PROVISIONING	
Food production	Production of plant or fungal-based food for human consumption
Game and fish production	Production of wild game and fish for human consumption

(*cont.*)

Table 5.3 (cont.)

Ecosystem Service	Description
Fiber production	Production of wood and other natural fibers for human use
Soil formation	Long-term production of soil and peat for support of vegetation and other uses
Biochemical production	Provision of biochemicals, natural medicines, pharmaceuticals, etc.
Genetic information	Genetic resources for medical and other uses, including those not yet realized
CULTURAL	
Recreation and ecotourism	Outdoor, nature-based experiences like hiking, birding, hunting, camping, etc.
Savings in community services	Savings in community services from not converting natural land to houses
Increase in property values	Provide attractive location for homes and businesses
Science and education	Existence of natural systems and areas for school excursions, advancement of scientific knowledge, etc.
Spiritual and aesthetic	Aesthetic enjoyment or spiritual or religious fulfillment
Bequest value	The value placed on knowing that future generations will have the option to utilize the resource
Existence value	The nonuse value of simply knowing that particular resources exist, even if they are not used

peak discharges, which can increase the amount of sediment and pollutants that enter waterways and increase sewer back-ups that can contaminate drinking water and create public health hazards. Natural systems such as wetlands, grass lands, and permeable surfaces are often the least costly and most efficient way to prevent damage from such conditions (Conservation Fund, 2013). This will be particularly important as municipal and state governments apply their already thin budgets to infrastructure needed to comply with stormwater-management regulations.

Green infrastructure provides multiple ecosystem services. They preserve and create permeable surfaces that ensure that water is absorbed into the ground to recharge aquifers rather than entering sewer and stormwater systems. The ability to absorb water and avoid runoff consequently reduces the amount of nonpoint-source pollution, sediment, nutrients such as nitrogen and phosphorus, bacteria, and other contamination from entering water supplies. And as a result, fewer water-treatment facilities must be built or replaced. Poor water quality also has a significant impact on recreation in terms of contamination and on transportation over waterways due to sedimentation. Groundwater recharge affects all living things. During recent droughts, a number of municipalities have faced the substantial challenge and cost of identifying and accessing new water supplies, and it can be more efficient economically to restore existing aquifers. Groundwater also contributes to the natural base flow of rivers and streams.

The geology of groundwater absorption, infiltration, and recharge is complex, but an essential element is minimizing the amount of impervious surfaces that divert water to sewers and other stormwater drains before it can soak into the ground. Green infrastructures provide permeable surfaces and prevent runoff water through plant cover, root systems, and various types of basins to store water.

Another important ecosystem service provided by green infrastructure is capturing and sequestering carbon from greenhouse gases such as carbon dioxide. Carbon is stored above ground in leaves and woody matter and below ground in roots and soil, and forests and urban trees remove sulfur dioxide, nitrogen oxide, ozone, carbon monoxide, and fine particles from the air, all of which are harmful to humans. Their leaves reduce air pollution by absorbing and intercepting the pollutants, and forest soils act as sinks that sequester carbon.

Table 5.4 *Common methods for valuing ecosystem services in monetary terms*

Method	Description
Avoided cost	Services allow society to avoid costs that would have been incurred in the absence of those services (e.g., natural flood control preventing property damages or natural waste treatment preventing health costs)
Replacement cost	Services could be replaced with human-made systems (e.g., natural waste treatment having to be replaced by costly engineered systems)
Factor income	Services provide for the enhancement of incomes (e.g., water quality increasing commercial fisheries catches and fishermen incomes)
Travel cost	Service demand may require travel, whose costs can reflect the implied value of the service (e.g., value of ecotourism or recreation is at least what a visitor is willing to pay to get there)
Hedonic pricing	Service demand may be reflected in the prices people will pay for associated goods (e.g., increase in housing prices due to water views or access to parks)
Contingent valuation	Service demand may be elicited by posing hypothetical scenarios that involve some valuation of alternatives (e.g., how much people are willing to pay for increased availability of fish or wildlife)

Methods for Valuing Ecosystem Services

The six methods commonly used to value ecosystem services in monetary terms (Farber et al., 2002) – avoided costs, replacement costs, factor incomes, travel costs, hedonic pricing, and contingent valuation – are described in Table 5.4.[2] Table 5.5 presents the available metrics and types of economic analyses that generally can be applied to seven ecosystem services – regulating and controlling water flows

---

[2] For more information on the economic methods and challenges of accurately measuring the value of ecosystem services, see the excellent reviews by Olander et al. (2017) and Johnston et al. (2017).

Table 5.5 *Ecosystem service metrics and economic analysis types*

Ecosystem Service	Metrics	Types of Economic Analyses
Water flow regulation/flood control	Reduction of flood damage, reduction of stormwater flows, reduction of peak discharges, reduction of combined sewer system costs, reduction of soil erosion	Avoided cost, replacement cost
Water purification	Reduction of N, P, Cl⁻, sediment, bacteria, and other pollutants for drinking water, swimming, fishing, aquatic life, and other uses.	Avoided cost, replacement cost
Groundwater recharge	Supply of water to groundwater rather than surface runoff	Avoided cost, replacement cost, price of public water supply
Carbon storage	Reduction of atmospheric CO_2 and associated climate effects	Avoided cost, market price of carbon
Air purification	Removal of SO_x, NO_x, O_3, CO, and PM_{10} from the air	Avoided cost, replacement cost
Native flora & fauna	Protection of wildlife habitat; maintenance of ecosystem functions and resilience	Willingness to pay (contingent valuation)
Recreation and ecotourism	Money spent on nature-based recreation (hunting, fishing, birding, hiking, etc.)	Surveys of money expended on nature-based recreation

Source: Adapted from Chicago Wilderness Green Infrastructure Vision 2.3: Ecosystem Service Valuation (2015), https://datahub.cmap.illinois .gov/lv/dataset/green-infrastructure-vision-2-3-ecosystem-valuation.

and floods, air and water purification, groundwater recharge, carbon storage, preservation of native species, and recreation and ecotourism. Using these services and techniques, the benefits of green infrastructure networks can be converted into spatially explicit maps.

Using these techniques, we have valued ecosystem services in numerous projects in the United States in the past 10 years using estimates of the per-acre economic value of landscapes and habitats that support such services from peer-reviewed studies. Our initial pilot project involved the Chesapeake Bay watershed in Cecil County, Maryland, where we found that forests and wetlands in the county provided more than $2.1 billion in ecosystem service value annually (Conservation Fund, 2008). We also mapped the green infrastructure network in Cecil County and found that it efficiently provided ecosystem services. Though the green infrastructure network covered only 37 percent of the county's land area, it provided 81 percent of the county's ecosystem services. In subsequent projects, we have found similar significant efficiencies.

In the Houston-Galveston region of Texas, we estimated the value of five important ecosystem services provided by prairies, tidal and nontidal wetlands, bottomland and upland forests, floodplains, and water bodies: water quality, air quality, water supply, flood protection, and climate regulation (Conservation Fund, 2013). We found, for instance, that the region's wetlands were particularly effective at absorbing stormwater; they were reducing flood damage by almost $8,000 per acre per year while also capturing water valued at as much as $9,000 per acre per year.

In our Chicago Wilderness study, we found that natural ecosystems were contributing considerably more than $6 billion per year in economic value to the seven-county Chicago metropolitan planning region just for the six ecosystem services that could be readily valued in the study: flood control, water purification, groundwater recharge, carbon storage, native species (i.e., biodiversity), and recreation and ecotourism (Conservation Fund, 2015). Our literature review indicated that one large tree could capture up to 5,400 gallons of stormwater runoff per year in the Midwestern United States and that an acre of wetlands could typically store between one and one and a half million gallons of floodwater (Conservation Fund, 2013). In a follow-up study of a single county in the Chicago Wilderness region (Lake County), we found that the extensive network of woodlands, wetlands, water bodies, and prairies provided more than $1.85 billion per year in flood control benefits (Conservation Fund and Lake County Forest Preserve District, 2016).

These numerous ecosystem service valuation projects have demonstrated that estimating the monetized social benefit of conservation and comparing it to the investment required to protect land is a scientifically valid and valuable process that provides critical information to decision-makers and the general public about the importance of green infrastructure for a region's quality of life and a greater understanding in various disciplines, including conservation and environmental economics, of the relationship between built environments and a region's ecological capital. In the next chapter, we delve more deeply into methods that allow us (and you) to transform conservation criteria into the greatest possible conservation benefits.

6   Transforming Criteria into Conservation Benefits

As the wine example described earlier in the book clearly illustrated, understanding trade-offs and opportunity costs is an important part of strategic conservation to help get the best bang for your buck. However, several key questions need to be answer to make this happen in a manner that is consistent with the core principles of strategic conservation.

- How can you effectively measure conservation benefits and make them understandable to decision-makers?
- How do you and your organization identify the best criteria when there are countless criteria that can be considered?
- How can a logical and transparent decision framework be developed to identify conservation priorities and ultimately select the best implementation projects?

To identify an optimal solution, reliable information on both costs and benefits is needed and the benefits must be quantified and measured to feed into optimization models. Thus, we need information to answer the following questions:

- What types of benefits are frequently used for strategic conservation projects?
- What are the best ways to quantify and measure those benefits?
- How can you ensure that you calculate and evaluate potential benefits in a way that is logically consistent and reflects the intent of the decision-maker?

The importance of a scientific approach when defining and quantifying benefits became clear in our earliest explorations into using optimization to select conservation projects. While it was not technologically difficult to assign numerical values to particular conservation objectives, we became very aware of the importance of ensuring that the calculation of quantified benefits was in line with the intuitive judgment of the local decision-makers. If these decision-makers did not intuitively find that our criteria and scoring systems made sense, they questioned the resulting optimized portfolios. As a result, we have invested significant resources over the last decade in selecting and refining methods that ensure development of transparent, defensible criteria that can be incorporated into decision-support tools.

Quantifying and measuring benefits is both an art and a science, with a significant amount of subjective human involvement, but there is also a robust literature in science and mathematics that demonstrates that combining objective and subjective information is a scientifically valid way to solve sophisticated conservation planning problems.

QUANTIFYING CONSERVATION BENEFITS

Land Suitability Analysis

In our ideal world, people would live in full harmony with nature and, as a result, natural resources, ecosystems, and ecological functions and processes would be maintained amidst all forms of human development. Alas, there will always be impacts on ecosystems used to support human communities by growing food, building infrastructure, or engaging in other economic endeavors. Therefore, it is crucial to understand the trade-offs associated with land-use choices in various locations.

Because Will is a regional planner by training, it is perhaps inevitable that our discussion uses a land-use-planning framework as the foundation for understanding strategic conservation. Thankfully, this framework is consistent with various existing definitions of land use planning, including ones from the American Planning Association and the Canadian Institute of Planners (those definitions specifically use the phrase "scientific, aesthetic, and orderly disposition of land"). The science of land use planning involves seeking to organize land uses in an efficient, equitable, and ethical way, often to manage competing needs and avoid conflicts. Systematic assessments of land uses are often integrated into comprehensive plans but also appear in other specialized planning documents addressing issues such as hazard mitigation, climate adaptation, and watershed protection. The specific needs and solutions addressed by land use planning vary based on the needs of the particular community or watershed being addressed, but all land-use analyses share some common goals and objectives. In strategic conservation programs, the focus is on environmental planning, a branch of planning that became prominent as the impacts of human development on ecosystems became better understood (Walters, 2007). As the field of environmental planning expanded, a number of specialized assessments were developed that were subsequently incorporated into comprehensive plans and into smaller conservation plans that addressed issues such as wetlands, endangered species habitat, flood zones, and coastal zones.

We understand intuitively that some places are better than others to develop (e.g., stable ground versus near the edge of an eroding cliff), and the same can be said for conservation (e.g., areas with rich biodiversity are better to preserve than areas without such resources). Sometimes the intrinsic value of the land identifies its suitability. At other times, the values that humans assign to activities or locations drive the suitability of a particular piece of land for the desired purpose.

A suitability analysis evaluates contributing projects or parcels in terms of their ability to deliver the resources or services required by stakeholders and/or decision-makers and is at the heart of every strategic conservation process. The earliest application of a suitability analysis for strategic conservation purposes most likely is Warren

Manning's (1923) national plan study brief in which he proposed a national network of parks and open spaces based on an assessment of landscape features. The most famous more-modern example of suitability analysis is Ian McHarg's influential book, *Design with Nature*, in 1967. McHarg pioneered the use of map overlays and suitability analysis to assess natural processes, asserting through his methodology that the intrinsic landscape attributes of a place should be the basis for land use planning.

Despite the limited technology available to McHarg for visualizing suitability (i.e., gray-scale transparent film sheets), he demonstrated the fundamental concepts for what would later become GIS. Thanks to the modeling capabilities offered by modern GIS systems and a wide array of available spatial data layers, McHarg's suitability-analysis framework can be applied with incredible sophistication and subtlety using geoprocessing frameworks such as Idrisi and Esri's ArcGIS.

Because of the heavy dose of human input associated with suitability analyses, they are inherently subjective to some degree, a reality that has often made natural scientists uneasy. Frequently when we taught them to use GIS-based suitability analysis, they worried about correlation between some of the model criteria. For instance, criteria used to evaluate the quality of wetlands near streams and the health of the aquatic system are often inextricably linked. To help solve this potential problem, one should turn to multicriteria decision analysis.

Multicriteria Decision Analysis

Ultimately, a land-use suitability analysis is a spatial form of a multicriteria decision analysis, a branch of operations research that provides systematic methods for analyzing complex decision problems, that explicitly incorporates the preferences of human decision-makers. Among the various multicriteria decision-support software applications available, GIS is the most commonly used platform because of the spatial nature of the conservation decision problems (Weistroffer et al., 2005). GIS-based suitability models create spatial visualizations of the ideal scenario based on multiple criteria simultaneously.

Consider the complexity of the average conservation project. Large blocks of forest, for example, provide numerous benefits for people, plants, animals, and ecosystems. A forest's interior habitat can provide refuge for neotropical migratory birds in the Americas while simultaneously providing clean water in streams and rivers that serve as human water supplies. Forests provide benefits that can be objectively measured, such as water quality in a stream, and benefits that are measured subjectively, such as the quality of scenery valued by people. And in terms of project selections, individuals making those selections often have both objective goals (e.g., projects located within one mile of a stream) and subjective goals (e.g., acquiring "prime" projects or parcels). Consequently, multicriteria decision analysis used for strategic conservation is a matter of uncovering all of the benefits associated with conserving a resource.

Inherent to multicriteria decision analysis is our fifth core principle of strategic conservation: *Acknowledge Limited Resources.* Through constraints come opportunities to protect what is most valued in communities. Because of the subjectivity inherent in conservation efforts, a primary objective is organizing and structuring the selection criteria to ensure that they reflect the decision-maker's intent and that they are tightly linked to the stated goals of the conservation project. In this case, we use the term decision-maker generally as the decision-maker could be rule makers for federal conservation programs, the board of directors of a nonprofit organization, or staff in a State or local government agency. Subjectivity does not invalidate or discredit the process, but its presence can make the process seem messy, inconsistent, and sometimes illogical. You can mitigate such concerns by using structured decision processes such as the Logic Scoring of Preference (LSP) method that have been established scientifically.

In decision theory, the weighted-sum model is the best-known and simplest method of multicriteria decision-making for evaluating alternatives (Triantaphyllou, 2000). A key requirement of the weighted-sum model is that it is valid only when all the data are expressed in the same unit. If not, the final result is equivalent to "adding apples and oranges." Therefore, a key challenge to multicriteria decision analysis is integrating a variety of objective and subjective measurement systems into a consistent, standardized system.

When using GIS, then, we need an efficient and effective method of transforming individual GIS layers that represent the landscape into a set of layers expressed in a single unit that can be overlaid. Consider a hypothetical decision framework in weighted-sum form: [Suitability = land cover + soils + land slope]. First, you have to know what you want the project or property to be suitable for – preservation of farm land, restoration of wetlands, creation of green space? So the first step is to thoroughly define the desired outcome of the suitability analysis.

For this simple example, let's assume that you are identifying potential wetland restoration sites. Certain land covers, soil types, and land slopes will be better than others for that goal. In terms of cover, grasses and agricultural crops would be preferable to impervious surfaces and areas already providing ecosystem services that existing wetlands offer. Hydric soils, which are effective at holding water, would be suitable since such areas may have been wetlands in the past, and slopes of less than three percent are most suitable because water would normally flow and settle on such slopes.

Until you decide on a mathematical formula to transform those three features into a quantitative system, you cannot create a layered GIS map that allows you to interpret the suitability of various areas based on all three criteria. One solution is to convert the suitability values for each feature into values on a numerical scale such as 0–100. Then, you can begin to characterize the suitability of each area using its value in terms of land cover, soils, and slopes. You could, for example, assign the highest suitability value (100) to grass lands, hydric soils, and no slope and a medium suitability value of 50 to agricultural lands, moderately hydric soils, and a 1.5 percent slope. In that case, an area of grass land consisting of hydric soils and a 0 percent slope would have a suitability value of 300: [Suitability (Wetland Restoration) = Land Cover (100) + Soils (100) + Slope (100)]. This weighted-sum model requires development of a standardized, structured criteria-evaluation system prior to evaluating the prospective areas.

When crafting a scientifically defensible suitability model and a multicriteria decision-making framework for strategic conservation, we find that the easiest way to get started is to organize your criteria into a simple matrix that clearly shows the connections between the goal to be achieved (e.g., wetland restoration), the specific measureable characteristic that can be quantified or mapped, the technical approach to measuring that characteristic, and the data sources that will be used to quantify them. We illustrate this process using our work with Missouri's Department of Conservation in establishing criteria for selecting properties for conservation.

Success Profile: Paul Zwick

Our global society constantly pushes to do things faster, easier, and overall better. When it comes to strategic land conservation … that is just what Paul Zwick has done. Dr. Zwick started as a professor at the University of Florida in the department of Urban and Regional Planning in 1986. With research interests in new paradigms for how to use GIS in planning, he worked with fellow professor Margaret Carr in designing LUCIS (Land-Use Conflict Identification Strategy), which uses land suitability analysis and attempts to identify land-use conflicts using suitability and community preferences.

Before GIS-based land suitability analysis, conservation professionals would create paper maps to help identify the best parcels of land to conserve. This process was slow and tedious and could only create one scenario at a time. Using GIS allows analyzing scenarios with remarkable speed and precision. Zwick's latest research is continuing to speed up the GIS analysis by using multiple processors at once. The technology we have today gives conservation professionals an edge to make sure they are selecting the best land to protect. One of LUCIS's most powerful benefits is it suggests what lands are highly appropriate for future development, what lands should be set aside for conservation, and what lands should be set aside for agricultural production (Carr and Zwick, 2007). But most importantly, LUCIS develops alternative land-use futures. Zwick has helped revolutionize technology when it comes to strategic land conservation and has greatly enhanced the process for everyone involved.

Criteria Design

The Missouri Department of Conservation (MDC) acquires parcels of land to protect forests, fish, and other wildlife in the state. We worked with the department to develop a structured decision-support system to assist the staff in identifying the highest priority parcels to acquire and to assist the realty committee in using its limited funds wisely to obtain the maximum possible conservation benefit. As part of this project, we convened a half-day workshop with the staff to refine their existing criteria and ensure that the process was scientifically based and as transparent as possible in quantifying and assessing the potential parcels. Then, over the following months, we coordinated development of a final field data sheet that would quickly provide a numerical benefit score for each project.

The first step in establishing the department's selection criteria was to establish a structured set of goals and objectives. That process produced three overarching goals for the conservation program and funds that were supported by three or four specific objectives for each goal (see Table 6.1). Then, we developed the structure shown in Table 6.2 to capture the importance of the objective and how it would be quantified, listing the goal, objective, rationale, approach, data sources, and process. Tables 6.3 and 6.4 present the outcome of that process for two of the criteria we developed using this framework.

Table 6.1 *Missouri Department of Conservation goals and objectives for land acquisition*

Attribute	Criterion	Description
Goal 1: **Acquire lands with the highest conservation values**		
Objective 1a	1	Protect habitats that maximize the aggregate value of the MDC property portfolio
Objective 1b	2	Protect high-quality habitat with a species composition that supports diverse and healthy natural communities
Objective 1c	3	Protect habitat with documented natural heritage occurrences of a federally or state-listed species
Objective 1d	4	Protect habitat that provides functional connectivity within the green infrastructure network
Goal 2: **Acquire lands most likely to retain natural resource and recreational values in perpetuity**		
Objective 2a	5	Protect lands where nearby land conversion is less likely
Objective 2b	6	Protect lands that support or enhance a wide range of public use activities
Objective 2c	7	Protect lands where minimal land management or restoration will be required
Goal 3: **Acquire lands where MDC land management is most feasible**		
Objective 3a	8	Protect lands within a priority geography of a Conservation Opportunity Area
Objective 3b	9	Protect lands that can be managed in an efficient and cost-effective manner
Objective 3c	10	Protect lands that are accessible via an existing public road and near existing MDC land holdings

Table 6.2 *Structured framework for criteria development*

Goal	Desired conservation goal
Objective	Metric to achieve goal
Rationale	Why is this objective important
Approach	Techniques for measuring the objective
Data sources	GIS layer(s) or other data source(s) needed to classify relative values
Process steps	Manipulation of GIS layer(s) or other data sources to create classes and scores

Table 6.3 *Criteria for acquiring high-value conservation lands*

Goal 1: **Acquire lands with the highest conservation values**	
Objective 1a	Protect habitats that maximize the contribution to the overall value of the MDC property portfolio
Rationale	Land should include habitats that have been identified as statewide priorities: prairies, grasslands, savannas, caves, wetlands, woodlands, forests, and river and stream corridors
	Also important to acquire habitats underrepresented in the MDC portfolio: sand prairie, bottomlands in the Ozark Highlands ecoregion, glades
Approach	Highest value assigned to acquiring MDC realty committee priority habitats
	High value assigned to acquiring underrepresented habitat in the MDC portfolio
	Low value to acquiring habitats that are currently well represented
	No value if the land does not expand habitats in the MDC portfolio
Data sources	Land cover GIS layer, aerial photography, MDC field surveys
Process steps	MDC staff assign a high value, low value, or no value after a review of the property

Table 6.4 *Criteria for acquiring lands for which MDC management is most feasible*

Goal 3: Acquire lands where MDC land management is most feasible	
Objective 3b	Protect lands that can be managed in an efficient and cost-effective manner
Rationale	Assess the contribution of the land to the MDC property portfolio; determine if property is a strategic inholding; determine if property is intended to be an expansion of an existing unit or a new stand-alone unit; determine if property is large enough to be a new unit
Approach	Highest value assigned to a significant expansion of an existing unit that provides high marginal value to the public and MDC mission or a strategically located, large, new stand-alone unit
	High value given to a strategic inholding that solves a boundary line or other management issue
	Low value given to expansion of an existing unit that does not significantly improve public access or expand MDC program activities
	No value given for an isolated area of insufficient size for a new unit
Data sources	Existing GIS layer for MDC lands, property boundaries, aerial photography, MDC staff field surveys
Process steps	MDC staff assign a high value, low value, or no value after a review of the property

DESIGNING LOGICALLY CONSISTENT MEASURES TO QUANTIFY BENEFITS

Note that the tables in the preceding example do not provide quantitative evaluations of the criteria. Before establishing a method for quantifying the benefits of proposed conservation projects, you must first identify the measurement system you will use when designing your criteria. Four types of data are commonly used in a strategic conservation project: *nominal, ordinal, ratio,* and *interval* (Stevens, 1946). All of the data that can be incorporated into the planning project will fall into one or more of those categories. This data classification system is important when designing and combining quantitative criteria to avoid logical inconsistencies in the suitability models.

With *nominal* data, a label that has no specific numerical value or meaning is assigned a value. Temperatures classified as hot, warm, cool, and cold are good examples of nominal data. In strategic conservation, information on land cover (agricultural, grass land, forest) is a source of nominal data. A tricky case of nominal data is the National Land Cover Database's classification system (Homer et al., 2015). Since it is a raster-based GIS format, each type of land cover has been assigned a numerical value; some types of forest, for example, are assigned numbers 41, 42, and 43. However, these numbers are only labels, and they would need to be reclassified to be used in a suitability analysis. All nominal data must be converted to a quantitative scale to be used in suitability and multicriteria decision analyses.

An *ordinal* data set ranks items but does not account for relative degrees of difference. For instance, in an Olympic race, there are first, second, and third place finishes but those rankings do not tell you how much faster the first place winner was than the second and third place athletes. Natural resource data sets are sometimes classified into an ordinal format such as tiers (i.e., tier 1, 2, and 3) in which the tier designations have no explicit mathematical relationship, requiring one to consult the layer's metadata (i.e., the file accompanying the GIS layer that explains how the data sets were created) to determine if tier 1 is better/worse or higher/lower than tier 2. Even then, you still have to make an educated judgment about how to transform the tier values into a numerical scale for a suitability analysis.

The Kelvin temperature scale is an example of *ratio* data, organized as a normalized scale with a meaningful zero value (absolute zero degrees Kelvin). Examples from strategic conservation are the ratio of stream miles to total land area in a watershed and the

Table 6.5 *Techniques for transforming levels of measurement to suitability classifications*

Technique	Description	Methods	Examples
Threshold ranges	Quantitative rules applied to divide area, distance, or landscape feature data into discrete ranges to differentiate suitability	Peer-reviewed scientific literature, convening of subject matter experts, and/or a specific regulatory environment governing land use planning activities.	Distance from streams, percentage slope, proximity to existing protected lands
Zone statistics	Mathematical calculation for subsets of specific geography based on computing area or distance to differentiate suitability	Zone often a watershed or hydrologic unit; specific calculation is made for each unit and then applied across the entire unit	Percentage forest, percentage impervious surface, stream miles per hydrologic unit
Nominal classifications	Assignment of relative suitability for nominal data based on landscape features	Peer-reviewed scientific literature, convening of subject matter experts, and/or a specific regulatory environment governing land use planning activities	Assignment of suitability values to specific land cover or soil attributes (e.g, hydric, drainage)

percentage a watershed covered by forest. Ratio data often can be put directly into a suitability analysis, particularly if it is already on a scale of 0 to 100.

A common example of *interval* data is temperature measured in degrees Celsius, which describes relative differences in values but not ratios; 40 degrees Celsius is not twice as hot as 20 degrees Celsius. Quantitative GIS models such as raster-based suitability analyses typically produce interval data (unless the metadata underlying the model explicitly state that the outputs represent ratios). In some cases, it makes sense to group interval scores into categories since the data are not in ratio form.

Several methods for converting nominal, ordinal, ratio, and interval data into a single format for GIS-based suitability modeling are presented in Table 6.5. We next present a set of case studies that illustrate how this concept of logically consistent measures of benefits has been addressed in a variety of settings.

Water Quality

The Upper Neuse Clean Water Initiative in North Carolina is a collaboration by The Conservation Fund, Ellerbe Creek Watershed Association, Eno River Association, Tar River Land Conservancy, Triangle Greenways Council, Triangle Land Conservancy, local governments, and state agencies and is coordinated by the Conservation Trust for North Carolina. Together with willing landowners, these partners protect natural areas that are critical to the long-term health of drinking water from the Upper Neuse River Basin by either purchasing parcels or establishing conservation easements on them. A large part of the initiative's funding comes from the City of Raleigh's Watershed Protection Fund, which charges customers of the city's water utility based on volume of use (the average fee for households is about 60 cents per month). Significant additional financial support is provided by other local governments, including the City of Durham, the City of Creedmoor, Durham County, Granville County, Orange

County, and Wake County, and by the state's Clean Water Management Trust Fund. This broad base of funding has been critical to the initiative's success (Upper Neuse Clean Water Initiative, 2015). In its first 10 years, the initiative acquired ownership or an easement for 88 properties, protecting 84 miles of stream bank across 7,658 acres. In 2015, the initiative set a goal of protecting 30,000 acres over the next 30 years.

We worked with the initiative to refine its original GIS-based model (Trust for Public Land, 2006) for identifying the most ecologically important locations in the Upper Neuse River Basin for investment. To begin to refine the model, the technical advisory team convened multiple times to evaluate available data, eventually selecting 12 GIS data layers that best represented the initiative's goals and objectives. The model was developed to help visualize four primary goals: (1) protect water sources and conveyances, (2) conserve upland areas, (3) promote water infiltration and retention, and (4) avoid development of vulnerable areas. Each goal also had three associated objectives, each with its own GIS layer that represented the relative suitability for achieving these goals. For example, to achieve goal 3, the technical advisory team felt that identifying opportunities to protect wetlands, floodplains, and groundwater recharge areas would best promote water infiltration and retention. Project staff members then collected and organized the best available GIS data so that new layers representing the entire watershed could be derived in a consistent form. Each of the 12 layers is described in greater detail in Table 6.6.

The GIS model examined every potential parcel in the watershed using multiple criteria and ultimately identified more than 17,000 parcels totaling more than 260,000 acres – approximately 15 percent of the total number of parcels in the watershed and 56 percent of the watershed's land area. The previous version of the model had identified a little over 20,000 parcels (about 18 percent) and close to 325,000 acres (about 69 percent). The refined model was more selective thanks to more-detailed geographic data; recent scientific data

Table 6.6 Objectives for the Upper Neuse Clean Water Initiative's selections and type of data used for each objective in the suitability analysis

Description	Data Type for Quantifying Benefit	Suitability Type	Criterion
Goal 1: Protect water sources and conveyances			
Objective 1a: Protect headwater streams	Interval	Threshold ranges – area	Smaller catchments denote source water areas. Technical advisors identified suitable headwater catchment size cutoff.
Objective 1b: Support connected high-quality water features	Ratio	Zone statistics – area	Protect land within intact catchments. Technical advisors selected thresholds for percentage of conserved land by catchment. Ratio data transformed to interval data classes for GIS modeling.
Objective 1c: Protect riparian areas	Interval	Threshold ranges – distance	Close proximity to stream equals higher-quality benefit. Technical advisors selected distance thresholds based on scientific literature and local knowledge.
Goal 2: Conserve upland areas			
Objective 2a: Protect uplands and pervious areas	Nominal	Nominal classifications – landscape	Pervious land cover reduces surface runoff. Technical advisors selected the relative suitability of cover types.
Objective 2b: Protect areas with minimal impervious surface	Ratio	Zone statistics – area	Higher water quality occurs in less impervious catchments. Technical advisors selected suitability classes based on scientific literature. Ratio data transformed to interval data classes for GIS modeling.
Objective 2c: Protect uplands with forest cover	Ratio	Zone statistics – area	Higher water quality in more highly forested catchments. Technical advisors selected thresholds based on in-state scientific study. Ratio data transformed to interval data classes for GIS modeling.

(cont.)

Table 6.6 (cont.)

Description	Data Type for Quantifying Benefit	Suitability Type	Criterion
Goal 3: Promote water infiltration and retention			
Objective 3a: Protect wetlands	Nominal	Threshold ranges – distance	Closer to wetlands equal higher value for water quality. Technical advisors identified distance threshold and wetland presence suitability values.
Objective 3b: Promote floodplain protection	Nominal	Nominal classifications – landscape	Undeveloped floodplains can absorb flood waters. Technical advisors identified floodplain suitability values.
Objective 3c: Protect underground recharge areas	Nominal	Nominal classifications – landscape	Infiltrate stormwater into the soil to increase groundwater supply. Technical advisors identified soil recharge suitability values
Goal 4: Avoid development of vulnerable areas			
Objective 4a: Protect wet and hydric areas	Nominal	Nominal classifications – landscape	Hydric soils capture and retain water. Technical advisors used soil survey hydric attribute.
Objective 4b: Protect steep slope areas	Ratio	Threshold ranges – landscape	Steeper slopes are more susceptible to runoff. Technical advisors selected thresholds based on scientific literature. Ratio data transformed to interval data classes for GIS modeling.
Objective 4c: Protect highly erodible soils	Nominal	Nominal classifications – landscape	Protect areas with higher surface runoff potential likely to export more sediment. Technical advisors selected thresholds based on soil survey erodibility attribute.

on the relationship between impervious surfaces, nonpoint-source runoff, and water quality; and updated model objectives and weights provided by the stakeholders. Thus, the new model does a better job of getting the most "bang for the buck" for the initiative's land-acquisition projects.

Once the types of measurements and suitability analyses were selected, staff members assigned suitability values to each spatial data layer associated with the criteria (see Table 6.7). To facilitate scoring later, all of the suitability values in the model ranged from 0 (lowest suitability) to 100 (highest suitability). Thus, this scale can be thought of as percent satisfaction in achieving a particular objective. Each GIS suitability layer had to have at least two values and could have an unlimited number of intermediate values. For example, the measure for objective 1c, protecting riparian areas, used thresholds for the distance to a stream with a distance of less than 300 feet scoring 100 percent, more than 300 feet scoring 0 percent, and 100 to 300 feet scoring 80 percent.

We convened a meeting of 26 stakeholders to provide input and feedback on the model's criteria weightings. There is a variety of established scientific methods for weighting criteria (Hajkowicz et al., 2000; Nutt, 1980). We used a simple "dot map" voting technique by which stakeholders established relative weights for the four watershed protection goals and each set of three related objectives. The results of that process are presented in Table 6.8. Note that the weights had to sum to 100 percent; thus, for the goal of conserving upland areas, for example, the weights assigned to objectives for that goal (32 percent, 32 percent, and 36 percent) sum to 100 percent, as does the weighting of the goals. The weight assigned to each objective in the model was calculated by multiplying the goal's weight by the objective's weight (e.g., 31 percent (0.31) for the goal of conserving upland areas multiplied by 32 percent (0.32) for the objective of protecting uplands and pervious areas = 9.9 percent (0.099).

Once the weighting system described in Table 6.8 was complete, we ran the raster GIS model using the suitability values and weights

Table 6.7 *Sample suitability values from the Upper Neuse watershed protection model*

Description	Suitability Type	Class	Suitability Score (Percentage)
Objective 1c: Protect riparian areas	Threshold range – distance	Less than 100 feet from stream	100
		100–300 feet from stream	80
		More than 300 feet from stream	0
Objective 2a: Protect uplands and pervious areas	Nominal classification – landscape	Forest, wetlands land cover	100
		Grassland, pasture	80
		Row crops, urban grass/pervious surface	50
		Developed	0
Objective 2b: Protect areas with minimal impervious surface	Zone statistic – area	0%–10% impervious surface	100
		11%–25%	70
		26%–60%	30
		61%–100%	0
Objective 3c: Protect underground recharge areas	Nominal classification – landscape	Soil drainage class A (highest infiltration)	100
		Class B (moderate)	80
		Classes B/C, C (low)	50
		Classes C/D, D (lowest)	0
Objective 4b: Protect steep slope areas	Threshold range – landscape	26%–100% slope	100
		13%–25%	50
		0%–12%	0

Table 6.8 *Watershed protection model criteria and weightings*

Goal	Goal Weight	Objective	Objective Weight	Model Weight
(1) Protect water sources and conveyances	29%	1a) Protect headwater streams	37%	10.7%
		1b) Support connected high-quality water features	21%	6.1%
		1c) Protect riparian areas	42%	12.2%
(2) Conserve upland areas	31%	2a) Protect uplands and pervious areas	32%	9.9%
		2b) Protect areas with minimal impervious surface	32%	9.9%
		2c) Protect uplands with forest cover	36%	11.1%
(3) Promote water infiltration and retention	19%	3a) Protect wetlands	36%	6.8%
		3b) Promote floodplain protection	36%	6.8%
		3c) Protect underground recharge areas	28%	5.4%
(4) Avoid development of vulnerable areas	21%	4a) Protect wet and hydric areas	18%	3.8%
		4b) Protect steep slope areas	35%	7.4%
		4c) Protect highly erodible soils	47%	9.9%

for each 30-meter pixel in the watershed to generate 12 GIS layers (one per objective). The model then combined those layers, creating the spatially explicit model (pixels of 30 meters by 30 meters) of each parcel's suitability score shown in Figure 6.1. The scores were generated using "zonal statistics as table" function in ArcGIS to attribute the parcel data layer.

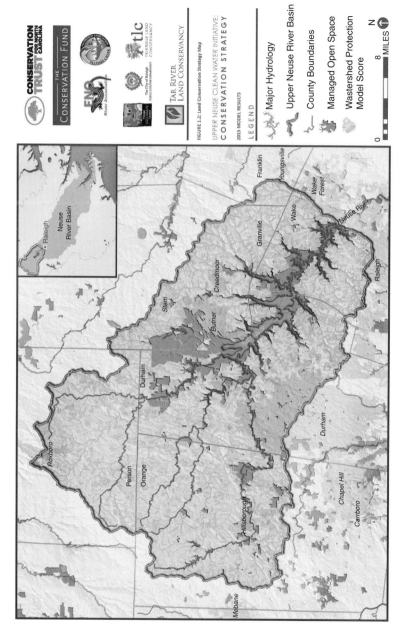

FIGURE 6.1 Upper Neuse Clean Water Initiative.

Agricultural Preservation

Part of protecting more with less is making sure that every dollar spent by an existing public conservation program is spent as effectively as possible. We were asked by Baltimore County's Department of Environmental Protection and Resource Management to build a GIS-based model to improve the effectiveness and efficiency of the department's decisions for the county agricultural preservation program. This work illustrates how strategic conservation can be implemented as part of a traditional conservation program that purchases easements using a combination of local and state funding.

The initial stage of the model-development process involved a variety of tasks designed to build Baltimore County's capacity to quantify the program's resource values, use decision-support tools, and measure the department's progress in achieving its agricultural preservation goals. The department convened a leadership forum addressing agricultural land preservation to obtain input from stakeholders on the criteria and weights that should be incorporated when quantifying the resource value of a potential project and constructing the GIS data layers in the model. This was the first time in the program's history that the contribution of an individual farm to maintaining and enhancing water quality was incorporated into the county's decision-making criteria.

To identify a weighting for each component of the model, we used the analytic hierarchy process, a structured technique for organizing and analyzing complex decisions based on mathematics and psychology (Saaty, 1982) that allows one to establish numerical scores that align with the decision-maker's intent. It is based on pairwise comparisons, which can be completed manually or electronically. Stakeholders compare the value of each criterion to the value of every factor in the decision-making criteria, generating a matrix that reflects the weights of all of the factors (Duke and Hyde, 2002). In a conservation planning process, the stakeholders compare the relative values of GIS layers and data sets for determining the weights used in a particular suitability model. For example, in an analytic hierarchy process exercise, when stakeholders are asked to compare the relative importance of three criteria (i.e., A, B, and C), they compare two at a time: A to B, B to C, and A to C.

In the Baltimore County project, we used a manual approach, creating a written questionnaire that presented the pairwise comparisons for each suitability model (Messer and Allen, 2010). The results from the forum members' questionnaires were tabulated the week following the meeting and entered into Expert Choice, specialized software that automates the weight calculations in the suitability model and ensures that the results from the pairwise comparisons are logically consistent with one another (Expert Choice, 2017). The software also allows for slight modifications to ensure that the consistency ratio falls below an appropriate threshold. The consistency ratio is a measure of ensuring logical relationships among criteria. For instance, if A > B and B > C, then it must be A > C. These final suitability weights were incorporated into raster suitability surface calculations in GIS to complete the analysis. The resulting selection criteria and weightings are presented in Table 6.9.

We also developed an optimization algorithm to increase the cost-effectiveness of the selections made using the suitability scores; it is described in greater detail later in this book. The optimization application used GIS data sets describing the program benefits provided by each applicant's parcel, information from a field survey of program applicants, and information on the cost of acquiring each easement to develop optimal easement-acquisition scenarios under various budgets and other model constraints. This allowed the department to explore project-selection scenarios using various criteria-weighting schemes and minimum acceptable values for a farm's soil quality, physical location, and benefits provided for water quality and other measures associated with the agricultural preservation program.

The weighted models are helpful, but sometimes decision makers want to incorporate criteria that do not fit neatly into numerical scales. You will see later in the book how the LSP method is able

Table 6.9 *Selection criteria used by Baltimore County, Maryland, to preserve agricultural land*

Goal	Goal Weight	Objective	Objective Weight	Model Weight
(1) Protect land most suitable for agricultural production	42.4%	1a) Protect high-quality soils	42.2%	17.9%
		1b) Protect highly erodible soils	7.4%	3.1%
		1c) Protect hydric soils	5.6%	2.4%
		1d) Protect steep slopes	11.2%	4.7%
		1e) Protect large blocks of agricultural land	33.6%	14.2%
(2) Protect farms in strategic locations	36.4%	2a) Close proximity to existing agricultural easements	47.8%	17.4%
		2b) Inside the county-designated Agricultural Preservation Area	26.0%	9.4%
		2c) Inside the State of Maryland's Rural Legacy Area	18.0%	6.6%
		2d) Close proximity to protected conservation and water supply reservoir protected lands	8.2%	3.0%
(3) Protect important nonagricultural environmental characteristics	21.2%	3a) Protect significant ecological resources	52.6%	11.2%
		3b) Protect lands important for water quality	47.4%	10.0%

to incorporate mandatory criteria into decision support models. Two mandatory requirements in Baltimore County's agricultural preservation model eliminated some parcels from consideration in the suitability model: applicant properties had to be designated as rural on the urban growth boundary map, known locally as the Urban-Rural Demarcation Line, and the proposed easement had to extinguish an entitled right to develop the property. The theory behind the policy was that public funds would be allocated most efficiently if used solely to prevent land that was highly suitable for agriculture from being developed. Donations of easements on agricultural lands that lacked additional entitled development rights were still accepted, and owners of those parcels were entitled to any tax rebates provided in the tax code.

Stream Restoration through Social Responsibility

In the United States, spending on capital projects and gray infrastructure is expected to rise to $1 trillion annually by 2025. These investments in pipelines, transmission lines, and clean energy sources provide significant economic benefits to the country but also can have significant negative impacts on the environment and local communities. Infrastructure developers avoid and minimize these impacts to the extent practical and provide compensatory mitigation for unavoidable impacts, but many of the impacts are not addressed by existing regulatory programs. Another avenue by which infrastructure developers can mitigate negative impacts and improve the environment is through corporate social responsibility programs. When providing philanthropic funds, they can address issues that are not directly related to infrastructure. In recent years, companies have been directing such purely voluntary efforts to local and community resource protection and stewardship needs in their project areas.

One such company is Williams, a pioneer in the concept of environmental stewardship as a proactive approach to planning and developing linear infrastructure projects. Williams operates the Transco pipeline, which transports natural gas from production areas to customers such as utility companies and power plants throughout the eastern United States. The pipeline is designed to supply enough natural gas to meet the daily needs of more than 7 million American homes by connecting producing regions in northeastern Pennsylvania to markets in the Mid-Atlantic and southeastern states. When Williams began planning for an expansion of their Atlantic Sunrise pipeline that would add 1.7 million dekatherms per day of capacity (Williams, 2017), proactive demonstration of its commitment to the communities and landscapes affected was a priority (Springer, 2016).

The idea of environmental stewardship by businesses is built on our emerging understanding of green infrastructure and the role it plays in communities. In addition to obvious impacts on landscapes, gray infrastructure projects often have less-visible negative impacts on human and natural environments that are difficult to quantify and are not regulated, such as degrading the aesthetic quality of a landscape and fragmentation of wildlife corridors. As a result, businesses are motivated to be good neighbors, particularly since they will be long-term partners with surrounding landowners in managing their rights of way. Environmental stewardship is way for businesses to keep an informal ledger of environmental and economic impacts and benefits associated with an infrastructure investment. It may never have the precision of "no net loss" incorporated into regulatory systems for wetlands, but the positive impacts of stewardship programs can be quantified and figured into the overall effect of an infrastructure project.

Most of the economic and environmental impacts of Williams's Atlantic Sunrise pipeline expansion affected eight Pennsylvania counties (Columbia, Lancaster, Lebanon, Luzerne, Northumberland, Schuylkill, Susquehanna, and Wyoming) that offer significant natural resources, including a portion of the Appalachian Trail and miles of stream frontage and riparian areas in need of restoration and reductions in nutrient pollution from agricultural runoff. Therefore, Williams was interested in establishing a program of stream restoration and protection. We designed a turnkey environmental stewardship program in which the company would obtain input from local communities and then we would help manage completion of several environmental stewardship projects on their behalf.

The planning process began with Williams identifying important stakeholders in the community and identifying some initial criteria by which to evaluate potential projects, including a desire for selected projects be "shovel ready" and requiring no more than about one year of funding. Williams also preferred projects associated with matching funds from local partners as a demonstration of local support. Using the resulting criteria, we developed a comprehensive set of GIS layers for the project area to ensure that all known natural resources and community assets were mapped and could be used when evaluating potential projects. We also assisted in development of an appropriate budget since environmental stewardship programs were relatively new and there was no established standard. Williams opted for approximately $3 million, which was about 1 percent of the infrastructure budget for the pipeline, a reasonable figure according to our research into comparable programs administered by public agencies.

Success Profile: Chris Springer

Coordinating a collaborative effort of engineers, survey crews, environmental scientists, and construction personnel for energy infrastructure installations is a major challenge. So is making sure that, in the process, natural and cultural resources are protected, unavoidable impacts are minimized, and affected communities are provided with environmental and economic benefits from the projects. Chris Springer, a project director at Williams, one of the largest energy infrastructure companies in the United States, emphasizes the importance of internal and external collaboration when addressing environmental stewardship.

Most of Williams's many infrastructure projects have adequate resources to minimize the impacts of new roads or pipelines, but

Springer recognized that the scale and complexity of the Atlantic Sunrise project in Pennsylvania would require a more powerful planning process. The Atlantic Sunrise Environmental Stewardship Program allowed the company to identify, rank, and select measurable, lasting projects important to wildlife and communities in the project area using LSP and optimization.

The program collaborated proactively with members of local communities affected by the pipeline project to identify opportunities for Williams to enhance the environment voluntarily, extending their contribution well beyond the mitigation that was legally required. Williams spent a year developing and implementing a formal approach to enhanced environmental stewardship and ultimately invested close to $3 million in 18 projects. Collectively, those projects resulted in restoration of 10 miles of stream frontage and 30 acres of riparian areas plus installation of 8 miles of new recreational trails benefiting 200,000 annual users. In addition, the projects stored 925 tons of agricultural manure annually, preventing harmful nutrients from entering waterways.

With the basic parameters in place, Williams convened community focus groups in the project area and asked local stakeholders to identify their priorities for the environmental stewardship program (e.g., aquatic resources, recreation) and the types of project activities that were most valuable to them (e.g., conservation, restoration, creation). More than 100 stakeholders attended the meetings over a one-week period and collectively contributed 539 ideas for environmental stewardship opportunities. Working with Williams over the next month, we distilled those ideas into 265 opportunities that fell into the broad categories of aquatic resource protection and restoration and recreation, were potentially feasible as "shovel ready," and were likely implementable within one year. We then reviewed the stakeholders' reported priorities for resources and project activities and narrowed the list to 60 projects that, as a group, represented a variety of project types, a broad distribution of projects over the affected region, and a manageable number of projects to evaluate within the one-month timeframe.

In establishing the selection process, we developed criteria using a structured decision-making LSP framework that organized the criteria for consistent evaluation. This structure facilitated scoring of the potential benefits from each project on a standardized 100-point scale so the projects could be appropriately and transparently compared. The objectives and respective weightings in the model are shown in Table 6.10. For aquatic restoration projects, the benefit scores were based on stream length and riparian area protected; for nutrient-reduction projects, tons of manure storage per year served as a proxy for quantifying reductions in nitrogen and phosphorus entering nearby streams. Projects related to creating recreational trails were evaluated for miles of trail enhanced, number of potential users, ability to increase access to existing public lands, and whether a new trail filled a key gap in the existing network.

We managed the project-solicitation process, which resulted in 48 proposals requesting a total of $13.6 million with one or more proposals addressing each of the priority project types: aquatic restoration, nutrient reduction, and creation of recreational trails. To select the best possible projects with the budget of approximately $3 million, we entered the information about the submitted projects into two online tools, LSPweb (an earlier version of LSP.NT) and ODST, which applied algorithms to select an optimal portfolio of projects based on the budget. This process ensured that all of the projects were evaluated fairly and that the maximum environmental and community benefits were obtained. The latest generation of these software tools are described in more detail in Chapters 11 and 12.

When the environmental stewardship project was completed, close to $3 million had been invested in stream restoration, nutrient reduction, and recreational trail projects in Pennsylvania communities through local organizations such as Trout Unlimited, the

Table 6.10 *Selection criteria for Williams's environmental stewardship project restoring aquatic resources*

Goal	Objective	Rationale	Model Weight
Select project with high value for aquatic restoration	Maximize stream length, measured in feet	Prefer projects with higher amount of stream length restored	18%
	Maximize riparian area restored, measured in acres	Prefer projects with higher amount of acreage restored, minimum 3 acres	12%
Select projects in strategic locations	Priority watersheds for Williams	Prefer projects in counties with higher number of stream crossings per mile for the proposed pipeline	4%
	Close proximity to existing protected lands	Prefer projects in close proximity to protected areas and easements	3%
	Avoid projects subject to pollution/ land-use change	Prefer projects where there is lower likelihood of impoundment for dams or land-use change through infrastructure and urban development	3%
Preferred site characteristics	Stream segment quality	Prefer projects in stream segments where there is no existing regulatory impairment	9%
	Resource designations	Prefer projects where there are exceptional value designations, such as scenic or fisheries	12%
	Catchment condition	Prefer projects in watersheds with better conditions based on slope, soils, percent forest, and percent impervious	9%

(*cont.*)

Table 6.10 *(cont.)*

Goal	Objective	Rationale	Model Weight
Stewardship focus area	Williams priority county	Prefer projects in counties with higher community impacts from the proposed pipeline	4%
	Long-term management plan	Prefer projects with high-quality management and monitoring plans	4%
	Adopted plan priority	Prefer projects identified in adopted state and local conservation and restoration plans	6%
	Funding leverage	Prefer projects with a high financing leverage from other funding sources, a sign of higher public support	6%
Green infrastructure network	Core areas GI Network	Prefer location with the interconnected green infrastructure network identified for Pennsylvania	7%
	GI network within 1 mile	Prefer higher amounts of green infrastructure within 1 mile of the project area	3%

Millcreek Preservation Association, the Wyoming County Conservation District, and the Rail-Trail Council of Northeastern Pennsylvania. Overall, 18 projects were funded: 9 for aquatic restoration, 6 for nutrient reduction, and 3 for recreational trails. The aquatic restoration projects resulted in over 10 miles of stream frontage restored and 30 acres of riparian area restored. Eight miles of new trails were installed that benefit annually over 200,000 trail users. The nutrient-reduction projects in Wyoming County resulted in 925 tons of manure stored annually that no longer enter the streams. In 2017, Williams received the Southern Gas Association's Environmental Excellence Award for its Atlantic Sunrise Environmental Stewardship Program.

Multiple Forest Benefits

This last case study in defining benefit criteria involves our work with Mid America Regional Council (MARC) to develop regional forest conservation and restoration models for its nine-county planning area, which covered five counties (Cass, Clay, Jackson, Ray, and Platte) in Missouri, and four counties (Johnson, Leavenworth, Miami, and Wyandotte) in Kansas. MARC is the Metropolitan Planning Organization for the Kansas City region, so it oversees investments in transportation infrastructure. MARC was interested in forest conservation and restoration opportunities in order to avoid and minimize potential impacts to forested lands and in order to identify strategic mitigation opportunities when impacts were unavoidable. To identify potential projects, we established a raster GIS suitability model for with the same resolution as existing regional land cover maps (2.5 meters). The resulting map provided a spatially explicit framework for MARC and other partner organizations to use to implement conservation and restoration projects and identify mitigation and environmental stewardship opportunities.

The criteria and weights were established in response to input provided by four webinar-based meetings with an ad hoc project-steering committee and an in-person, half-day staff workshop. Once the criteria were established, we organized them into two suitability models, one for restoration and one for conservation, as shown in the partial list presented in Table 6.11.

Both suitability models used a benefit-driven approach to identify a potential project's suitability. Each model used four primary benefit categories: clean water (quality and quantity), clean air (carbon storage, pollution), quality of life (recreation, protected lands), and

Table 6.11 *Forest conservation and restoration criteria for the Mid-America Regional Council*

Goal/Objective	Conservation Weight	Restoration Weight	Conservation and Restoration Notes
Water quality/ water purification service	22	15	Protecting existing forest cover is an effective method to maintain high water quality
Water quality/ floodplain location	16	23	Restoring undeveloped land to forest is an effective method to enhance water quality
Water quantity/ hydric soils	20	20	The ability of hydric soils to store water does not change based on the desired conservation objective
Clean air benefit/ carbon storage service	37	21	Protecting existing forest cover is an effective method at storing more carbon in trees
Wildlife benefit/ proximity to forest patches	23	37	Most suitable to implement reforestation adjacent to existing forest patches
Wildlife benefit/ forest patch size	32	24	More effective strategy to maintain large blocks of existing forest and avoid fragmentation

Note: The model weightings in the table do not add up to 100 since this is only a sampling of the criteria in the model and the values correspond to a specific subset of benefits.

wildlife habitat (green infrastructure network). The attributes considered in the trees were the same but we adjusted some of the weightings and elementary criteria ranges to suit each type of activity. And in a couple of situations, the suitability values were reversed – for instance, high suitability for conservation was treated as low suitability for restoration. The table highlights some distinctions in weightings for the conservation and restoration models and why it is important to clearly communicate your exact goals to stakeholders.

In the selection process, GIS-based models analyzed the mean, median, and mode for each weight, and a final weight was selected based on expert judgment. In most cases, we selected the mean; in a few, we selected the mode based on the statistical distribution of the values. The maps and associated GIS layers and models were developed using Esri's ArcGIS geoprocessing framework so they could be updated over time (Esri, 2017).

This section has illustrated how water quality, agricultural preservation, stream restoration, and forest conservation and restoration can be incorporated into multicriteria decision analysis to support strategic conservation. There are many other strategic conservation objectives that can be achieved using the same methods as long as there is available data to support identifying the important resources.

MOVING TO THE SELECTION PROCESS

Our goal in this chapter has been to provide you with a variety of examples of on-the-ground projects illustrating how to effectively develop, organize, and prioritize the criteria by which you and your organization can evaluate projects for strategic conservation using GIS layers to inform your choices, input from stakeholders and other concerned parties about the types of projects and activities they value, and methods for converting diverse measures into a single scale. In the next chapter, we take up the selection process and the benefits of using optimization algorithms to select the best possible suite of projects and get the most bang for the buck.

7 Enhancing the Evaluation of Choices

Suitability analysis and multicriteria decision analysis are essential building blocks to help protect more with less. But to use them effectively, a structured decision-making process is needed for identifying the best criteria and models to use – one that accounts for both the intricacies of how humans make decisions and the limitations of our brains in evaluating multiple criteria. This idea is an important seventh core principle of strategic conservation – *take advantage of the idiosyncrasies of human decision-making*. In the realms of science and economics, human idiosyncrasies are often seen as something to weed out of the process. However, by emulating the natural, intuitive way in which people make decisions in actual situations, we can create more effective criteria and models. Models that "think" like the stakeholders can successfully achieve the stakeholders' goals in a complex environmental program in which numerous factors contribute to the "quality" of a proposed project or parcel.

Structured decision-making has been applied to many complex environmental management problems. It is not so much a technique as a collection of methods and a way of thinking – an approach to organizing a complex, multifaceted problem to reach decisions that are clearly focused on achieving the stated goals. The concept combines cognitive psychology with analytical methods drawn from decision sciences (US Fish and Wildlife Service, 2008) to achieve a primary aim: engage stakeholders, experts, and decision-makers in a process that capably handles complexity, uncertainty, and trade-offs and thus provides a rigorous, inclusive, defensible, and transparent process (Gregory et al., 2012). So the first step is to assemble a decision-support team consisting of (1) stakeholders who are focused on the end results, (2) analysts who convert the stakeholders' goals into decision-support models, and (3) experts in the various domains associated with planning and completing the project (such as landscape ecologists, conservation biologists, environmental planners, and geospatial analysts) who are tasked with verifying that the proposed criteria and models address the stakeholders' expressed goals.

HUMANS USE SOFT COMPUTING AND FUZZY LOGIC

In the preceding chapters, we discussed simple weighted-sum models that relied on "hard computing" and oversimplified the way humans make decisions. Hard computing requires a discrete solution for every computational problem and offers no way to address uncertainty, imprecision, or approximation. If you use hard computing to sink a putt in golf, for example, you have to map the topography of the ground between the ball and the hole, definitively measure the amount of force needed to propel the ball just to the hole and no further, and identify the speed and direction of the wind so you can predict how it will affect the ball's movement. It would be a pretty slow game!

Instead, golfers use "soft computing" because they have incomplete information about the various conditions that affect the putt. For instance, they may have played this hole before so have a general idea of the topography of the ground or are looking it over for the first time to see how much it slopes and whether the surface is smooth or breaks. Wind is considered only insofar as it is generally calm, gusty, or gale force. As a golfer thinks about the best approach, she is keeping four or five fuzzily measured factors in mind and relies on her experience, observations, and estimates to determine where and how to strike the ball with the club in those circumstances. That is, she is using soft computing and "fuzzy logic." Expand this case to an environmental conservation project and the degree of complexity and incomplete information increases dramatically, but the concepts are the same.

The complicated logical relationships that underpin humans' decision-making processes cannot be adequately represented by simple models, and the discrete solutions required by hard computing can make it a poor choice for measuring the overall "quality" of

Table 7.1 *Criteria summary for strategic conservation projects*

Project Name	# Criteria	# Categories to Evaluate	Maximum Criteria per Category
Missouri Department of Conservation	10	3	4
Upper Neuse Watershed Protection Model	12	4	3
Baltimore County Agricultural Preservation	11	3	5
Williams Atlantic Sunrise Environmental Stewardship	14	5	4
Mid-America Regional Council	19	5	5

something. Consequently, our ability to use soft computing and fuzzy logic is an advantage in decision-making. It allows us to make effective decisions despite having imprecise and incomplete information.

The disadvantage of human decision-making is the limited number of criteria our brains are capable of considering simultaneously. Cognitive psychologist George Miller (1956) demonstrated that, on average, we can hold only about seven considerations in working memory at one time (seven plus or minus two). As shown by the projects we have discussed in previous chapters (summarized in Table 7.1), most conservation projects involve considerably more than seven criteria and the relationships between those criteria are complex.

One way to compensate for this limitation is by organizing a large number of criteria into logical categories containing no more than five criteria each. Breaking the task down in this way makes it relatively easy to prioritize the criteria in each category and assign meaningfully different scores to each criterion to sum to 100 for the category. It also makes it easier for stakeholders to determine whether the criteria and any weightings associated with them are valid, ensuring that the stakeholders will be comfortable implementing recommendations made based on the models.

DEGREES OF SATISFACTION AND SUITABILITY

In soft computing, objects (such as parcels proposed for conservation) are assessed for the *degree* to which they satisfy various criteria. As a simple example of soft computing and fuzzy logic, consider a common attribute: the temperature in whatever space you are currently occupying. Is it cold, cool, neutral, warm, or hot? You instinctively and subjectively assign those qualitative descriptions to various ranges of degrees Fahrenheit (or Celsius) that you could choose to define numerically in a formal analysis. An example of the value of soft computing in terms of conservation is soil mapping. Soil survey maps typically show hard boundaries between various types of soil when, in fact, soil exists as gradations in which most of the characteristics of the soils are the same and two adjacent soils vary primarily in the degree to which the characteristics are present. Thus, when making soil conservation selections, a detailed map of erodibility values may be less useful to you than a map of general regions of qualitative categories: highly erodible, moderately erodible, and mildly erodible.

Fuzzy logic systems similarly work on the concept of degrees of membership in a set. In fuzzy logic, truth values range from completely true to completely false, and a value that is partially true is interpreted as fuzzy membership in the set (Klir and Yuan, 1996). Consider a set of "tall" people; in that case, the degree of membership of a professional basketball center might be 100 percent and everyone shorter than him would have some lesser degree of membership. In the context of conservation, a conservation suitability analysis uses LSP to compute the overall suitability score for each proposed project, which represents the degree of truth of a statement asserting that the project fully satisfies the stakeholders' requirements – in other words, the degree to which it is a member of a fuzzy set of ideal/perfect choices.

The term fuzzy logic was coined by Lofti Zadeh (1965), and the concept has been applied in countless fields, including electronics and artificial intelligence. As demonstrated in the golf analogy, we use fuzzy logic all the time in our everyday lives. Standard logic requires a Boolean answer – yes or no – but few situations involve exact or complete knowledge about the variables that affect the decision.

Success Profile: Jozo J. Dujmović

Humans instinctively rate and compare new things we come across so we can put them in a frame of reference we can easily understand. We rate other people, houses, food, and even the weather. Jozo Dujmović (Figure 7.1), a professor of computer science at San Francisco State University, founded System Evaluation and Selection (SEAS) in 1997 to expand the use of LSP software solutions when making complicated decisions. Prior to coming to the United States, Dujmović applied the LSP method to evaluate and select among 25 mainframe computer systems, saving the purchaser millions of dollars while ensuring that computing requirements were met. SEAS's advanced decision logic system allows for rapid and reliable evaluation and selection processes that save money for companies by negotiating the best possible prices for goods and services.

Jozo has enjoyed applying the LSP method to conservation: "Land conservation processes generate a variety of complex evaluation decision problems. For example, evaluation and selection of the best habitat locations for endangered species is a major component of mitigation projects. In Canada, we used LSP for evaluation of land suitability for agriculture and for suitability maps in geography. A recent LSP project was done by a group in Spain for the analysis of nitrate contamination of groundwater." Regardless of the application, "whoever develops or uses LSP evaluation methods must never forget

FIGURE 7.1 Jozo J. Dujmović.

that decisions are human mental activities. Consequently, trustworthy decision models cannot be developed without relating them explicitly to observable patterns of human decision making."

LOGIC SCORING OF PREFERENCE

The LSP method was pioneered by Jozo Dujmović and was designed with observable properties of human reasoning in mind. As noted in Hatch et al. (2014, p. 65), LSP is

> [A] method for analyzing complex trade-offs between choice alternatives based on precise modeling of human evaluation reasoning... LSP criterion functions can use any number of input attributes and generate an overall suitability score which is defined as a degree of truth of the statement that all requirements are perfectly satisfied. The structure of each... function is based on a set of attributes, the corresponding attribute criteria, and a soft computing logic aggregation of attribute suitability scores.

This proprietary methodology was originally developed for evaluating the complex requirements of computer mainframe systems but has since been expanded to numerous biological and environmental applications. Our recent review of the literature identified more than 60 publications describing use of LSP for selecting everything from software components to conservation priorities and agricultural land uses, and we and others have developed specialized tools using it as a platform. In some cases, LSP was used to effectively compare proposed projects using hundreds of criteria. The LSP method illustrates well our sixth principle of strategic conservation: Embrace complexity but strive for simplicity.

The selection models described earlier, which used simple weighted sums to calculate suitability values, have been popular because they are easy to implement in GIS software and allow for each suitability value to be calculated independently. LSP also can be incorporated directly into GIS models but has the advantage of using soft computing functions that include all of the necessary logic relationships between the attributes to create suitability surfaces (Dujmović et al., 2010; Dujmović and Scheer, 2010). The tools provided with the LSP software allow you to develop and edit the criteria, combine multiple evaluation projects, evaluate and compare your choices, produce documentation, perform sensitivity analyses and optimization, and reliably analyze the results. Chapter 12 provides an opportunity to explore LSP software tools, and Appendix A provides an overview of the mathematical foundations of the LSP method.

STRUCTURED DECISION-MAKING USING ATTRIBUTE TREES

We use LSP in strategic conservation to apply soft computing and fuzzy logic to a set of criteria that is too large for our brains to process effectively. It uses the same basic structure for criteria and weightings as simpler suitability analyses but provides a more robust logic structure. Another advantage is that the evaluation process is performed in small steps that evaluators can easily understand and control. This "decomposition" process systematically organizes large numbers of attributes and their associated criteria into a hierarchical "tree." Tables 7.2, 7.3, and 7.4 present *attribute trees* for several of the projects discussed in previous chapters. Briefly, the steps involved in constructing the attribute tree are:

- Collaborate with stakeholders to identify all of the qualitative *attributes* that must be accomplished or acquired to achieve the program's goals and expressly state the justification for their inclusion.
- For each attribute, identify a numerically measurable *elementary criterion* that can be used to determine the degree to which a project satisfies a required attribute.
- Identify a *numerical scale* that can be applied to all of the measurable criteria to provide valid same-unit comparisons.
- Establish the *logical relationships* between criteria in terms of whether and how they can be met – mandatory versus desirable, substitutability.

In this strategic decision-making process, you first need to identify the goals that you want your suitability analysis to achieve. Table 7.2 illustrates the Missouri Department of Conservation's

Table 7.2 *Missouri Department of*
Conservation attribute tree for land-
acquisition priorities with logic neutrality

11 High Conservation Value
    111 MDC property portfolio value
    112 Species composition
    113 Natural heritage occurrences
    114 Functional connectivity
12 Protection in Perpetuity
    121 Land conversion probability
    122 Public use activities
    123 Adaptive management and restoration
13 Agency Land Management
    131 MDC Conservation Opportunity Area
    132 Management efficiency
    133 Accessibility

interests in acquiring land with a high conservation value that can be protected in perpetuity and be managed efficiently by department staff. Table 7.3 illustrates the same criteria as Table 7.2, but it has been restructured using the LSP method by organizing criteria by mandatory requirements and desired characteristics. The suitability scores for projects will be different for each attribute tree based on their different logic structures. Table 7.4 provides another example of mandatory requirements where the project will be considered unsuitable if it does not meet the mandatory criteria, regardless of how many desired characteristics it has.

After identifying goals, you then identify all of the *attributes* that must be considered to determine whether a submitted project is suitable (e.g., the size of the parcel, the diversity of species occupying the parcel, and the risk of the parcel being developed) and a *criterion* for each attribute (e.g., the number of acres, the number of species present in an area, and a rating of the development risk) that allows you to measure numerically the degree to which the project is suitable. As previously noted, it is important to establish the rationale

Table 7.3 *Missouri Department of Conservation attribute tree for land-acquisition priorities with mandatory/desired logic structure*

11 Mandatory Requirements
    111 MDC property portfolio value
    122 Public use activities
    133 Accessibility
12 Desired Characteristics
    121 Ecological Value
        1211 Species composition
        1212 Natural heritage occurrences
        1213 Functional connectivity
    122 Land Management
        1221 Land conversion probability
        1222 Adaptive management and restoration
        1223 MDC Conservation Opportunity Area
        1224 Management efficiency

Table 7.4 *NiSource Take Species attribute tree*

11 Habitat Mitigation Needs
    111 Mandatory requirements
        1111 Mitigation units
        1112 Site assessment
        1113 Physical conditions
        1114 Species occurrence
        1115 Project location
    112 Desired characteristics
        1121 Protection in perpetuity
        1122 Listed species protection
            11221 NiSource HCP take species
            11222 Federal & state listed species
12 Strategic Conservation Goals
    121 Green infrastructure network
    122 Adopted plans and leverage
        1221 State Wildlife Action Plans
        1222 Other adopted state/federal/local conservation plans

for including each attribute (see the sample rationales provided in the tables in Chapter 6).

You likely will need to identify basic categories of nonredundant attributes that represent at least two and no more than five attributes. These categories can relate to various conservation projects or can differentiate mandatory and desirable attributes. In Table 7.2 (a simple case of logic neutrality), those categories are high conservation value, protection in perpetuity, and agency land management. This first level of "branches" in the tree, therefore, consists of attributes and/or categories of attributes.

The attribute trees in the tables demonstrate various ways that the logic relationships and weighting and penalty/reward systems can be used. Table 7.4 demonstrates how an attribute tree can incorporate multiple logic structures. The model used for NiSource included a penalty for a low suitability value and a reward for a high suitability value for desired characteristics (you will get to see how this works when you do the LSP.NT™ exercises). It considered the habitat mitigation and strategic conservation goals simultaneously but the mandatory attributes under habitat mitigation first eliminated any project that failed to provide those benefits.

The Mid America Regional Council forest prioritization attribute tree shown in Table 7.5 illustrates a multiple-benefit approach in which the overall suitability score was highest when all four of the goals were satisfied simultaneously. Weights were used to differentiate the relative value of each benefit based on the region's stakeholder preferences. The criteria used for the Greater Baltimore Wilderness Coalition shown in Table 7.6 provides one or more mandatory attributes and one or more desirable attributes weighted with a penalty/reward system for each category.

After identifying the primary attributes required for the project and the evaluation criteria, the next step in the process is to assign values that represent the "least suitable" (i.e., 0 percent) and "most suitable" (i.e., 100 percent) conditions for each attribute. Once those values have been established, you can create breakpoints or interpolation functions (see Table 6.7 for an example of breakpoints) to establish partial degrees of satisfaction.

Table 7.5 *Mid-America Regional Council forest prioritization attribute tree*

11 Clean Water Benefits
  111 Water quality
      1111 Water purification ecosystem service
      1112 Erosion control ecosystem service
      1113 Steepness of slope
      1114 Proximity to drainage network
      1115 Floodplain location
  112 Water Quantity
      1121 Water flow regulation ecosystem service
      1122 Water retention/hydric soils
      1123 Groundwater recharge ecosystem service
      1124 Groundwater transmission rate
12 Clean Air Benefits
  121 Air quality enhancement
  122 Climate mitigation
      1221 Carbon storage service
      1222 Microclimate regulation ecosystem service
      1223 Proximity to impervious surface
13 Quality of Life Benefits
  131 Proximity to existing bikeway/trail corridors
  132 Proximity to existing protected lands
14 Wildlife Benefits
  141 Forest patch size
  142 Forest interior habitat
  143 Proximity to existing forest patches
  144 Forest patch percentage by watershed

In conservation and other contexts, it is common to have some mandatory and some desirable but not mandatory attributes. Those logic aggregators can be used to organize the attribute tree. The trees in Tables 7.3 and 7.4 have been categorized according to whether the attributes are mandatory or desirable. The mandatory attributes would be considered first and any project that failed to meet a mandatory requirement would be dropped from consideration.

Table 7.6 *Baltimore Wilderness resiliency goals with LSP logic aggregations*

Resiliency Goal	Goal Description	Mandatory Criteria	Reward/Penalty Criteria
Natural resource protection	Preserve, restore, or enhance valuable and vulnerable land and water resources providing hazard mitigation and other cobenefits; specific types include floodplains, wetlands, forests, stream systems, steep slopes, hydric and highly erodible soils, and important habitat areas	Not developed (pervious surface) Not already protected (with fee simple or easement restrictions)	Prefer areas of overlap between regional and statewide green infrastructure networks Prefer areas of overlap between local/county scale resource priorities and regional/state green infrastructure
Tree canopy enhancement and restoration	Maintain, enhance, and restore tree canopy in urban and suburban communities to reduce stormwater runoff, ameliorate the urban heat island effect, and improve air quality	Areas not currently classified as tree canopy Focus restoration work in areas below tree canopy targets Focus maintenance/enhancement in areas above tree canopy targets	Prefer urban grass land cover (easiest/most feasible areas for reclamation) Prefer already protected – fee simple or easement restrictions or in public right-of-way (easiest/most feasible for implementation)

(cont.)

Table 7.6 (cont.)

Resiliency Goal	Goal Description	Mandatory Criteria	Reward/Penalty Criteria
Multibenefit green stormwater infrastructure	Retrofit developed areas to reduce impervious surface and incorporate best management practices such as bioretention areas, green streets, and green roofs in order to restore water infiltration and storage and reduce vulnerability to flooding and associated pollution	Available menu of best management practices: bioretention, constructed wetland, dry pond, grassed swale, infiltration basin, infiltration trench, porous pavement, sand filter (both surface and nonsurface), vegetated filter strip, wet pond	Areas with high percentage imperviousness and no installed best management practices rank highest Prefer already protected – fee simple or easement restrictions or in public right-of-way or other public ownership (easiest/most feasible for implementation)
Critical infrastructure protection	Use green infrastructure to reduce extreme weather risks to critical infrastructure, including key transportation corridors, power production and transmission facilities, hospitals, and emergency management centers, water supply reservoirs, and wastewater-treatment facilities	Area within storm-surge/sea-level-rise influence area Area within 100/500 year floodplains Areas within USGS modeled flood areas	Prefer areas adjacent to existing green infrastructure
Coastal defense	Preserve, restore, or enhance natural habitat and introduce nature-based practices (e.g., living shorelines) to buffer from impacts of coastal flooding, storm surge, and sea level rise	Area within storm-surge/sea-level-rise influence area	For restoration priorities, prefer areas where forest, marsh, or other natural ecosystems are not currently present Prefer areas adjacent to existing green infrastructure

Table 7.7 presents a fully completed set of evaluation criteria for an attribute tree that includes the criterion values and breakpoints. Once the attribute tree, such as Table 7.7, is completed, the next step is to compare the characteristics of the proposed projects to the criteria and assign suitability scores to the project for each attribute. For the parcel size attribute, for example, the criterion could be a 5.0-acre minimum; projects smaller than that requirement would be given a suitability score of 0 percent regardless of the value of the desired characteristics and parcels equal to or greater than that requirement would be given a suitability score of 100 percent. The resulting data set represents the degree to which the projects meet each individual requirement.

ESTABLISHING WEIGHTING SYSTEMS AND LOGIC RELATIONSHIPS

Before proceeding with the analysis, you must establish (1) any relative weights you want to assign to prioritize some attributes over others and (2) rule-based, mathematical logic relationships between the attributes that will be used in the model to compare the proposed projects. Weights and rewards (penalties) are typically percentages added (subtracted) to increase (decrease) the suitability score for particular attributes. For instance, you can provide a 20 percent reward for a high suitability value and a 15 percent penalty for a low suitability value.

The logic relationships refer to how multiple criteria must be satisfied. Mandatory attributes must be satisfied, a condition known as *simultaneity*. If a project fails to provide any of the mandatory attributes, its overall suitability score is 0 percent and it is rejected as an option. In *substitutability* logic relationships, satisfaction of one desirable (but not mandatory) attribute (e.g., proximity to a water source) can make up for lack of satisfaction of another desirable attribute (e.g., presence of forest cover) and a penalty/reward system can adjust the scores to control how the substitutions occur. Standard weighted-sum models use *logic neutrality* and provide a good balance between simultaneity and substitutability.

Table 7.7 *Elementary attribute criteria for the Indiana bat summer habitat protection criterion*

111		Maternity colony location
Value	%	Evaluated parcel is expected to be close to the maternity
0	100	colony location (inside the circle with the radius of 2.5
2.5	0	miles). Evaluation is based on the distance measured in
		miles (a distance of 2.5 miles or more is not acceptable).
1121		**Parcel size**
Value	%	The size of evaluated parcel is measured in acres. Parcels
5	0	of five acres or less are considered unacceptable. Parcels
20	60	of 46 acres (or more) are considered completely
46	100	satisfactory.
1122		**Parcel shape**
Value	%	The parcel shape can be contiguous (what is the most
1	100	desirable) or fragmented (what is less desirable).
2	80	Evaluation is based on the number of distinct fragments.
3	50	The maximum number of fragments that can be
9	0	tolerated is 8.
113		**Forest cover**
Value	%	Evaluation is based on percentage of the 2.5-mile
19	0	maternity colony circle that is forest land cover. Perfect
20	10	satisfaction is achieved if the forest covers 80% of the
30	40	evaluated area.
80	100	
1211		**Proximity to perennial water source**
Value	%	Availability of a perennial water source (river, lake, or
0	100	other) is important characteristic of the analyzed parcel
2	0	location. Evaluated as a distance from the parcel to the
		closest water source, and measured in miles.
1212		**Connected forest**
Value	%	Percentage of the 2.5 miles circle around the maternity
0	0	colony location that includes the following:
100	100	– Green infrastructure core forest
		– Green infrastructure forest corridors

Table 7.7 (cont.)

1221		**Risk of forest conversion**
Value	%	Risk of forest conversion (e.g., conversion to agricultural
1	100	land) is evaluated according the following risk rating scale:
5	0	1 = None; 2 = Low; 3 = Medium; 4 = High; 5 = Very high
1222		**Risk of hydrologic alteration**
Value	%	Risk of hydrologic alteration (e.g., draining of wetland) is
1	100	evaluated according the following risk rating scale:
5	0	1 = None; 2 = Low; 3 = Medium; 4 = High; 5 = Very high

USING THE LSP MODEL TO DETERMINE OVERALL PROJECT SUITABILITY AND COST-EFFECTIVENESS

Using the logic relationships and weighting schemes you establish, the LSP model simultaneously considers all of the individual suitability scores. The end result is an aggregate *project suitability score* on a scale of 0 to 100 that takes all of the mandatory requirements and trade-offs into account. And in the final phase of the analysis, the LSP model simultaneously considers the *project suitability scores* and the *cost of each project* to identify the most cost-effective conservation projects.

Here, we have provided an overview of selection using LSP in a conservation context. Appendix A describes the mathematical foundations of the LSP method using an example involving a purchase of an automobile, and Chapter 12 provides hands-on exercises for exploring the online LSP.NT platform. For information on the detailed mathematics of the LSP methodology, see Dujmović (2007, 2018), Dujmović and Nagashima (2006), and Dujmović and Larsen (2007).

THEORY INTO PRACTICE: CASE STUDY OF A PROGRAM TO PROTECT INDIANA BAT HABITAT

To transition from theory to practice, we next describe the complete process involved in developing and using structured decision-making and LSP in a simplified version of an existing program designed to protect summer habitat in the United States for the Indiana bat (*myotis sodalis*), an endangered species. We developed the necessary LSP criteria using the software tool LSP.NT.

Protection of the bats' habitat was a goal of both the NiSource Habitat Conservation Plan (HCP) discussed in Chapter 5 (Allen et al., 2011) and an HCP being developed for the wind energy industry in the Midwest (US Fish and Wildlife Service, 2017). Therefore, the attribute tree (Table 7.7) had to incorporate the regulatory requirements from the HCPs to ensure that projects selected would comply as well. In this case study, we have incorporated specific mitigation requirements recently outlined by the US Fish and Wildlife Service.

The mitigation requirements for Indiana bat involved habitat for roosting and foraging and intact forests that provided functional corridors between those habitats, and any land acquired from private owners for mitigation had to be protected in perpetuity through either fee purchases or permanent conservation easements. Scientific studies indicated that a minimum of 46 acres had to be protected and/or restored per maternal colony for each site to support one female bat. This area estimate is based on the known average home range of female Indiana bats around a roost tree (US Fish and Wildlife Service, 2014). Additional requirements were that proposed mitigation projects had to be located within a 2.5-mile-radius circle around the estimated center of a known maternity colony (roost trees in which the female bats raised their young) and the circle also had to (1) contain known occupied habitat, (2) serve as a known corridor that sustained the bats' movement to various patches of occupied foraging habitat, or (3) connect to an occupied portion of a maternity colony to provide a new corridor. Those and other requirements are presented in the criteria shown in Table 7.7.

Constructing the Attribute Tree, Criteria, and Suitability Values

Suppose that five parcels have been submitted for consideration as protected summer bat habitat and our problem is to evaluate the parcels and identify the most suitable one based on the attributes

Table 7.8 *Attribute tree showing mandatory*
and nonmandatory characteristics

1 **Indiana bat summer habitat protection**
11 **Mandatory characteristics**
111 Maternity colony location
112 Parcel size and shape
1121 Parcel size
1122 Parcel shape
113 Forest cover
12 **Desired (nonmandatory) characteristics**
121 Green infrastructure network
1211 Proximity to perennial water source
1212 Connected forest/green areas
122 Human disturbance level
1221 Risk of forest conversion
1222 Risk of hydrologic alteration

each parcel provides and the cost to acquire it. The first step is to construct an attribute tree. The core structure of the tree is presented in Table 7.8. Note that the two major categories in this case are the mandatory requirements established by the HCPs and other desirable attributes.

Table 7.9 isolates the eight attributes under consideration: location of maternity colonies, parcel size, parcel shape, forest cover, proximity to a perennial water source, connection to forests or other green areas, risk of conversion of forest to agriculture, and risk of draining of wetlands (hydrologic alteration). The first four are mandated by the HCPs and must be satisfied. Any parcel that fails to satisfy any one of those attributes will be rejected. The other four attributes are desirable but not mandatory. If a parcel fails to satisfy one or more of those attributes, it would not necessarily be rejected. However, penalties might be applied in calculating the suitability score. The stakeholders ultimately determine which attributes are mandatory and which are optional, and their decisions affect the aggregation structure in the LSP model.

Table 7.9 *List of input attributes:*
Four mandatory and four
nonmandatory attributes

1. Maternity colony location
2. Parcel size
3. Parcel shape
4. Forest cover
5. Proximity to perennial water source
6. Connected forest/green areas
7. Risk of forest conversion
8. Risk of hydrologic alteration

The second step involves analyzing the role of each attribute (with the assistance of experts in those domains) and defining corresponding criteria that will be used to measure potential parcels' suitability. Table 7.7 presents the criteria for the completed tree, which describes the eight attributes in the case study, the criterion associated with each attribute and the unit of measure used, and the suitability values and breakpoints that will determine the suitability scores.

Consider attribute 111 (Maternity Colony Location) in Table 7.7, which specifies that an ideal parcel is adjacent to the location of a maternity colony. Desirable parcels can be somewhat separated from the maternity colony (less than 2.5 miles based on scientific observations of Indiana bats). Therefore, adjacent parcels (distance of 0) are assigned the maximum value of 100 percent and parcels 2.5 or more miles away are assigned the minimum value of 0 percent. In this case, we specify only the minimum and maximum values and use linear interpolation for distances in between (80 percent for 0.5 miles, 60 percent for 1.0 miles, 40 percent for 1.5 miles, and 20 percent for 2.0 miles). Using this criterion, we can easily answer a variety of related questions. For example, we may be interested in the range of distance that will satisfy more than 50 percent of our requirements. Using the interpolation, we determine that all parcels located within a 1.25-mile radius are at least 50 percent suitable.

Most of the criteria (111 through 1212) evaluate measurable quantities, and we have assigned suitability scores to each breakpoint using linear interpolation. Attribute 1221 (risk of conversion of forests) and attribute 1222 (alteration of hydrology), on the other hand, require some additional steps to compute. In such cases, we use rating scales and adjust the number of levels based on the level of precision expected. For Indiana bat habitat, we use five nominal degrees of risk: 1 for none or negligible, 2 for low, 3 for medium, 4 for high, and 5 for very high. To assign the ratings, experts in those fields work with the stakeholders to investigate the amount of risk associated with each parcel. Once the experts have rated each parcel, the ratings are mapped to the suitability score. A parcel rated as having a low risk of conversion might be assigned an attribute suitability score of 75 percent.

Assigning Attribute Suitability Scores

The third step in the process is to assign the attribute suitability scores for the parcels under consideration. The five parcels in this case study are designated P1, P2, P3, P4, and P5. Table 7.10 presents the cost of each parcel and the results of the numerical evaluation process that determined each parcel's contribution to the eight attributes. P1, for example, is located within a 1-mile radius of a maternity colony, consists of 41 acres divided into two fragments, has 79 percent forest cover, is 1.5 miles from a perennial water source, is 70 percent green infrastructure, and is at low risk of conversion to agriculture and draining of wetlands.

Tables 7.11 and 7.12 depict the attribute suitability scores (as percent satisfaction) based on each parcel's characteristics. These tables allow us, to the extent possible, to visually compare the parcels' individual strengths and weaknesses. Table 7.13 provides a side-by-side comparison of the numerical evaluation and conversion of those values into suitability scores for P1-P5.

Table 7.10 *Raw scores for criteria of five competitive parcels*

ID	Attribute	Parcel 1	Parcel 2	Parcel 3	Parcel 4	Parcel 5
	Cost	100	93	122	90	84
111	Maternity colony location	1	0.4	0.58	0.55	0.2
1121	Parcel size	41	35	45	44	33
1122	Parcel shape	2	1	9	2	2
113	Forest cover	79	72	35	91	28
1211	Proximity to perennial water source	1.5	0.3	0.2	0.6	0.7
1212	Connected forest/ green areas	70	68	25	85	18
1221	Risk of forest conversion	2	1	4	3	2
1222	Risk of hydrologic alteration	2	1	3	1	1

Table 7.11 *Suitability values for criteria of five competitive parcels*

ID	Attribute	Parcel 1	Parcel 2	Parcel 3	Parcel 4	Parcel 5
111	Maternity colony location	60.00	84.00	76.80	78.00	92.00
1121	Parcel size	92.31	83.08	98.46	96.92	80.00
1122	Parcel shape	80.00	100.00	0.00	80.00	80.00
113	Forest cover	98.80	90.40	46.00	100.00	34.00
1211	Proximity to perennial water source	25.00	85.00	90.00	70.00	65.00
1212	Connected forest/ green areas	70.00	68.00	25.00	85.00	18.00
1221	Risk of forest conversion	75.00	100.00	25.00	50.00	75.00
1222	Risk of hydrologic alteration	75.00	100.00	50.00	100.00	100.00

Table 7.12 *Sample evaluation of individual parcel evaluation results*

System: Parcel 1 Cost: 100   Overall score: 64.08%

ID	Attribute	Value	Score [%]
111	Maternity colony location	1	60.00
1121	Parcel size	41	92.31
1122	Parcel shape	2	80.00
113	Forest cover	79	98.80
1211	Proximity to perennial water source	1.5	25.00
1212	Connected forest/green areas	70	70.00
1221	Risk of forest conversion	2	75.00
1222	Risk of hydrologic alteration	2	75.00
122	Human disturbance level		75.00
121	Green infrastructure network		49.92
112	Parcel size and shape		87.20
12	Desired (nonmandatory) characteristics		59.95
11	Mandatory characteristics		66.05
1	Indiana bat summer habitat protection		64.08

The tables demonstrate that, even with a small number of attributes (eight attributes and five parcels), it is essentially impossible to simultaneously compare the relative benefits of the parcels without the assistance of a decision-support tool. Weighted sums cannot take important trade-offs, simultaneity, and substitutability of the attributes into account. Therefore, the next step in the process is to aggregate each parcel's eight attribute suitability scores into a single overall suitability score using logic relationships incorporated into the LSP model.

Handling Partial Suitability Using Conjunction and Disjunction

To understand how to establish logic relationships in LSP, we have to further explore simultaneity and substitutability, which often occur

Table 7.13 *Evaluation results of five competitive parcels*

ID	Attribute	Parcel 1	Parcel 2	Parcel 3	Parcel 4	Parcel 5
1	Indiana bat summer habitat protection	64.08	86.20	0.00	80.18	48.67
11	Mandatory characteristics	66.05	86.12	0.00	83.10	43.44
12	Desired (nonmandatory) characteristics	59.95	86.36	52.06	74.12	60.15
112	Parcel size and shape	87.20	87.73	0.00	89.52	80.00
121	Green infrastructure network	49.92	77.27	64.06	78.12	43.86
122	Human disturbance level	75.00	100.00	34.06	68.11	84.59
1222	Risk of hydrologic alteration	75.00	100.00	50.00	100.00	100.00
1221	Risk of forest conversion	75.00	100.00	25.00	50.00	75.00
1212	Connected forest/ green areas	70.00	68.00	25.00	85.00	18.00
1211	Proximity to perennial water source	25.00	85.00	90.00	70.00	65.00
113	Forest cover	98.80	90.40	46.00	100.00	34.00
1122	Parcel shape	80.00	100.00	0.00	80.00	80.00
1121	Parcel size	92.31	83.08	98.46	96.92	80.00
111	Maternity colony location	60.00	84.00	76.80	78.00	92.00

as degrees rather than as yes/no extreme values. We will be using Table 7.8, which illustrates the concepts of conjunction and disjunction, and these are described in more detail in both the hands-on exercises and Appendix A.

- *Simultaneity* is a *conjunctive* "and" relationship, and the degree of simultaneity between two objects or factors is called *andness*.
- *Substitutability* is a *disjunctive* "or" relationship, and the degree of substitutability between two objects or factors is called *orness*.

Hard conjunctions and disjunctions represent the maximum degree for the relationship. Therefore, in an attribute tree, the relationship is a hard conjunction when two or more attributes are all mandatory and must be satisfied. A suitability score of 0 percent on any one of those attributes results in an overall suitability score for the parcel of 0 percent. An example of hard conjunction in Table 7.8 is the parcel size attribute (1121), which has a minimum acreage requirement in order for the parcel to be considered suitable. Likewise, for *hard* disjunctions, the extreme case of maximum *orness* in which suitability of one attribute can completely compensate for 0 percent suitability of another attribute.

Soft conjunctions and disjunctions represent the relationships between lesser degrees of simultaneity and substitutability.

- In *logic neutrality*, the degrees of simultaneity and substitutability are equal. The mathematical model of *logic neutrality* is a simple arithmetic mean: $z = (x + y)/2$.
- In a *soft conjunction*, simultaneity has a higher value than substitutability.
- In a *soft disjunction*, substitutability has a higher value than simultaneity.

The human disturbance level attribute (122) in Table 7.8 is an example of soft conjunction where the suitability values for the risk of forest conversion and the risk of hydrologic alteration need to be simultaneously satisfied since a negative impact in one cannot make up for the other. The green infrastructure network attribute (121) in Table 7.8 is an example of soft disjunction where proximity to a perennial water source can help substitute for forest connectivity.

Finally, LSP uses asymmetric *simultaneity aggregators* that allow mandatory attributes to completely or partially "absorb" the impact of optional attributes. The adjustable partial aggregators provide for a *conjunctive partial absorption* relationship (Dujmović, 2014). In this relationship, the mandatory attribute must be satisfied to avoid rejection of the parcel. The optional input does not have to be satisfied and can apply a penalty/reward system. In Table 7.8, the mandatory and desired characteristics are set up as *conjunctive partial absorption* where there is a 35% penalty on the mandatory suitability values when there is a low suitability value for desired characteristics and a 25% reward on the mandatory suitability values when there is a high suitability value for desired characteristics. You will find these penalty and reward values in the hands-on exercises in Chapter 12.

The results of the LSP analysis are presented in the first line of Table 7.13. Note that P3 has been assigned a suitability score of 0 percent. The nonlinear properties of the LSP criteria result in rejection of P3 because it fails to satisfy a mandatory requirement limiting the number of fragments in a parcel's shape to eight (attribute 1122). It is important to emphasize that this result cannot be obtained if we use simple additive scoring or strictly soft aggregators. The hard aggregators are indispensable for making sure that the parcels satisfy all of the mandatory requirements.

Cost-Benefit Analysis: Selecting the Most Suitable Parcels

Once LSP has been used to determine the overall suitability score for each parcel, a final LSP analysis simultaneously compares the overall suitability score *and* the cost to acquire each parcel (as raw data or as normalized values) to identify the most cost-effective selections. The resulting cost-effectiveness ranking of the parcels and the contributing attribute scores are presented in Tables 7.14 and 7.15. Though the table includes P3, that parcel has been eliminated from consideration by its 0 percent suitability score. The *overall value* of each parcel shown in the last column in Table 7.15 is a conjunctive aggregation of relative affordability and relative preference: that is, we want low cost and high quality *simultaneously*. The maximum overall value

Table 7.14 *Ranking of competitive parcels in decreasing overall suitability*

Rank	Parcel	Suitability
1	Parcel 2	86.20%
2	Parcel 4	80.18%
3	Parcel 1	64.08%
4	Parcel 5	48.67%
5	Parcel 3	0% (rejected)

that can be obtained this way is 100 percent, and in our case the highest overall suitability score is 86.20 percent (P2).

An important advantage of this LSP aggregation approach is that decision-makers can adjust the relative importance of a high score and the complementary relative importance of low cost. If, for example, extra weight needs to be given to the overall quality of the parcels' contributions and there is less concern about the cost, the parcels can be selected using one of columns that emphasizes the suitability score, such as the 70 percent column, which ranks the parcels as shown in Table 7.16. In that case, P2 is once again the most cost-effective choice, ranking 100 percent satisfaction.

At the end of the LSP evaluation process, the values of attributes are fixed and the overall suitability value of each parcel cannot be changed. However, prices can still be negotiable. Consider what happens when the normalized price of P4 is reduced from 90 percent to 95 percent, as shown in Table 7.17. When the relative importance of high suitability scores is 50 percent or less, P4 is the first choice; for relative importance of a high suitability score of 60 percent to 100 percent, P2 is the best choice. Examining the effects of changes in price provides a useful sensitivity analysis.

Using Data Sets with Missing Values

LSP.NT can be used to select the best parcel despite some missing data. Suppose that it is not possible to reliably assess P4 and P5 for

Table 7.15 Cost preference results of five competitive parcels

System	Cost	Relative Importance of High Score (w)											Overall Score (%)
		0%	10%	20%	30%	40%	50%	60%	70%	80%	90%	100%	
Overall value: $100 * (Score_k/Score_{max})^w (Cost_{min}/Cost_k)^{1.w}$ [%]													
Parcel 1	100	84.00	82.98	81.97	80.98	79.99	79.02	78.06	77.11	76.17	75.25	74.34	64.08
Parcel 2	92	90.81	91.69	92.58	93.48	94.38	95.29	96.22	97.15	98.09	99.04	100.0	86.20
Parcel 3	122	68.85	0.00	0.00	0.00	0.00	0.00	0.00	0.00	0.00	0.00	0.00	0.00
Parcel 4	90	93.33	93.30	93.27	93.24	93.21	93.18	93.15	93.11	93.08	93.05	93.02	80.18
Parcel 5	84	100.0	94.44	89.20	84.24	79.56	75.14	70.97	67.02	63.30	59.78	56.46	48.67
Normalized Value													
Parcel 1	100	84.00	87.86	87.89	86.63	84.75	82.92	81.13	79.37	77.66	75.98	74.34	64.08
Parcel 2	92	90.81	97.08	99.26	100.0	100.0	100.0	100.0	100.0	100.0	100.0	100.0	86.20
Parcel 3	122	68.85	0.00	0.00	0.00	0.00	0.00	0.00	0.00	0.00	0.00	0.00	0.00
Parcel 4	90	93.33	98.79	100.0	99.75	98.76	97.78	96.81	95.85	94.89	93.95	93.02	80.18
Parcel 5	84	100.0	100.0	95.63	90.12	84.30	78.85	73.76	68.99	64.53	60.36	56.46	48.67

Table 7.16 *Final ranking of parcels by suitability score using normalized value (70 percent – relative importance of high score)*

Rank	Parcel	Normalized Value
1	Parcel 2	100%
2	Parcel 4	95.85%
3	Parcel 1	79.37%
4	Parcel 5	68.99%
5	Parcel 3	0% (rejected)

the risk of forest conversion and hydrologic alteration. Thus, the risk values are known for P1, P2, and P3 but not for P4 and P5. Instead of having to eliminate P4 and P5, the LSP software is able to insert values for P4 and P5 based on the most likely substitutes: values that are consistent with the values assigned for the other parcels.

The results using the estimates of risk are shown in Table 7.18. The overall suitability of P4 increases insignificantly from 80.18 percent to 81.49 percent and the suitability of P5 decreases from 48.67 percent to 43.58 percent. These results are fully consistent with the previous ranking and therefore can be used to support decisions about parcel selection despite missing data.

LESSONS FROM THE CASE STUDY

Our sample structured decision-making and LSP process points to three useful conclusions. First, even the smallest decision problem requires a methodology that supports sophisticated logic aggregators and logic decision models that provide soft and hard partial conjunction and disjunction. Without those aggregators, it is impossible to build justifiable criteria that reflect the complex properties of human reasoning. It is also impossible to automatically reject options that do not satisfy some of the mandatory requirements.

The second conclusion is that the project evaluation and selection processes must simultaneously consider both the quality of each proposed project in terms of conservation (the benefit) and the cost.

Table 7.17 Normalized cost/preference results after price reduction of Parcel 4

System	Cost	Relative Importance of High Score (w)											Overall Score (%)
		0%	10%	20%	30%	40%	50%	60%	70%	80%	90%	100%	
Parcel 1	100	84.00	84.48	83.96	83.44	82.93	82.42	81.13	79.37	77.66	75.98	74.34	64.08
Parcel 2	92	90.81	93.35	94.82	96.32	97.84	99.39	100.0	100.0	100.0	100.0	100.0	86.20
Parcel 3	122	68.85	0.00	0.00	0.00	0.00	0.00	0.00	0.00	0.00	0.00	0.00	0.00
Parcel 4	85	98.82	100.0	100.0	100.0	100.0	100.0	99.05	97.50	95.99	94.49	93.02	80.18
Parcel 5	84	100.0	96.15	91.36	86.81	82.48	78.37	73.76	68.99	64.53	60.36	56.46	48.67

Table 7.18 *Evaluation results and cost/preference analysis in the case of missing data*

ID	Attribute	Parcel 1	Parcel 2	Parcel 3	Parcel 4	Parcel 5
1	Indiana bat summer habitat protection	64.08	86.20	0.00	81.49	43.58
11	Mandatory characteristics	66.05	86.12	0.00	83.10	43.44
12	Desired (nonmandatory) characteristics	59.95	86.36	52.06	78.12	43.86
112	Parcel size and shape	87.20	87.73	0.00	89.52	80.00
121	Green infrastructure network	49.92	77.27	64.06	78.12	43.86
122	Human disturbance level	75.00	100.00	34.06	*****	*****
1222	Risk of hydrologic alteration	75.00	100.00	50.00	*****	******
1221	Risk of forest conversion	75.00	100.00	25.00	*****	*****
1212	Connected forest/green areas	70.00	68.00	25.00	85.00	18.00
1211	Proximity to perennial water source	25.00	85.00	90.00	70.00	65.00
113	Forest cover	98.80	90.40	46.00	100.00	34.00
1122	Parcel shape	80.00	100.00	0.00	80.00	80.00
1121	Parcel size	92.31	83.08	98.46	96.92	80.00
111	Maternity colony location	60.00	84.00	70.80	78.00	92.00

		Relative Importance of High Score (w)											Overall
System	Cost	0%	10%	20%	30%	40%	50%	60%	70%	80%	90%	100%	Score (%)
Parcel 1	100	84.00	88.79	87.60	86.43	84.75	82.92	81.13	79.37	77.66	75.98	74.34	64.08
Parcel 2	92	90.81	98.11	98.94	99.77	100.0	100.0	100.0	100.0	100.0	100.0	100.0	86.20
Parcel 3	122	68.85	0.00	0.00	0.00	0.00	0.00	0.00	0.00	0.00	0.00	0.00	0.00
Parcel 4	90	93.33	100.0	100.0	100.0	99.40	98.57	97.75	96.94	96.13	95.33	94.53	81.49
Parcel 5	84	100.0	99.95	93.24	86.98	80.65	74.61	69.02	63.85	59.07	54.65	50.55	43.58

The decision process evolves in an environment of collaborative contact among the stakeholders, analysts, and domain experts, and financial negotiations are a vital part of this process. The cost should not be used as an attribute. It reflects the overall expense, which must be compared with the overall suitability for conservation as shown in the iterative cost/preference analysis in our case study.

The third conclusion is that the LSP method and its decision-support software (including LSP.NT) offer a verified methodology that can efficiently solve the complex evaluation and selection problems faced by conservation organizations and fully justify those decisions to stakeholders even when some data are missing.

Now, what happens when we have $10 million worth of projects submitted to provide summer habitat for the Indiana bat but only $3 million in the budget? Once we have established the overall value of the proposed parcels using LSP, we can use optimization tools to evaluate every potential suite of projects for funding and select the portfolio that provides the greatest overall benefit with our budget. That is, we can use optimization to recognize opportunity costs and trade-offs – the focus of the next chapter.

8   Getting the Best Bang for Your Buck

At its core, acquiring parcels of land for conservation projects using a finite budget is a fundamental economic problem where difficult choices are made with limited resources. As discussed in Chapter 2, a number of economic studies in the past couple of decades have analyzed this problem and cautioned that a process that fails to consider the cost of acquiring and maintaining these parcels will inevitably be economically inefficient whenever a property provides significant ecological value but is also relatively expensive and when the costs to acquire the parcels varies more than the level of benefits they provide (Ferraro, 2003). In response, resource and environmental economists have developed models that use mathematical programming, also known as "optimization," to identify the best set of acquisitions given the budget.

Mathematical programming is a branch of operations research and computational science designed to identify what is "best." In this case, the word "programming" does not refer to software, although computer algorithms have greatly enhanced our ability to analyze complex, multicriteria problems. Rather, programming refers to a hierarchical set of activities required to solve a particular problem when the goal is to find the optimal solution given certain criteria and limits. The limits are defined by the context, which can be essentially any type of human endeavor, including businesses, scientific endeavors (physical, chemical, and biological), engineering, architecture, economics, management, and agricultural and natural resources. An example of optimization is a mix of crops and livestock chosen by a farmer that maximizes the farmer's profit given the resources (land, labor, machinery, animal stocks, and capital) available to produce them. Ride-sharing apps, such as Uber and Lyft, use optimization to identify available drivers to assign to pick you up as quickly as possible. In the context of environmental economics, a farmer who has agreed to restrict her farm's emission of carbon needs to identify the optimal level of production of crops and livestock that will meet the carbon requirement and maximize the farm's profit. These farmers are optimizing their operations to deliver the best profit possible under the circumstances.

Mathematical programming has its roots in the 1940s when Leonid Kantorovich (linear programming), George Danzig (the simplex method), and John Von Neumann (duality) developed procedures for linear programming, an analytical technique in which various requirements are represented by linear relationships. Linear programming was used extensively by the US military during World War II, primarily to minimize various costs associated with the war effort, and after the war, the procedures and applications were rapidly adopted by the private sector, academics, and government agencies as a quantitative technique to handle a variety of problems. Today, mathematical programming is one of the most widely used quantitative approaches in decision analysis.

In his textbook with Harry Kaiser (Cornell), Kent wrote about key four features of mathematical programming models. There is an *objective* (such as total environmental benefit) that is to be maximized or minimized, *activities* or *decision variables* that describe how the objective will be achieved, the *objective function coefficient* translates the overall numeric values into the objective through its interaction with the values from the activities, and a set of *constraints* that model the restrictions within which the decision-maker must operate (Messer and Kaiser, 2011). The programming problems are modeled as a set of linear and/or nonlinear equations that define the decision-making environment. The model then calculates the quality of an answer (such as a collection of parcels for conservation) in numerical terms. Likewise, optimization models traditionally consist of an objective function and a set of constraints, which are incorporated into the model using a system of equations or inequalities. Such models are used extensively for decision-making in sectors ranging from engineering to stock trading. In particular, optimization models have proven useful for selecting one or more conservation projects that will provide the greatest cumulative benefit given their cost – that is, optimizing the aggregate benefit of a set of projects or parcels.

As computers have become more powerful and heuristic methods for solving complex analyses have advanced (Higgins and Hajkowicz, 2008), conservationists have been able to employ sophisticated mathematical programming models for problems associated with efforts to reconnect fragmented parcels in a region (Williams and Snyder, 2005), allocate land to various projects (Mallawaarachchi and Quiggin, 2001), protect sensitive watersheds (Ferraro, 2003), and conserve agricultural soils (McSweeny and Kramer, 1986), among others.

APPLYING OPTIMIZATION TO CONSERVATION SETTINGS

In conservation contexts, using Binary Linear Programming (BLP) follows the three important principles of strategic conservation: *Consider both the benefits and the costs; Recognize opportunity costs and trade-offs; and Acknowledge limited resources*. BLP identifies the set of projects (one, a few, or many) that maximizes the overall aggregate benefits to the environment using binary variables, where a one means the project is funded and a zero means the project is not funded. The analysis is driven by data describing the estimated benefits offered by each potential project, each project's cost, and relative priorities (weights) assigned to various characteristics, such as adjacency to other parcels or the habitat quality of a parcel, by the organization. These models compare high-cost, high-benefit "budget sponge" projects that consume most of the budget and make relatively small contributions to overall goals with "best buy" projects that collectively provide a significant aggregate benefit by, for example, protecting many times more acres of wetlands than the budget sponge project.

The emphasis of optimization methods is on the overall benefit achieved collectively by the suite of projects. As described previously, traditional Benefit-Targeting processes (also referred to as rank-based models) examine each candidate project separately, valuing them without information about costs or the ability to compare the cost-effectiveness to other candidate projects. As a result, their process ignores the potentially large cumulative benefit of a suite of solid but not spectacular projects and instead solely selects the highest-ranked projects (often budget sponges) until the funds are exhausted.

Consider a project undertaken by the Maryland State Highway Administration to improve US Highway 301 near the town of Waldorf. The transportation agency was considering whether to upgrade the existing highway or construct a new bypass and had incorporated environmental stewardship into the planning process with the goal of improving both transportation and the environment. Using this innovative approach, the agency not only met but surpassed the amount of mitigation required by the National Environmental Policy Act to offset impacts from construction and related activities (Weber and Allen, 2010). The agency set out to identify sets of projects providing environmental stewardship under several funding scenarios to identify the one that would provide the greatest benefit (Allen et al., 2010). Messer (2010) compared the outcome of optimization and a simple BT approach for the highway project and found that optimization provided a 69 percent larger area of green infrastructure, resulted in a 68 percent greater aggregate environmental benefit score, and protected 1,641 acres that would not have been protected by a BT approach under a hypothetical $15 million budget.

Decades ago, a supercomputer would be required to run this type of optimization model and it would take days for this analysis to be run. Today, however, the computer on your desk has both enough raw computational power and the standard spreadsheet software, a Microsoft Excel add-in called "Solver," needed to complete the analyses in seconds. This simple Solver program can process models that include up to a couple hundred parcels. Larger and relatively complex models can still take hours of run time so optimizations involving a large number of parcels typically are conducted using the more-powerful Solvers that are commercially available through Frontline Systems. For readers of this book, we have developed a custom optimization tool. It employs the most current and powerful optimization processes but presents them in a user-friendly interface mostly involving point-and-click selections. This software, referred to as an online Optimization Decision-Support Tool (ODST) has been customized to conservation contexts and includes the functions discussed in this chapter. You will have the chance to explore using the ODST through some exercises (with step-by-step instructions and answers) in Chapter 11. Thanks to these developments, most conservation organizations can adopt optimization techniques without having to invest in significant computing upgrades.

BENEFIT–COST TARGETING

The simplest method that follows the core principles of strategic conservation is Benefit–Cost Targeting (BCT) (also referred to as Cost-Effectiveness Analysis) – selection of as many of the highest-ranked projects according to their benefit–cost ratios as the budget allows.[1] Note that this is similar to Benefit Targeting (BT) since it continues to use a ranking in an iterative process to make selections and buys only top-ranked projects. However, the key element of BCT is that it follows the third core principle of strategic conservation – because it accounts for both benefits and costs. By using a ratio (dividing the total benefits by the total costs), the approach effectively ranks the projects based on their *benefits-per-dollar*. The projects are then selected using that ranking until the budget is exhausted. This approach allows conservation organizations and funders to allocate their financial resources more efficiently. It also allows them to select and rank potential projects using a process that is scientifically and

---

[1] Variations of BCT have been developed to account for complexity (Ando et al., 1998; Costello and Polasky, 2004; Machado et al., 2006; Abbitt et al., 2000). For example, Newburn et al. (2005) developed a framework to account for a net loss of benefit prevented per unit of cost. Wu et al. (2001) and Wu (2004) looked at the conditions related to total net social benefit and sought to account for impacts on commodity output prices and slippage.

economically sound. Thus, BCT ensures that each project selected will offer the greatest benefit per dollar and will achieve results that are no worse – and usually dramatically better – in terms of cost-effectiveness than BT (Babcock et al., 1996). Consequently, many economists have been promoting BCT (Ferraro, 2003; Duke et al., 2014), and a number of federal programs in the United States, including the Conservation Reserve Program and Environmental Quality Incentives Program, have adopted a version of BCT in an effort to optimize their selection processes for economic efficiency (Wu et al., 2001).

CASE STUDY: BALTIMORE COUNTY, MARYLAND

Baltimore County, Maryland, first introduced optimization approaches in 2006 as part of a reinvigorated effort to preserve agricultural land. Acres of farm land in Maryland had dropped from 4.0 million to 2.2 million between 1950 and 2000 as large swaths of property were developed for residential and commercial uses (Lynch and Musser, 2001). The state's population, on the other hand, was growing rapidly. The state was expected to gain about 1.1 million residents between 2010 and 2040 (Maryland Department of Planning, 2014a, 2014b). The growing number of residents combined with shrinking average household sizes and communications technologies that would allow people to telecommute was expected to lead to a sharp increase in development and decline in agricultural properties. In fact, the county lost 24 percent of its farm land to development between 1987 and 2012, when there were only 640 farms remaining, 15 percent fewer than in 2007 (Maryland Department of Planning, 2014a, 2014b).

The losses could have been much greater without Baltimore County's preservation program, which ranked as one of the top 12 local programs nationwide in 2003. The county introduced BCT as a pilot program in 2007 to identify the least costly projects by computing a ratio of each potential parcel's acquisition price (its cost) to the monetary value of the estimated nonmonetary benefit it would provide.

As detailed in Messer et al. (2016), Baltimore County started using strategic conservation as a pilot program in 2007. The county found that the use of BCT was responsible for an 11.2 percent increase in the aggregate conservation benefit delivered, which translated into an additional $5.8 million in value, and preserved 17.2 percent more acres of farm land (596.3 acres valued at $4 million based on the average cost per acre) than the county's traditional BT selection system. The significant measurable gains in conservation benefits and acres preserved as a result of using a relatively simple optimization method convinced the county to formally adopt BCT as its selection process. In 2012, the county acquired an additional 852 acres and a 10 percent gain in overall conservation benefit compared to what would have been achieved under the same budget using BT (data provided by Baltimore County's Department Environmental Protection and Sustainability).

How did Baltimore County accomplish this transition? We developed decision-support tools that could evaluate many different types of agricultural programs and parcels, including the program proposed by Baltimore County's Agricultural Land Preservation Program. The county's farm land preservation program had been established in 1979, and in 2006, it had reached a major milestone: preservation of 40,000 acres, representing half of its long-term goal of preserving 80,000 acres. Members of the county's staff and the program's advisory board wanted to test the ability of optimization techniques to improve how the program distributed its limited financial resources and maximize its return on those resources by picking the worthiest projects. A significant portion of the funds came from the Maryland Agricultural Land Preservation Foundation, and the state had established guidelines for agricultural preservation and relied on LESA models to help its own officials make wise investments. Baltimore County also used a LESA model to evaluate applications and wanted to refine their models of water quality by incorporating GIS and taking other factors (such as the presence of forests) into account. Members of the staff applied an early version of the ODST to their applicant pool so they could learn to use it and make operational adjustments to adapt it to their program.

The gains identified from use of cost-effective conservation techniques suggested that Baltimore County's return on its investment in the optimization method during just the first three years was nearly 60 to 1 – that Baltimore County received more than $60 in *additional* conservation benefits for every dollar it spend on strategic conservation techniques.

Success Profiles: Robert Hirsch and Wallace Lippincott
Baltimore County, Maryland, was the first land conservation program in the United States to adopt Cost-Effectiveness Analysis as its primary selection method. This method provided a simple and transparent way for Baltimore County specialists and planners, Robert Hirsch (Figure 8.1) and Wallace Lippincott (Figure 8.2), to select the best lands for conservation. Between 2007 and 2014, Baltimore County was able to purchase 5,680 acres of land with the cost-effectiveness approach. If they had used Benefit Targeting instead, they would have had to spend an additional $6.3 million to get the same acreage.

FIGURE 8.1 Robert Hirsch.   FIGURE 8.2 Wallace Lippincott.

Wallace Lippincott is the Northern Sector Planner in Baltimore County's Department of Planning. He has been working for Baltimore County for 27 years. His work focuses on zoning, development review, and land preservation. Baltimore County has a mixture of urban, suburban, and rural areas that can make planning and preservation a complex operation. Robert Hirsch is now a Natural Resource Specialist of Baltimore County. He has been working for the county for 13 years. His work now focuses on progress of water-quality protection and restoration, but his work on Baltimore County's optimization strategies for land preservation still lives on today.

Baltimore County operates on a two-year cycle with the state of Maryland. They are making about 5–10 new project investments each cycle. At the present time, Baltimore is not doing any county easements. One of the county's other roles in land preservation comes in the form of assisting the local land trusts.

Utilizing BCT in Baltimore County has been a major success. One of the greatest benefits of the BCT comes from its simplicity. The math is easy; anyone can do it. It is just the ratio of conservation benefit to the cost. This method may seem a little too simple, but it still approaches an optimal outcome. The public and conservation stakeholders are able to do the math and understand the ranking of projects on their own. BCT involves subjective and objective preference analysis. Complex mathematical strategies for optimization may provide better scenarios for land protection in more complex situations, but Wally and Rob felt it may also lead to more unhappy people because it can be difficult to explain why certain parcels are selected over others – and ultimately relationships with landowners was a key to their success in a county preservation program.

BINARY LINEAR PROGRAMMING

True optimization methods, such as BLP and Goal Programming (GP), stand apart because of their ability to identify the optimal solution in complex selections involving multiple projects and criteria using algorithms that can analyze every potential combination of selections. An conservation organization may, for example, need not only maximize the overall benefit provided but preserve as many species as possible, enroll a minimum number of acres from a particular area, or meet two or more disparate goals (Underhill, 1994; Sarkar et al., 2006; Balmford et al., 2000; Kaiser and Messer, 2011). These algorithms can identify optimal selections when ecological complexities such as thresholds introduce complexity into the selection process. In addition, the techniques can provide a slight advantage over iterative techniques such as BCT by adjusting to account for budget remainders (Messer, 2006).

Budget remainders are a significant problem for many conservation organizations. A large remainder is most likely when the budget is so small that only a few parcels can be selected, the projects' costs are relatively high, the agency can implement only parts of a project, and/or the budget cannot be carried over to the next year. The ability to take budget remainders into account is a key benefit of optimization methods, which take advantage of the ability of computers to compare thousands of potential solutions to a problem. A simple example illustrates this problem and why BLP guarantees an optimal solution. Remember, BLP takes the benefits and costs of each parcel into account when evaluating all of the combinations of projects possible given the budget and selects the portfolio that yields the greatest possible conservation value in aggregate. BCT selects parcels based solely on their individual benefit–cost ratios.

Consider the ten-parcel scenario illustrated in Table 8.1 in which the parcels are lettered A to J, which represents their rank from highest (A) to lowest (J) based on the benefit–cost ratio each parcel provides. With a budget of $2,500, BCT selects the highest-ranking parcels (A, B, C, and D) plus parcel J (ranked tenth) with the funds remaining. This selection provides an aggregate benefit score of 9.64. BLP selects parcels B, C, E, and F, yielding an aggregate benefit score of 10.48. The benefit score is maximized by forgoing A (ranked first), D (ranked fourth), and J (ranked tenth) and instead selecting E and F,

Table 8.1 *Ten-parcel example for Benefit–Cost Targeting and Binary Linear Programming*

				Benefit–Cost Targeting			Binary Linear Programing		
Parcel	Benefits	Cost	B/C	Selected?	Cost	Benefits	Selected?	Cost	Benefits
A	2.26	$450	0.0050	Yes	$450	2.26			
B	2.43	$500	0.0049	Yes	$500	2.43	Yes	$500	2.43
C	2.60	$600	0.0043	Yes	$600	2.60	Yes	$600	2.60
D	2.10	$500	0.0042	Yes	$500	2.10			
E	2.65	$650	0.0041				Yes	$650	2.65
F	2.80	$700	0.0040				Yes	$700	2.80
G	2.05	$700	0.0029						
H	1.10	$650	0.0017						
I	0.85	$900	0.0009						
J	0.25	$450	0.0006	Yes	$450	0.25			
Budget	**$2,500**			**Total**	**$2,500**	**9.64**		**$2,450**	**10.48**

Source: From Messer (2006).

which are ranked fifth and sixth. Furthermore, the BLP selections cost less ($2,450 versus $2,500) and reduce transactions costs by selecting four parcels instead of five.

What's more, BLP's efficiency relative to BCT is even greater when the selection process involves two or more constraints. For many conservation organizations, for example, the number of parcels selected is often an additional concern, especially since labor is often fixed in the short-term for conservation organizations such as state preservation programs and land trusts.

When we applied BLP and BCT to the data from the Catoctin Mountain region of Maryland, imposing the additional restraint on number of parcels selected reduced the aggregate benefit achieved by both methods. However, BLP still identifies the optimal solution to the problem in terms of aggregate benefit while BCT's inefficiency increases under the parcel constraint. As shown in Figure 8.3, BLP's ability to compare potential projects using multiple constraints drives the difference in efficiency of the portfolios selected by the two

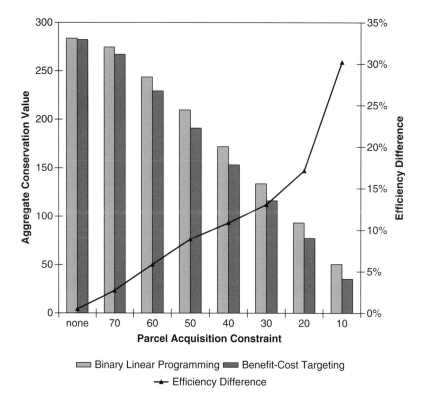

FIGURE 8.3 Efficiency difference between Binary Linear Programming and Benefit-Cost Targeting.

techniques. Under a $2.5 million budget and a parcel limit of 60, BCT is 5.9 percent less efficient than BLP. Likewise, when the parcel limit is 20, BCT is 17.1 percent less efficient. You will get a chance to replicate this finding in the exercises in Chapter 11.

The number of situations in which optimization is valuable is nearly endless. In our experience, optimization has proven to be particularly useful when priority weights used to evaluate projects or action depend on future actions, such as changes to land use regulations, and when a variety of additional factors must be considered, such as the relative urgency of the potential projects. Optimization methods also facilitate sensitivity analyses, such as exploring how a change in the budget or an organizational priority would affect the optimal set of projects. In general, optimization is most effective when the following types of information are readily available:

- Clearly identified project opportunities
- A set of objectives or priorities by which to evaluate the projects (criteria, factors, values, weights).
- Numeric normalized scores indicating how each project addresses the objectives and priorities (benefits).
- Estimates of the financial investment required to complete each project (direct and indirect costs).
- A realistic overall budget for each project and thresholds for determining whether a project is viable (budget and decision constraints, scenarios).

BINARY LINEAR PROGRAMMING CASE STUDY: MARSH BIRD HABITAT PROTECTION

Conservation of salt marsh habitats currently is a high priority worldwide because of threats from rising sea levels (Douglas, 1991; Intergovernmental Panel on Climate Change, 2007; Rahmstorf, 2007) so organizations dedicated to preserving such marshes urgently need to use their resources efficiently. The pressure is particularly great in the United States because one-third of all tidal marshes in the world in area – 4.5 million hectares – are located there along the Atlantic and Gulf coasts (Greenburg, 2006). And the stakes are high for a number of species; 21 of the 25 vertebrate species that depend on salt marshes for habitat are considered endangered, threatened, or otherwise of heightened concern (Greenburg, 2006). In particular, several avian species – including clapper rails, willets, saltmarsh sparrows, and seaside sparrows – spend their entire annual life cycles in tidal marshes, nesting near or directly on the marsh surface. Both rising sea levels and increasingly frequent floods associated with climate change pose a severe threat to such birds (Gjerdrum et al., 2005, 2008; Shriver et al., 2007).

Wiest et al. (2014) compared selections of salt marsh habitat in the United States for preservation using BT and BLP with three levels of sea rise (0.5, 1.0, and 1.5 meters) and three budgets ($10 million, $15 million, and $20 million) and found that BLP selected greater numbers of parcels, protected larger areas of marsh, and conserved a larger number of tidal-marsh-obligate birds than BT. Under a $10 million budget, the BLP model selected 18 parcels of previously unprotected salt marsh supporting four bird species. By selecting the most efficient combination of parcels, BLP conserved an additional 77 hectares of marsh and 319 tidal-marsh-obligate birds relative to the parcels selected by BT. Furthermore, nearly $2.9 million in supplementary land-acquisition funds would have been required for BT to achieve the conservation benefit secured by the optimization model. Similar patterns were found for the $15 million and $20 million budgets. Under those budgets, BT would have required an additional $2.70 million and $1.75 million, respectively, to match the overall conservation outcome of BLP. The improvements in area conserved by BLP varied from 7.2 percent to 9.6 percent and the improvements in bird densities ranged from 7.3 percent to 12.8 percent.

The evaluation of the three levels of potential sea level rise showed that water would inundate more than 95 percent of the wetland areas of the parcels. The least inundated type of land cover was agricultural – from 79.9 hectares under the $10-million budget and 1.5 meters of sea rise (82.0 percent of the total portfolio area) to 648.7 hectares under the $20 million budget and 0.5 meters of sea rise (70.8 percent of the total portfolio area). In light of these results, the authors concluded that migration of marshes to adjacent agricultural land would provide the best opportunity for preserving tidal marshes and their bird populations when the marshes could not accrete enough additional material to remain unflooded.

HYBRID LINEAR PROGRAMMING

As previously discussed, a significant challenge for conservation organizations is accurately and fully capturing the value of the benefits potentially provided by a project. The benefits do not come with price tags already attached, and the metrics available to value them are frequently imperfect. As we have shown, selections made using BLP and BCT can provide less than the maximum possible benefit – as much as 30 percent less if the grading metric tends to normalize scores from a skewed distribution of underlying value (Fooks et al., 2017). This problem is most acute when some of the potential projects offer a large, signature-level of benefit but are expensive.

Another issue is that some benefits associated with a project, such as prestige and public opinion, are difficult to measure and may only exist for a handful projects. These types of "signature" projects may be important for the overall public relations of the conservation effort. The challenge is that these signature projects can also be budget sponges. Thus, since strategic conservation is ultimately an approach to have conservation groups do a better job meeting their mission with a limited budget, we developed an approach to deal with signature projects that enables groups to get the best bang for their buck with their remaining funds.

To address this issue, we developed a Hybrid Linear Programming (HLP) method that combines the best of BT and BLP, thereby enabling organizations to select a few signature projects and then use optimization to select the remainder of the portfolio (Fooks et al., 2017). With this hybrid approach, conservation organizations and funders can keep a foot in both camps, the most realistic option in many cases. They sacrifice some strict cost-effectiveness in exchange for intangible benefits from the signature projects but still have a more cost-effective process than BT or BCT alone.

Our hybrid optimization heuristic is intuitive, easy to implement, and, based on computer simulations involving different sets of assumptions (including correlation between a parcel's cost and its benefits). Hybrid optimization recovers a substantial portion of the maximum available conservation value relative to BT and BCT – 20 percentage points or more of BLP's shortfall relative to a full-information benchmark (Fooks et al., 2017).

These types of hybrid approaches can be incredibly useful tools for conservation organizations and funders. In addition to being intuitive and easy to use, they provide flexibility. The organization chooses how many signature projects to fund before applying optimization to make the most of the remaining budget. Furthermore, hybrid models can serve as a bridge, both within the organization and for stakeholders, in the process of adopting cost-effective selection methods that rely on mathematical programming.

HYBRID CASE STUDY: DELAWARE COMMUNITY FOUNDATION'S FUND FOR WOMEN

One of Delaware Community Foundation's programs is the Fund for Women, a $2.8 million permanent endowment created using private contributions in 1993. The fund provides grants for programs that promote "the education of girls and women in health, wellness, and life skills that lead to future economic self-sufficiency" and for projects that help women and girls avoid abuse, improve their physical and mental health, achieve financial independence, and receive prenatal and medical care. As of 2016, it had awarded more than $1.4 million in grants to 242 nonprofit programs statewide. The grants are awarded annually in a competitive process with applications submitted in January and the grant recipients announced in July.

Leaders of the fund's grant selection committee established a partnership with us to determine how to improve their selection process by moving from a rank-based BT approach to optimization. In the existing selection process, projects were selected solely by benefit scores assigned by the 11-member committee. Each member reviewed the submitted projects and assigned a score of 1 to 100 to each. The individual scores for each project were then averaged to arrive at the final project score used in the ranking. Similar to the selection process of conservation groups, the Fund for Women based its selections solely on the resulting ranked list (same as BT), beginning with the highest-ranked project and working down the list until the budget was exhausted. Projects' costs were considered only when more than one project received the same score and the budget prevented the committee from approving all of the projects.

In 2010, Fund for Women received 93 applications and had a budget of $136,219. The fund was also interested in whether their selections were equitably benefiting Delaware's three counties since New Castle has a much larger population than other two counties (keep in mind Delaware is a small state that only has three counties). Of the 93 proposed projects, 44 applied to New Castle County, 14 to Kent County, and 15 to Sussex County; 27 applications were for statewide projects (some projects served women in multiple counties). We compared the selections made using BT in 2010 with selections that would have been made using BLP and a number of hybrid optimizations in terms of overall benefit provided, the number of projects funded, the distribution of the selections by county, and the number of people served by the projects (Wu et al., 2017).[2] The results of that comparison are presented in Table 8.2; note that the hybrid-10 model is the same as using BT since the 10 parcels exhausted the budget) and that the hybrid-0 model is the same as using BLP.

Naturally, all of the optimizations led to lower total project scores than BT, which automatically selected the highest-ranking projects. For organizations used to maximizing the overall benefit, this result tends to be discouraging since optimization may pass over signature projects that have a moderately higher benefit score but also cost significantly more. In general, the optimization models selected only one or two highly ranked projects that were relatively inexpensive, a large number of mid-quality projects, and a few low-quality projects. The variation in emphasis between BT and BLP results in an average project score of 70 or less using optimization versus 86 using the rank-based process.

The committees, after reviewing the analysis, chose to adopt a hybrid optimization process for 2012 in which they first selected a few budget signature projects based solely on the benefit ranking and then selected the rest of the projects using BLP. The fund's leaders were

[2] Wu et al. (2017) also looked ath the impact of applying HLP to the USDA Forest Legacy program and also showed impressive environmental improvements with the methods.

Table 8.2 *Results from each selection model*

Selection Model	Number Chosen by Ranking	Number of Projects Selected	Total Project Score	Average Project Score	Number of Women Served	Total Cost
Binary linear programming (Hybrid-0)	0	31	2,122	68.46	16,132	$135,887
Hybrid-1	1	30	2,081	69.38	17,044	$135,887
Hybrid-2	2	29	2,059	71.02	16,958	$135,887
Hybrid-3	*3*	*28*	*1,997*	*71.32*	*16,966*	*$135,902*
Hybrid-4	4	27	1,923	71.26	18,286	$135,777
Hybrid-5	5	26	1,892	72.79	18,161	$135,977
Hybrid-6	6	24	1,793	74.74	19,821	$135,677
Hybrid-7	7	22	1,647	74.87	19,739	$135,677
Hybrid-8	8	19	1,460	76.86	11,192	$136,074
Hybrid-9	9	17	1,320	77.68	10,969	$136,124
Benefit-Targeting (Hybrid-10)	10	10	862	86.24	10,194	$136,219

understandably concerned that a strict BLP process would reduce the average score too much and felt that the hybrid approach was a good compromise.

All of the hybrid models' total project scores (see Table 8.2) were significantly higher than the total project score achieved with BT while remaining within the budget and serving a greater number of women. Consider the hybrid in which three projects were chosen by rank. It generated a 180 percent improvement in the number of projects funded (increasing from 10 to 28). The aggregate benefit score rose from 862 under BT to 1,997 (132 percent) and the number of women served increased from 10,194 to 16,966 (66 percent). Furthermore, in this hybrid version, the average project scores for the selected projects were higher as well. Also important is the relatively small decrease in the total project score – the normal BLP process achieved a score of 2,122 while the hybrid-3 model achieved a score of 1,997, a 5.9 percent decrease. The number of projects selected decreased from 31 to 28 (just 9.7 percent), and the number of women served rose from 16,132 to 16,966 (5.2 percent) compared to a BLP-only process.

GOAL PROGRAMMING

If you want it all, then *Goal Programming* (GP) may be for you. GP can help overcome concerns about the inability of standard programming methods to weight one characteristic relative to another (Nijkamp, 1977). GP provides a solution to that problem as it can analyze the diverse interests of agencies, partners. donors, the community, and the environment simultaneously by incorporating secondary objectives and typically minimizes a weighted sum of deviations from certain goals (Kaiser and Messer, 2011).

Several studies have applied GP to conservation programs that need to simultaneously consider economic and biological objectives over the short and long term in a number of different contexts: forest protection (Fooks and Messer, 2013); fishery management (Drynan and Sandiford, 1985; Mardle and Pascoe, 1999; Mardle et al., 2000); energy production (Silva and Nakata, 2009); forest management Önal (1997); and public water resources (Neely et al., 1977; Ballestero et al., 2002).

GOAL PROGRAMMING CASE STUDY: HABITAT PROTECTION AT US MILITARY BASES

Many of the US Department of Defense's (DoD's) 513 military installations are located on the Atlantic, Pacific, and Gulf coasts and/or include major rivers and other wetland sites. Despite representing a relatively small share of all federal lands in the United States (the federal government controls approximately 28 percent of the nation's federally own land), the military's properties in 2015 accounted for approximately 25 million acres (US Department of Defense, 2015) that support an unusually large number of rare flora and fauna and the greatest densities of threatened and endangered species of any federal lands (Stein et al., 2008; Boice, 2014). Thus, DoD is responsible for establishing sound environmental policies for its bases while simultaneously ensuring the nation's military capabilities.

The Readiness and Environmental Protection Integration (REPI) program is a large federal conservation fund for military installations designed to address those dual goals. REPI partners with conservation organizations and other government agencies in cost-sharing agreements that maintain and preserve surrounding lands. At the end of 2013, the program had protected 315,000 acres using $890 million in combined funds (REPI, 2014). The codes that established the fund specifically require it to function cost-effectively:

1 DoD shall manage its natural resources to facilitate testing and training, mission readiness, and range sustainability in a long-term, comprehensive, coordinated, and cost-effective manner...
2 ...protecting and enhancing...biodiversity conservation, and maintenance of ecosystem services.

REPI funding is designed to serve as a catalyst for financial investments by project partners and to provide substantial financial and technical support for joint conservation efforts (REPI, 2015). In doing so, REPI seeks to address interdependent interests of the military, environmental groups, and the community (REPI, 2014, p. 1):

> Under the REPI Program, DoD works with stakeholders to find solutions to military-community-environmental encroachment issues and enters into unique cost-sharing agreements with conservation organizations and state and local governments to maintain compatible land uses and preserve habitats around military installations.

An example of the types of problems facing military bases in the United States, the military installation at Fort Bragg, North Carolina, harbors a large number of endangered red cockaded woodpeckers that thrive in the longleaf pine habitat on and around the base. In the 1990s, a surge in private development surrounding the base was threatening both the military installation and the birds' habitat, and the US Fish and Wildlife Service issued a biological opinion that military training and testing at Fort Bragg would likely jeopardize the woodpeckers' survival and restrict military activities. Thus for the base to remain active, DoD had to address both problems by preserving land surrounding Fort Bragg from development. In 2001, DoD established the Sustainable Ranges Initiative, and REPI was a key component. The Office of the Secretary of Defense worked with local land trusts and local, state, and federal agencies to develop solutions to the encroachment problem.

To test the applicability of optimization to the REPI program, we compared the ability of BT and GP to allocate REPI's funds cost-effectively (Messer et al., 2016b). A data set provided by DoD consisted of 44 projects REPI considered funding in 2010 with a budget of $54 million – 9 for the Air Force, 23 for the Army, and 12 for the Navy. First, experts from each service branch, other service branches, and the Office of the Secretary of Defense scored the proposed projects in three categories established by REPI:

> *Encroachment threat*: The greater the encroachment threat, the more important the project was in terms of military readiness. *(R)*

> *Justification used under the statute (incompatible development / habitat preservation)*: This is the term used by REPI to refer to environmental protection. *(E)*

> *Viability of agreement (V)*: This score included anticipated contributions of non-REPI funds and the likelihood of execution of the project.

We then calculated an average score for each project from the individual scores submitted by the military branches and the Office of the Secretary of Defense with all of their scores weighted equally. As a group, the Army projects received the highest average score (80.1) followed by the Air Force (71.5) and Navy (66.1) projects. The total

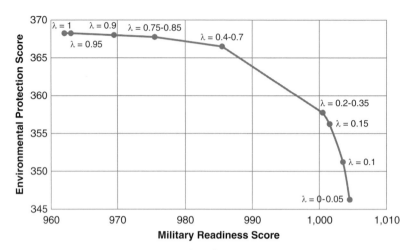

FIGURE 8.4 Sensitivity analysis between goals of environmental protection and military readiness. λ shifts weight between environmental protection and military readiness, with λ = 0 indicating that all weight is given to military readiness, while λ = 1 indicates that all weight is assigned to environmental protection.

anticipated cost to fund all 44 projects ($293.5 million) was more than twice the amount of cost share requested by REPI ($125,986,097) and 5.4 times the total REPI budget of $54 million. The average per-project funding request was $2.8 million and the average project size was 2,845 acres.

We found that using BLP rather than BT raised the military readiness benefit by 23.8 percent, the environmental protection benefit by 19.1 percent, and the viability of agreement by 18.2 percent. From a potential saving perspective, the total acquisition cost for BLP was $13,013,473 less than requested under BT. This is a substantial difference! BLP achieved a greater total benefit while saving more than $13 million. Furthermore, GP optimization led to a 21 percent increase in military readiness and environmental protection and could achieve the level of benefit provided by BT with 37 percent less money!

Figure 8.4 demonstrates how GP can conduct sensitivity analysis to show the relative trade-offs between the program objectives.

This can be helpful information to decision makers as they decide on which projects to fund.

The study dramatically demonstrated that BLP and GP would provide significantly greater benefits than BT, allowing REPI to operate cost-effectively and fulfill DoD policy of achieving multiple objectives. BLP increased the cost-effectiveness of REPI's allocations by achieving a 21 percent greater total benefit score. Put another way, using REPI would have to spend an additional $20.1 million (37.2 percent of its preservation budget) to achieve the same total benefit scores that either BLP or GP could achieve with the original budget.

GOAL PROGRAMMING CASE STUDY: USDA FOREST LEGACY PROGRAM

The USDA's Forest Legacy Program supports state efforts to preserve forest land by providing funds for acquiring partial ownership or conservation easements that prohibit development of environmentally important forest parcels. Conservation easements also typically require private owners to use sustainable forestry practices to protect existing stands and related ecosystem services. Forest Legacy Program administrators considered moving from BT to optimization for its funding selections and requested a study to compare their rank-based model to optimization using 82 requests for funds for projects ranging from 5 to more than 100,000 acres and a $53 million budget (Fooks and Messer, 2012a).

The BT selection process had recommended funding 18 projects, with a total environmental benefit score of 1,396. A simple BLP optimization that aimed to increase project benefit scores recommended funding 45 projects with a total environmental benefit score of 3,024, which is a 117 percent increase. The BT and BLP models agreed on the value of five of the top projects. Both the number of projects selected and the total environmental benefit scores achieved increased substantially and would therefore be attractive to project managers, but meanwhile, both in-kind cost share and number of acres protected decreased. Applying even basic BLP optimization to the Forest Legacy

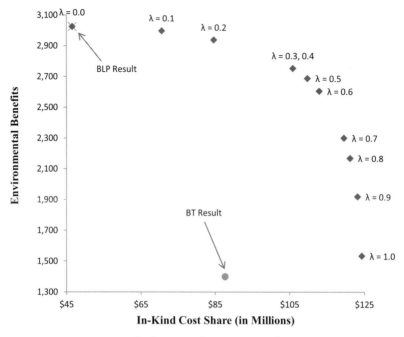

FIGURE 8.5 Results from Benefit Targeting and Binary Linear Programming and the result set from the two-objective goal-programming problem.

Program's selection process would significantly shift the types of projects selected, increase how rapidly conservation occurred, and, ultimately, influence states' priorities when conserving forests by driving them to consider costs in their proposals.

Subsequently, Fooks and Messer (2012) applied GP to the same Forest Legacy Program scenario to incorporate both conservation benefits and partner contributions of in-kind cost-sharing (see Figure 8.5). The GP algorithm maximized a weighted function incorporating both objectives. Our models demonstrated that a 127 percent increase in in-kind cost-sharing required only a 9 percent reduction in the maximum possible benefit. GP also increased the amount of environmental benefit by 120 percent and increased the number of projects funded by 155 percent.

By moving from BLP to the more flexible GP format, the program could achieve a 127 percent gain in in-kind cost share while suffering only a 9 percent reduction in benefits. Alternatively, the Forest Legacy Program could use a three-dimensional GP model to maximize the environmental benefit, in-kind cost share, and number of acres, a solution that provides more than 80 percent of the maximum possible levels of those benefits. Thus, using GP, the Forest Legacy Program's program managers would gain a significant amount of flexibility, allowing them to knowledgably select projects based on multiple priorities. In the next chapter, we switch gears from optimization tools to even more cutting edge techniques involving the harnessing of markets and behavorial nudges.

9 Harnessing the Power of Markets and Behavioral Nudges

In this chapter, we introduce some new and emerging tools that can be used along with optimization and LSP approaches to pursue conservation objectives. As with optimization, these approaches provide an opportunity to increase the level of on-the-ground conservation in a cost-effective manner. In particular, we discuss the importance of developing markets for ecosystem services and using behavioral "nudges" to improve the effectiveness of voluntary conservation programs. These approaches follow the seventh principle of strategic conservation: *Take advantage of the idiosyncrasies of human decision-making*. Nudges are small changes in the "architecture" of the financial incentives in choice presented to decision-makers (Sunstein and Thaler, 2008). Such nudges are attractive to designers of conservation programs because they cost little to implement, do not require potentially disruptive changes to existing programs, and preserve participants' voluntary actions by landowners. Note that these markets and nudges are designed to *complement* rather than *replace* the optimization and LSP approaches discussed previously in this book. In fact, as shown in the following example regarding agricultural preservation, using a combination of these approaches can be highly effective.

THE IMPORTANCE OF MARKET COMPETITION

Many programs have used fixed payments – a set amount of money per acre, for example – when compensating owners for delivering a given management practice or easement. Conservation efforts by government programs have often used fixed prices, offering a fixed number of dollars per acre to all of the potential sellers, who can "take it or leave it." However, environmental economists have advocated for establishing competitive mechanisms such as auctions instead. They have long argued that auctions in voluntary conservation programs could increase how efficiently the program's funds are spent (Ribaudo et al., 2008; Latacz-Lohmann and Van der Hamsvoort, 1997; Stoneham et al., 2003).[1] In theory, fixed prices tend to perform less efficiently than auctions (Schilizzi and Latacz-Lohmann, 2007). Evidence by Horowitz et al. (2009) suggests that auctions can outperform fixed-price approaches and provide more acres of conservation. The intuition behind the theory and the empirical results is that some owners are willing to deliver a level of conservation for less than the fixed payment, which consequently provides them with excess profits (also referred to in economics as 'rents').

Consider, for example, USDA's Conservation Reserve Program (CRP) auctions. This voluntary program for agricultural landowners addresses broad environmental objectives and requires that all funds be allocated on a competitive basis, a condition that is satisfied with an auction. Under CRP, landowners submit offers indicating the amount of compensation they require (will accept) to enroll their properties in the program for usually for a 10–15 year time period. Since the start of the program through June 2017, CRP had conserved 23.5 million acres from 358,589 farms and was paying approximately $1.8 billion per year (US Department of Agriculture, 2017). According to USDA's Farm Service Agency in 2012, the CRP had led to annual reductions in soil erosion of more than 308 million tons from pre-CRP levels, restoration of 2.1 million acres of wetlands and adjacent buffers, a 49 million metric ton reduction in carbon dioxide emissions, and protection of 170,000 stream miles and had increased populations of ducks, quail, and other wildlife by restoring habitats and corridors. In the CRP auction, the potential sellers submit offers representing how much compensation they require to enroll their land and the conservation methods they are willing to adopt for the duration of the program (reflected in the Environmental Benefits Index score).

---

[1] The same goes for negotiating with individual landowners. Such negotiations typically require considerable time and they also lack the competitive market pressures provided by auctions (Hackett and Messer, 1998).

Reverse auctions are now commonly used by government agencies when purchasing environmental and ecosystem services. They are called reverse auctions because, unlike traditional auctions where there is one seller and multiple buyers, they involve multiple sellers (such as landowners) and one buyer (such as a conservation organization).[2] Use of such reverse auctions reflects a general trend toward market-based policy instruments that attempt to bring some of the efficiency associated with private markets to environmental contexts (Horowitz et al., 2009), and in recent years, environmental economists have compared the efficiency of reverse auctions to other procurement approaches (Hanley et al., 2012; Messer et al., 2017; Fooks et al., 2015; Arnold et al., 2013; Fooks et al., 2016; Messer et al., 2014; Duke et al., 2017).

A key reason for government programs' use of reverse auctions is to prevent sellers from gaining *excess profits* (economists aren't against profit; only excess profit (or "rents") is a concern when it comes from strategically gaming a government program that expends the taxpayer money) and thereby achieve the greatest possible fiscal efficiency. In other words, government programs use such auctions in an effort to maximize, cost-effectively, the environmental benefits acquired given the available budget. In the ideal case, then, projects or parcels are enrolled in the program at the price of their unobservable (and heterogeneous) opportunity costs, leaving zero rents to the sellers, where "rents" are defined as excess profit – profits that are above the levels necessary to conduct an agricultural operation that operates successfully in a competitive market. This principle is illustrated in Figure 9.1, which shows what can happen when "ownership returns" from owning land are heterogeneously distributed. Ownership returns can be thought of as the value that an individual landowner gets from owning a piece of land through either working lands production and/or passive uses of the land (such as the enjoyment that comes

---

[2] Alternative terms for reverse auctions include "competitive tenders," "buying auctions," and "procurement auctions." For a review of conservation auctions, see Latacz-Lohmann and Schillizi (2005).

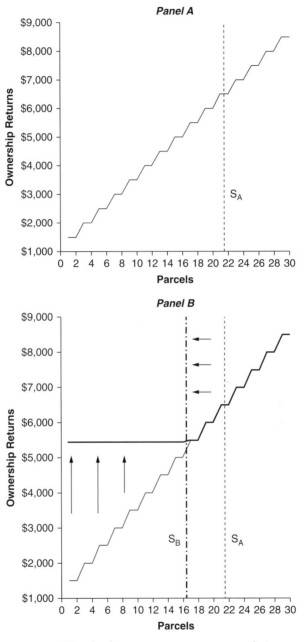

FIGURE 9.1 How landowners can secure excess profit in conservation markets.

from birdwatching). In this case, if a conservation buyer can perfectly pay each landowner the amount equivalent to her ownership return, the buyer can secure a greater quantity of conservation land (S_A) than it can if the sellers secure excess profits, which reduce the amount of land the conservation group can afford to only S_B, a 27 percent reduction (16 units instead of 22) in this example.

Conservation auctions have been used throughout the world, and the results of a number of studies of those auctions have shown that they generally are more cost-effective than other mechanisms for procuring conservation services. For instance, the CRP's auction structure was adopted by conservation agencies in Australia for trial in its Bush Tender program (Stoneham et al., 2003) and a pilot effort by the Auction for Landscape Recovery (Gole et al., 2005). In a study of the first round of auctions by the Bush Tender program in Victoria, Stoneham et al. (2003) found that fixed-payment approaches would have cost seven times more than the auction to obtain the same amount of biodiversity benefit. A study by CJC Consulting (2004) of a reverse auction mechanism used in Scotland under a Challenge Fund scheme found that fixed payments would have cost 33–36 percent more to achieve the same benefit. And in another study of an Australian program, Connor et al. (2008) concluded that, under the same budget, a fixed-payment plan would have produced only 56 percent of the benefits achieved using auctions by Catchment Care Australia in 2004. Other studies have measured the advantages of auctions in terms of doing more "good" within the limits of a budget constraint, such as a greater reduction in emissions (Latacz-Lohmann and Van der Hamsvoort, 1997) and conservation of a greater number of acres (Horowitz et al., 2009).

Success Profile: Delaware Agricultural Lands Preservation Foundation
Delaware is a small state (second smallest in the nation at 1.25 million acres) and a population of less than a million people. More than 60 percent of those residents live in the northernmost county of

New Castle, which includes the state's historic business center, Wilmington, and the University of Delaware in Newark. Projections suggested that Wilmington's population will decrease over the next 30 years while the state's overall population will grow by more than 177,000 (Delaware Population Consortium, 2016). Consequently, most of that increase in population will require conversion of farm land in the southern part of the state to residential and commercial uses. Because so much development is expected to occur, the American Farmland Trust has designated the Mid-Atlantic coastal plain, which incorporates all of the state of Delaware, as "endangered" (American Farmland Trust, 1997). Meanwhile, agriculture is Delaware's largest industry; it produced $1.2 billion in value in 2012 and has employed approximately one of every seven residents directly or in related industries (US Department of Agriculture, 2016). Nationally, the state ranks fifth in percentage of area used as farm land (41.2 percent) despite losing 600 farms comprising about 70,000 acres to development between 1997 and 2007, largely because of urbanization. Delaware's average elevation is also one of the lowest in the country, and its green infrastructure areas generally are located in the low-lying coastal areas.

As the State worked to address numerous environmental and land-use concerns, Delaware established (in 1991) one of the nation's largest and most successful programs for preserving agricultural land. The Delaware Agricultural Lands Preservation Foundation (DALPF) is a hybrid organization in which staff members from the state's Department of Agriculture administer the program with guidance from a nongovernmental advisory board. The program is funded by state taxes and local and federal matching funds.

DALPF generally has defined parcel "benefits" solely using the prices offered by owners through sealed bids in a reverse auction mechanism. Participation in the program is voluntary and is established through annual funding cycles. As detailed in Messer and Allen (2010), DALPF provides for appraisals to determine the value an easement on each parcel offered by qualifying landowners interested in participating. Each interested landowner reviews the appraisal and then chooses whether to submit a sealed "bid" that consists of a "percentage discount" on the appraised value of the easement (how much of the value they are willing to forgo) in a reverse auction. Thus, an offer of a 40 percent discount on an easement appraised at $1 million means that DALPF will pay only $600,000 for it. DALPF ranks the bids by the percentage discount offered and then acquires easements from the owners who offered the *greatest* discounts until there is not enough left in the budget to acquire the next best parcel.

This type of system is a "receive what you offer" auction – also referred to as a discriminative auction; the amount paid per acre is based on the amount of discount offered. An advantage of the DALPF auction is that cost is, by definition, the sole determinant in the algorithm. The program's goal is to maximize the total value of the set of easements acquired rather than the number of acres protected. However, DALPF's system does not guarantee that the parcels acquired have the highest value in terms of ecosystem and/or other related services. That occurs only if, by chance, the owners of those highest-quality parcels offer the greatest discounts.[1] Of particular concern to DALPF is the possibility that owners of land that is only marginally valuable for agriculture will offer relatively large discounts since they likely have few other options for obtaining income from those parcels. Similarly, when parcels are located near growing urban areas, there is significant potential for development. In that case, DALPF could wind up acquiring particularly expensive easements if both the discounts and the appraised values are high. Parcels that are not prime targets for development would have lower appraised values that could more than compensate DALPF for offers of relatively small discounts.

After two decades of operation, DALPF had acquired easements that protected 110,954 acres from 754 properties (21.3 percent of the state's agricultural land) and spent $198,780,209 (Delaware Department of Agriculture, 2013). DALPF's auction had spent over $93 million to obtain a total easement value of more than $162 million. As shown in Figure 9.2, DALPF's reverse auction clearly outperformed a traditional BT approach, protecting a greater number of farms (386 vs. 237) and slightly more acres.

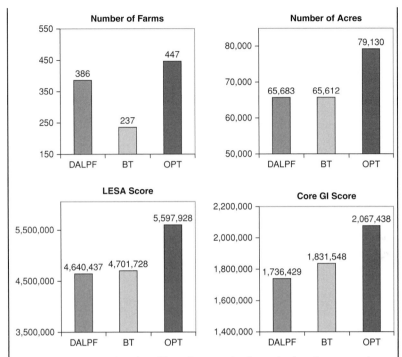

FIGURE 9.2 Results of benefit scenarios for agricultural preservation in Delaware.

To make DALPF's algorithm even more effective, the cost of projects could be appropriately incorporated into the selection process. Figure 9.2 shows how combining DALPF's reverse auction *with* optimization techniques such as BLP could provide for preservation of even more farms, more acres, and greater benefits – measured using either Land Evaluation/Site Assessment (LESA) or Core Green Infrastructure (GI) scores. For example, if DALPF had used a selection process that included BLP, it would have preserved an additional 13,518 acres for the same cost. The gain in cost-effectiveness in this case comes from preserving additional acres of agricultural land that have an estimated market value of $20.7 million.

Next, consider Figure 9.3, which shows the differences in efficiency between the Optimization Model (OM), the Benefit Targeting/Rank-Based Model (RBM), and the DALPF selection method from an analysis by Messer and Allen (2010). The percentage of the budget of

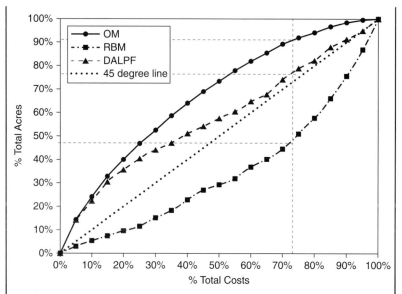

FIGURE 9.3 Lorenz curves for DALPF historical analysis.

$128 million dollars spent is shown on the horizontal axis and the vertical axis shows the percentage of the total number of offered acres (87,407) protected. All of the curves start with a base case in which no parcels have been protected and no cost has been incurred. They also converge when all of the submitted parcels can be protected and, therefore, 100 percent of the potential cost is incurred. The 45-degree line denotes reference situations at which the percentage of the budget expended equals the percentage of the potential benefit obtained. For example, when 30 percent of the budget ($38.4 million) is expended, 30 percent of the total potential acres (26,222) are conserved. By comparing the Lorenz curves, we can estimate the degree of efficiency for various scenarios; the higher a curve is on the vertical axis, the more efficient the selection method is. And the degree of horizontal distance between the curves represents the degree to which efficiency is improved.

In the study, 21 iterations of the model were conducted, allowing for 5 percent budget intervals. As shown in Figure 9.3, the OM and DALPF curves always exceeded the reference level of 45 degrees. The two curves initially were nearly identical – they did not significantly diverge until the cost represented 15 percent of the budget. By 55 percent, the DALPF curve begins to parallel the 45-degree line while the OM curve maintains a high trajectory, indicating that optimization sustains efficiency in most of the budget levels. RBM, on the other hand, starts at less than 45 degrees and drops further until reaching nearly 80 percent of the budget, at which point the curve begins to rise again.

At given budget points, the spaces between the lines measure differences in efficiency. For example, the $93 million budget in our earlier scenarios represents 73 percent of the budget in the figure of $128 million. Looking at the point in Figure 9.3 at which 73 percent of the budget is spent, one can see that the OM would acquire approximately 90 percent of the total potential acres while DALPF's auction would acquire 78 percent and the RBM only 48 percent.

[1] Selecting parcels strictly by the percent discount offered is analogous to shopping for food and buying only items that are most on sale even if you do not want to eat them. Furthermore, the greatest price reductions could be for the most expensive items (for truffles or aged organic filet mignon). In that case, even with large discounts, their prices could be higher than the undiscounted prices for similar foods that are nearly as good.

Success Profile: Mike McGrath

Discounts of 20 percent, 30 percent, 50 percent! When we're shopping sales, we naturally gravitate toward the stores offering the best discounts, and percentage markdowns make it easy to see which stores to hit first. In the conservation field, it isn't easy to find those best deals, but Mike McGrath found a way. As a planner for DALPF, McGrath developed a selection process that uses a reverse auction to clearly determine which sellers are offering the most bang for DALPF's buck.

McGrath (Figure 9.4), who retired from the Delaware Department of Agriculture in 2011 as chief of planning, has been an exceptional pioneer and leader in preservation of farmland in Delaware for 28 years. Thousands of acres, nearly one-third of the state's farm land, have been preserved thanks to his efforts and to the reverse auction program he developed.

FIGURE 9.4 Mike McGrath.
Photograph by Lindsay Yeager.
© University of Delaware.

In the 1970s, Delaware was largely an agricultural state, and, as McGrath notes, "There was a perception that farmland preservation wasn't really a pressing issue." McGrath was one of a handful of people who disagreed. The state was slow to pursue preservation – neighboring states such as Maryland had already established programs – and that delay provided Delaware with a unique opportunity to analyze existing programs and then to create something better. McGrath felt that the existing programs were not as effective as they could be. In his work with DALPF, he created a preservation selection program that used a competitive reverse auction to reap greater benefits for the first state. "Delaware defied what state programs should look like," McGrath said. The auction creates a market in which owners of farms of various sizes and conservation values compete to sell their development rights.

Delaware's reverse auction is an innovative design in which agricultural landowners submit sealed bids consisting of a percent discount on the appraised value of their land, reducing the price Delaware must pay for a conservation easement. The farms are ranked for preservation not by their appraised values or stated discounts in dollars; instead, they are ranked by the size of the percentage offered. An owner who offers a 50 percent discount ranks higher than an owner who offers a 30 percent discount, leveling the field for farms of various sizes and agricultural value. A large farm might easily be able to offer a $100,000 discount while a small family farm might be priced out at $20,000. By ranking selections by the percent discount, DALPF leverages the association between a farm's size and the discount offered to give Delaware's taxpayers the best deals possible.

The program has been so successful because it incorporates considerations from all stakeholders. According to McGrath, "The program we had using auctions took away the argument from the farm side of the equation that there was some bureaucrat deciding how much money they got." Traditional farmland preservation programs had declared a price that would be paid to the owners, and, as it turns out, farmers didn't like the idea of some unknown person telling them how much their farms were worth. McGrath took note of this friction and sought to create a selection process that could make everyone happy and still save money while doing more.

As McGrath notes, the farm owners respond to the reverse auction strategically by "trying to figure out how they can discount the least and still win the auction." They want to get the best deal, but their need to compromise results in a great deal for the public as well.

Will Markets Always Work?

The answer to the question posed by this heading is that the "devil is in the details." If the United States is to address its major environmental challenges, including water and air pollution, policymakers will have to design and implement competitive market processes for selecting and funding those important works (Shortle, 2013). The best-known example of a successful environmental market is the federal program aimed at reducing sulfur dioxide (SO_2) pollution. The program arose from an amendment to the 1990 Clean Air Act and had, by 2014, reduced sulfur dioxide pollution by 12.6 million tons to

20 percent of the level of pollution in 1990 (Environmental Protection Agency, 2016).

In addition, tradable permit, market systems such as the one established for fireplaces in Telluride, Colorado, can further promote reductions in air pollution. Reducing air pollution is an important goal for the popular ski resort there, which is located in a small box canyon that traps polluted air. Under tradable permit systems, the first step is to establish an overall goal for reducing the unwanted activity (such as local air pollution). The government then assigns a limited number of permits (or rights) to entities that contribute to the targeted pollution to reach that goal (in the case of Telluride, the number of permits for wood burning fireplaces[3]). Finally, the government establishes a market in which the firms can buy and sell permits. In the context of land conservation, the undesirable activity is development of environmentally important areas, and the government's goal is to limit the number of parcels that can be developed.

A study of Calvert, Howard, and Montgomery counties in Maryland by Lynch and Musser (2001) pointed to a challenge associated with programs that transfer development rights. They found that voluntary programs usually performed worse than the state program of purchasing development rights in terms of protecting areas that offered the greatest agricultural value. The reason? The number of acres conserved was the sole measure of the benefit of the program. Because the voluntary programs failed to consider the *quality* of the acres conserved, they tended to acquire development rights to mostly poor-quality properties while the state program generally acquired high-quality agricultural lands. That one factor in how the market was established led to a less-efficient outcome under the voluntary programs. One way to avoid such problems is to test the design of a competitive auction market for conservation before implementing it.

---

[3] In Tellulride, if you did not have a permit for a wood burning fireplace you could still install a fireplace that burned natural gas.

Using Economic Experiments to Test Conservation Auction Designs

Since the use of reverse auctions to achieve conservation objectives has so far been relatively rare, economists have increasingly turned to experimental methods to test potential reverse auction mechanisms. Economic experiments allow one to establish laboratory controls when testing the behavioral resources to incentives and different designs. Then these results can be verified by other studies (replicability) when exploring important economic questions. As traditional economic theories have been increasingly challenged and behavioral economics has risen in prominence, economic experiments have become a critical tool for testing and developing new understandings of human behavior and designing cost-effective approaches to benefit the environment.

Modeling real world behavior presents challenges that are difficult to address in many settings, particularly when aspects of individuals' decision are unknown to the researchers. This is usually the case in conservation settings. This is why Kent has spent considerable time studying auction behavior as director of the Center for Experimental and Applied Economics at the University of Delaware. In such experimental settings, participants make decisions that directly affect their payoffs (paid in cash). Thus, the results tend to be more robust and reliable than hypothetical responses that come from traditional questionnaire-based research.

Another advantage of experiments is that since they permit a significant amount of control they can be used to isolate key behaviors, which is important in understanding how and when reverse auctions are effective. In an uncontrolled environment, it is difficult to identify causality and the researcher cannot change a single condition to determine its marginal impact on participants' decisions. When an experiment is conducted, the investigator can design the institutional context, know the real monetary payoffs (i.e., the payment scheme), and examine the implications of one change one attribute at a time, through the use of experiment treatments. This allows one to test policies at a fine scale and consequently to suggest the mix of institutional rules and approaches that will lead to the best conservation outcome.

Replicability also contributes to the popularity of experimental methods. Early in the development of the field, Smith (1987) suggested that progress in the discipline of experimental economics depended on the replicability of one's experiments. As in other scientific disciplines, the ability to replicate the results of an economic experiment proves the robustness of its findings, and investigators sometimes replicate the same experiment multiple times. This allows them to test the results with different sets of participants to determine similarities and differences for different pools and potentially for different social groups. By publishing the experiments' instructions and protocols along with the papers, they open the door for other researchers to attempt to replicate the experiment to verify the results or use the design to aid in university teaching.

Increasingly, experiments are being used to test the potential impacts of policies, including reverse auctions designed for conservation. As Shogren (2004) noted, "like a wind tunnel to test airplane design, lab experiments provide a testbed for what is called *economic design* – the process of constructing institutions and mechanisms to examine resource allocation." Experiments as testbeds are particularly useful in settings in which implementation of a policy change would be difficult or costly; initially testing alternative policies in the laboratory can be highly cost-effective.

Figure 9.5 illustrates the trade-offs generally associated with designing experiments to test the effectiveness of market mechanisms in conservation settings. The details of those trade-offs, which are described in Messer et al. (2014), exceed the scope of this chapter, however several key results can be gleaned from that research and are described below.

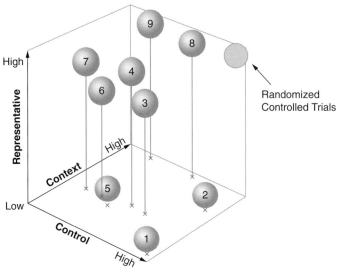

Point	Source of Values	Representativeness of Participants	Context of Instructions	Description
1	Induced	Students	Neutral	Experimental market in a university lab
2	Induced	Students	Specific	Experimental market in a university lab
3	Induced	Landowners	Specific	Experimental market in a university lab
4	Induced	Landowners	Specific	Experimental market in a university lab
5	Endogenous	Students	Neutral	General market in university lab
6	Endogenous	Landowners	Neutral	General market in university lab
7	Endogenous	Landowners	Neutral	General market in mobile lab
8	Endogenous	Landowners	Specific	Land-related market created in the field
9	Endogenous	Landowners	Policy Rules	Natural experiment

FIGURE 9.5 Trade-offs in experimental control, context, and representativeness. Modified from Messer et al. (2014).

Carefully Designing Auctions

Reverse auctions can be conducted using various rules, and experimental research has clearly shown that the rules matter. Thus, if you are trying to get great results like those of DALPF and the SO_2 air pollution program, you want to give careful consideration to the rules you establish and the incentives they create.

One popular reverse auction mechanism is discriminatory price auction. In this case, discriminatory is not related to bias against something. It simply means that the auction discriminates individuals' willingness to accept a payment in exchange for selling something in the auction. This type of auction is also known as a "pay what you bid" auction. This mechanism has been popular among conservation organizations such as DALPF because it ostensibly sorts sellers by their opportunity costs by first paying the individuals who make the least expensive offers. Theoretically, discriminatory price auctions are efficient as long as the projects vying to be enrolled are similar in quality or the auction incorporates a mechanism that correctly adjusts the offers to account for quality (Glebe, 2013).

However, a number of studies have shown that actual seller behavior is more complicated. Sellers consider both the price they are willing to accept and their chances of winning when deciding whether to participate and how much to offer, and sellers may choose to inflate their offers if they are uncertain about their chances of winning. They may also act strategically if they believe they have a good chance of winning by inflating their offers (trying to secure excess profits), which thus will not reflect their true opportunity costs. There is little opportunity to obtain an excessive profit when the sellers' opportunity costs and other land-ownership values are relatively similar. However, if there are relatively large differences in the value of their parcels and/or their opportunity costs, strategic behavior becomes much more likely, as shown in Figure 9.1 (Messer et al., 2017).

Studies (see Glebe, 2013) have found that excess profits secured from auctions in which the individual parcels are relatively diverse in value are higher than rents secured from auctions when most of the parcels are similar in value (Messer et al., 2014). In other words, when the parcel values are highly diverse, such as the Mid-Atlantic of the United States that faces significant differences in development pressure, there is a larger number of low-cost parcels so those sellers have a greater incentive to inflate their offers. In many areas of the Midwest or Great Plains of the United States, differences in returns for various parcels are typically relatively small, giving landowners little opportunity to inflate their offers. As a result, using reverse auctions in those regions should have a greater ability to be cost-effective.

The Power of Public Information: A Goldilocks Story

The economic efficiency of a reverse auction mechanism is strongly affected by how often the auction is conducted and the type and amount of information provided, directly and indirectly, in the process to the potential sellers. Consider energy auctions, which typically occur frequently and involve a small number of savvy sellers who can use their experience to optimize the prices they receive using complex dynamic strategies (Rassenti et al., 2003; Vossler et al., 2009; Shawhan et al., 2011). The sellers benefit from information about the auction and the buyer that they accumulate over time while the buyer can obtain better deals from the seller by giving them information that motivates them to reduce their prices. Consequently, the cost-conscious conservation buyer is left with a "Goldilocks Problem" (Messer et al., 2014) – determining what information is "too much," "too little," and hopefully "just right."

A number of studies of conservation auctions have found that sellers' experience with an auction and its mechanism and the information they can glean about the buying organization's objectives and the market as a whole can significantly affect their bidding behavior. How it influences that behavior varies with the particular set of circumstances. Some studies (Duffy and Feltovich, 2002; Devetag, 2003; Ferraro, 2008; Krishna, 2010; Glebe, 2013; Messer et al., 2014, 2017) have found that carefully disclosing information about the auction can increase the auction's efficiency while others have found that efficiency increased when some types of information remained hidden (Vincent, 1995; Vukina et al., 2008; Rolfe et al., 2009). Ferraro (2008), for example, found that complete disclosure enhanced participants' perceptions of the fairness and transparency of the auction and that those positive perceptions could increase their participation and compliance over the long term. Most of the studies, however, found that iterative bidding allowed sellers to learn enough about the auction and the buyer to gradually inflate their offers. Schilizzi and Latacz-Lohmann (2007), for example, examined auctions constrained by targets and budgets. They determined that auctions were more effective than fixed payments under one-time, single-period scenarios but that repetitive bidding rapidly reduced the auction's advantage. Rolfe et al. (2009) determined that providing information could increase transparency for sellers but could also increase their competitiveness and, in reality, give them information they could use to bid strategically and capture excess profits. Krishna (2010) found that any element of an auction that deterred competition had a negative effect on efficiency.

Other types of information are important as well. Banerjee et al. (2011) found that conservation auctions tended to be sensitive to the amount of information possessed by the sellers. As additional information was revealed, the sellers increased the amount required for them to enroll in the program and cost-effectiveness declined. An earlier study of common-value auctions by Vincent (1995) found that the auctioneer should not reveal all of its information. Cason et al. (2003) also found that conservation organizations could obtain better (less expensive) offers by not divulging information about how the environmental services of each parcel in the auction had been scored. They conceptualized information as whether or not participants knew the buyer's value for the landowner/participant's project. Their results showed that participants tended to inflate offers particularly when the projects were of relatively high value to the buyer. Consequently, less information about buyer value may increase auction efficiency. This result has important implications for ecosystem service markets since the buyer's preferences, such as habitat for endangered species, are often well publicized. Additionally, priorities, such as only acquiring land that is adjacent to already protected land may lead to higher offers from sellers to conservation programs.

In a subsequent study, Cason and Gangadharan (2004) compared the effect of information on discriminatory and uniform-price auctions. Their results showed that offers were more likely to exceed the true valuations and thus to increase excess profits when sellers knew relatively more about how the environmental benefits of the properties were assessed. Both types of auctions led to inflated offers but the discriminatory auction was more cost-effective than the uniform-price auction. Banerjee et al. (2011) found similar evidence of inflated offers in an iterative auction process as greater information became available.

In terms of the type of information provided, an experiment by Haruvy and Katok (2013) showed that revealing the program's objectives for the auction reduced cost-effectiveness, and Banerjee et al. (2011) found that rent-seeking increased with the amount of information provided. The information gave sellers a greater understanding of the auction's mechanism and allowed them to develop strategies for extracting excess compensation.

Another type of information that can affect bidders' behavior is details about the conservation organization's budget and its use of reserve prices. Bajari and Hortacsu (2003) found that announcements regarding the presence or lack of a reserve price had no effect on the offers received. Sellers who were given minimal information tended to be concerned about the auction's fairness, an issue that can be particularly important when the market for the auctioned item is quite small, as is usually the case with environmental services. Katkar and Reiley (2007) also found that revealing the reserve price could limit participation, making the bidding process less competitive. Using a simulation, Hailu and Schilizzi (2004) found that bidders' required prices increased if they received information about the auction.

A study by Latacz-Lohmann and Van der Hamsvoort (1997) noted an association between the relative cost of a set of purchases in an auction and bidder uncertainty, suggesting that a high level of bidder uncertainty could lead to strategic bidding and an inefficient outcome. Likewise, Cummings et al. (2004) found that a high degree of uncertainty could lead to strategic rent-seeking. Klemperer (2002) reported that sellers were able to obtain higher excess profits when they were allowed to discover others' valuations in a multiround auction. That information tended to make them feel more comfortable about identifying the optimal bidding strategy and less conservative about inflating their offers. Several other studies found that owners tended to offer the maximum bid set by a conservation agency after the first few rounds of the auction (Shoemaker, 1989; Khanna and Ando, 2009).

The take-away from these studies is that the frequency of a conservation auction and the information made available to sellers can have a significant effect on the outcome. Determining the "just right" type and amount of information to disclose regarding the organization's budget, objectives, and evaluation processes is both complicated and critical to designing an effective auction mechanism.

Budget Size and Variability

Large budgets and availability of information about the market allow sellers to obtain relatively large rent premiums. Studies involving experimental auctions have found that successful sellers were able to increase their offers by nearly 0.5 percent for every 1 percent increase in the budget when they knew how much the buyer had to spend (Messer et al., 2017). Potential sellers clearly took advantage of the information and adjusted their offers when the budget appeared to be relatively larger.

Experimental research has also shown that unpredictable variability in a program's budget in the presence of market information diminishes the effect of learning and inflation of offers. Thus, variable budgets are likely to achieve better results than fixed budgets. In other words, variation in a budget over time takes away some of sellers' strategic opportunities because they don't know when the best opportunity to inflate their offers will occur.

The Problem of Adverse Selection in Markets

As mentioned in Chapter 4, adverse selection occurs in conservation markets because sellers (landowners) typically possess private information about their cost to deliver the services offered. A planner, for example, typically cannot observe the cost required to convince an owner to expand riparian buffers without a policy incentive; some owners may be willing to provide riparian buffers for a minimal cost as a way of contributing to the health of the environment while others will not. Voluntary programs naturally tend to attract the owners who are already the most likely to deliver conservation services. If owners who would already be willing to supply a conservation service participate in a conservation program, some of the benefits ultimately provided are erroneously attributed to the program. Likewise, conservation gains can be overstated when they are not compared to the outcome in the absence of the program. In these cases, analyses based on an observed benefit and the program cost are not valid. The problem of adverse selection is further exacerbated when programs use cost targeting or a reverse auction (Arnold et al., 2013). While the owners' costs are not observable, the owners who will most likely offer a low price for providing conservation services in a reverse auction, again are already the owners most inclined to establish conservation measures on their own.

Arnold et al. (2013) argued that, because of program budget constraints, conservation markets are subject to an extreme adverse-selection problem in which some landowners should optimally be excluded from the market entirely but that hidden information precludes that outcome. In addition, by effectively assigning property rights to externalities of privately informed owners, conservation markets create informational rents for owners that might be avoided by alternative conservation programs, such as a basic tax on converting natural lands to development.

A number of recent efforts by conservation programs have tried to address adverse selection using additionality. Under some carbon programs, landowners who are already pursuing sequestration using no-till production methods are not allowed to sell carbon credits. Planners have focused mostly on challenges associated with implementing programs – costly monitoring, questions about equity – because early adopters are sometimes punished, and complex dynamics such as farmers who till one year so they can enter a program the following year.

The unfortunate problem with adverse selection is that despite spending billions of dollars, these programs may not be positively altering land-use patterns or other environmental outcomes as much as they hope. As mentioned in Chapter 4 in the discussion of how Pennsylvania has paid Amish people to protect farms that they were already highly likely to keep in agricultural production, these policies can wind up just transferring billions of dollars from the government and nonprofits to landowners who were the most likely to deliver the desired conservation services in the absence of a policy. Among the drivers of this problem are the mechanisms used, which seek to select the lowest-cost providers of the service and, in the case of discriminatory reverse auctions, allow landowners to "name their own price." When these selection techniques are combined with constrained program budgets, only a small subset of potential landowners will be selected, and that subset will likely include the owners who were least likely to sell their land to a developer in the absence of the conservation buyer.

Dynamics of Timing of Entry: Getting Something for Nothing

There is some potential good news about dealing with adverse selection in auctions that comes from research on multiple-round actions and combining optimization and reverse auctions. For instance, McAfee and McMillan (1987) argued that interdependencies among offers or combinatorial benefits are introduced by multiple rounds. Information can be gained by sellers about the suitability of their proposals (Rolfe et al., 2009). Klemperer (2002) found that sellers became more comfortable with their own ability to assess the value of their properties and less conservative in their bidding when they were allowed to learn about others' valuations through multiple rounds. Other arguments for repeat-auction designs are that participants need more than one round to understand the auction mechanism and how to offer true valuations, as well as to learn from market feedback (List and Shogren, 1999).

Dynamics arise in that there are multiple repeating cycles (or rounds), often occurring on an annual budget basis, making the landowner's decision problem more complicated than typically posed.[4] Owners may submit offers in any year that the program exists and, if they are not selected, may then decide to develop the land, reenter the auction the next year, or continue the land's current use. Further complicating decision-making, the future continuation and budget level of the program are uncertain. Significant behavioral implications are introduced when researchers recognize entry dynamics (Rolfe et al., 2009). Consider, for instance, competing predictions about the effectiveness of conservation auctions under dynamic entry. It may be that owners will "over enter" early, worrying that the program will end or eagerly seeking a new opportunity to make money. In this story, the program sees a high level of competition initially and, thereby, reduces rents – at least initially. A contrasting story is that owners hesitate because the program is unfamiliar or they see opportunities to "strategically wait," choosing to delay their participation because they anticipate a thin market (few participating sellers), greater buyer demand in future periods, and obtaining additional information about the market (as in Hailu and Schilizzi (2004)) – all giving them the opportunity to extract higher excess profits. This would trigger a dynamic sorting process in which greater profits could be extracted in the future. Finally, one may simply question whether owners have the capacity to optimize dynamically when the budgetary future of the conservation program is uncertain or they offer low-cost offers in the face of stochastic shocks such as illness, a significant family change, or financial distress.

One thing to consider in multiple-cycle auctions is that the conservation organization can benefit from sellers who wait for a future round to submit an offer. In several experimental studies (Fooks et al.,

---

[4] Here, we use "dynamic" to specifically describe reverse auctions where an agency is seeking to repeatedly procure services from a pool of potential sellers, where a seller's success or failure in past rounds affects their ability to participate in future rounds as in the case of long-term conservation contracts.

2015), the presence of an auction caused landowners to delay convert-ing their land from agriculture to other uses as they considered the conservation auction and attempted to participate. While they wait, their lands continue to provide ecosystem services that the conser-vation organization *does not have to pay for*. As a result, programs that involve multiple rounds secure some advantages just by delay-ing having to make payments while landowners hope for better deals in the future and forgo being paid immediately. We referred to these as "unpreserved benefits" since they accrue without compensation (Fooks et al., 2015).

Resolving Adverse Selection (Partially) by Combining Markets and Benefit-Cost Targeting

Research has shown that including optimization methods, such as Benefit-Cost Targeting (BCT), enables a reverse auction to outperform a discriminatory price auction in a multiple-round setting because it protects both more parcels and higher-quality parcels. In our research, we showed that parcels with a large social benefit were approximately 5 percent more likely to enter a BCT auction than a traditional reverse auction that paid owners what they bid (Fooks et al., 2015). A BCT auction can act as a sorting mechanism that leads owners of high-value properties to respond to the auction incentives and participate, thus providing a larger number of high-quality parcels from which to choose. Thus, BCT auctions can potentially increase the benefits achieved by making the selection process more efficient and by induc-ing entry by owners of higher-quality parcels, giving the conservation program better choices. The magnitude of the performance improve-ments tended to be in the range of 5–15 percent (Fooks et al., 2015).

THE POWER OF BEHAVIORAL NUDGES

Conservation scientists have become increasingly aware of the role human behavior plays in conserving nature and its services and the need to use behavioral economics to understand the choices landown-ers make and their impacts on the environment (Cowling, 2014).

Tapping into the power of nudges can help conservation professionals follow the seventh core principle of strategic conservation: *Take advantage of the idiosyncrasies of human decision-making.* Unlike the standard economic model that assumes that people and firms always make rational utility-maximizing and profit-maximizing decisions, behavioral models of economic behavior have demonstrated that people's decisions are often influenced by psychological factors and can also be influenced by nonfinancial means in predictable ways. This approach is generally known as behavioral economics, and the 2017 Nobel Prize in Economic Sciences was awarded to Richard Thaler for his pioneering working in this area. Thaler's research and that done by other behavioral economists has shown that concepts such as nudges can be effective in improving the parcels and services offered by sellers in a variety of conservation applications ranging from one-time, life-changing decisions to everyday behavioral habits.

The use of economic experiments has exploded in economics as a way to test theories and investigate how humans behave under different institutions (Harrison and List, 2004; List and Price, 2016). Shogren and Taylor (2008) noted that numerous empirical studies using experiments had challenged the rational choice theory as a guide to predicting behavior. Subsequent studies have shown that behavioral interventions can influence behavior and be highly cost-effective because they cost little to implement (Allcott and Mullainathan, 2010; Garcia-Sierra et al., 2015; Kahneman and Tversky, 2000; Metcalfe and Dolan, 2012).

In recent years, government agencies and NGOs in a number of countries have begun to incorporate insights from behavioral economics and psychology into their programs, including several cities and countries that have established full-time "nudge squads" of behavioral economists and psychologists to facilitate their efforts. For example, the United Kingdom's national government created a Behavioral Insights Team with the goal of improving the cost-effectiveness of their programs and policies. In the United States, the Obama administration created the Social and Behavioral Science Team and mandated that federal programs incorporate behavioral science and be evidence-based. These nudge squads have been embedding behavioral insights into programs to formally test the effect of nudges on choices ranging from tax compliance to educational performance.

Application of such behavioral insights into conservation programs and policies is still in a nascent stage. In 2014, the USDA Economic Research Service provided funds to establish a national Center for Behavioral and Experimental Agri-Environmental Research (CBEAR), the organization that Kent co-directs with Paul Ferraro from Johns Hopkins University. CBEAR catalyzes efforts to apply these behavioral insights and tests the approaches experimentally to improve the performance of conservation programs. CBEAR develops evidence-based approaches conservation programs can use to select projects or parcels and spend their limited funds cost-effectively.

Ferraro et al. (2017) outlined four characteristics of nudges that make them particularly appropriate for incorporation in conservation policies and programs:

1 Their ability to change policy-relevant behaviors is supported by a growing body of empirical evidence.
2 They are well-suited for programs that encourage voluntary actions, such as adoption of new technologies and practices.
3 They typically require only small adjustments to a program so they are often politically feasible, cost-effective ways to solve problems.
4 Their effectiveness can be easily tested in randomized controlled trials prior to being implemented on a large scale, thereby providing evidence regarding the nudges that work best under specific conditions.

Describing all of the creative ways that nudges can be incorporated into conservation is a lengthy endeavor worthy of another book. Here, we introduce a number of key behavioral nudges that have been documented as effective in other contexts. We hope that by introducing the idea of nudges, describing some of the evidence for the benefits, and suggesting how they can be incorporated into conservation programs can interest readers in learning more about this exciting and emerging area of strategic conservation.

Framing of Information

When considering how to nudge environmental actions in a particular direction, an obvious place to start is altering the types of information provided about the program. Note that nudges go beyond the basic idea of educating sellers or donors in the hope of influencing their choices or providing public information as described earlier in this chapter. Those approaches have long been used in conservation. *Informational nudges* generally are less oriented toward "educating" people and are designed instead to appeal to other human motivations and even emotions that affect behavior.

An example of an informational nudge comes from recent experimental research we conducted in which adults were asked how much they would pay for various water-conservation technologies their households could use, such as soaker hoses, soil test kits, and environmentally friendly fertilizers (Weigel et al., 2017). Half of the participants were given standard scientific information about why adoption of the technologies could improve local water quality. The other half were given a description of a retired police officer who had recently died after being infected by flesh-eating Vibrio bacteria while washing out a crab trap with bay water. The information cited a prominent conservation group that linked the abundance of the Vibrio bacteria to excess nutrient pollution from various locations, including lawns. The research question was which of these two messages would most motivate people to pay for the conservation technologies. Interestingly, the message that incorporated an identifiable victim was more effective in motivating the experiment participants to invest their money in a technology that could improve water quality.

Another interesting question relates to "the messenger" – what happens when identical information is provided by different types of messengers (e.g., scientists versus government representatives). Marketers clearly believe that the messenger – whether a celebrity, "real people," or a trusted official – makes a difference, and a number of studies have found that conservation groups should be similarly strategic and identify the best person or entity to deliver messages related to environmental issues. In a study of UK consumers regarding genetically modified foods, for example, Hunt and Frewer (2001) found that consumers most trusted university scientists and departments of health and the environment. And in the context of climate change, Arbuckle et al. (2015) conducted a study that compared Iowa farmers' trust in six environmentally oriented interest groups, finding that scientists were trusted most and mainstream media outlets were trusted least. However, when it came to potential food safety related to the use of recycled water to irrigate food, we found that consumers were more likely to follow advice that came from newspapers rather than advice from scientists, perhaps because they believed that food safety problems were most frequently reported in the news in a manner that protects the public (Schmidt et al., 2017). The results of these studies are mixed. On one hand, they show that who the messenger is matters. On the other hand, in some contexts, scientists or the news media are most trusted while the reverse seems to be true in other contexts. Thus, the take-home message is that conservation organizations would be wise to consider carefully who the most appropriate messenger would be for their stakeholders.

Scientific information in particular can be intimidating to people so both the *who* and the *how* of delivering such information are important. The information can be presented in many different forms, and conservation groups should determine how to present the information to target audiences in a readily accessible and understandable way. The faster the audience can comprehend and analyze the information, the more they can adjust their behavior to achieve environmental improvements. We tested this idea in recent research in which we showed people information about environmental outcomes resulting from their collective actions. When the information was presented as a gauge (like ones used by the US Forest Service to indicate fire risk), people took more conservation actions than when the same information was displayed numerically even when the financial incentives were identical (Butler et al., 2017).

Gain and Loss Framing

Have you ever noticed how inexplicably losing a $20 bill can cast a shadow over your whole day but that finding a $20 bill on the sidewalk makes you happy only for a couple of minutes and is easily overshadowed by later events? If so, you are not alone. In general, people focus much more on losses than on gains, and that tendency affects how they make choices. For example, Tversky and Kahneman (1991) asked people if they were willing to accept a bet based on a flip of a coin. If the coin turned up heads, they won x dollars; if the coin turned up tails, they lost y dollars. On average, to accept the bet, people requested about twice as much of a gain as they accepted as a loss. In other words, people were more concerned about what they could lose than what they could win. Behavioral economists refer to this tendency to prefer avoiding losses to acquiring gains, which has been observed in a variety of settings, as loss aversion.

Conservation efforts can be framed in different ways. Do we want to take actions that provide "greater ecosystem services" or are we working to "prevent damage to ecosystem services?" Activists chain themselves to an ancient redwood not to get more services but to prevent the loss of a service of an old-growth forest. We rarely see people express a similar level of passion when creating gains by planting trees or working on habitat enhancement projects.

Consider how this tendency plays out in a program designed to reduce pollution created by agricultural land. Those programs mostly provide financial incentives – a gain in the form of a payment – to motivate farmers to adopt pollution-reduction practices. Since the incentive is structured as a gain, perhaps these programs could increase the practices adopted and implemented by using a loss-based negative frame instead. For instance, instead of advising farmers of how much money they gain from adopting each practice, the program could let farmers know how much would earn from adopting all of the practices and the amount they would lose for each practice they rejected and/or failed to implement. This same concept can be

FIGURE 9.6 Picture of Kent with Rare's Meloy Jr. (left) and the University of Delaware's YouDee mascot.

applied to a variety of programs in which people are compensated to complete a series of tasks to improve conservation outcomes in which they would reduce nonpoint-source pollution, conserve water, or enhance habitat. This type of approach could be implemented in the context of a local land trust or a large federal program like CRP.

The influence of loss framing was recently connected to the influence associated with the messenger when we tested whether mascots could be used to motivate environmentally friendly behaviors (see Figure 9.6). This research was inspired by the nonprofit conservation group Rare, which frequently uses location-specific mascots as part of its public pride campaigns around the world to encourage more conservation. The study showed that, in general, encouragement from mascots that presented a local connection improved people's conservation efforts. And in line with the theory of risk aversion, the effect was most pronounced when the mascots presented negative emotions (i.e., disappointment and shaming) when participants did not take sufficient conservation actions (Butler et al., 2017).

Social Comparisons

Social comparisons refer to the idea of influencing people's behavior by informing them about how they compare with their peers. It originates from the social-comparison theory set forth by Festinger (1954), who proposed that humans judged the appropriateness of their behavior based on the behavior of others. Several studies have demonstrated that social comparisons can be used to promote environmental conservation. You may be familiar with how utility companies provide in the monthly bill comparisons of your energy use to your neighbors. Whether you knew it or not, you probably participated in an economic experiment! These comparisons may have been been accompanied by smiley faces or different colors if you are doing well compared to your neighbors. Allcott (2011) demonstrated that informing people how their household power use compared with others in their area reduced their consumption. In the context of water conservation, Ferraro and Price (2013) showed that incorporating a message based on social comparisons reduced water use. Importantly, several studies have also demonstrated that the impacts of such social comparisons last for years afterward (Allcott and Rogers, 2014; Bernedo et al., 2014).

A conservation group's communications can be developed to focus on "descriptive norms" rather than simply comparing behaviors. In this case, the social-comparison information communicates how "most people" behave in specific situations with a goal of nudging others to behave the same way in that situation.

Research has shown this approach to be effective (Cialdini et al., 1991), especially in situations in which the circumstances are relatively unfamiliar to the potential participant and the group providing the social comparison is similar to potential participants. Consider a study of efforts to conserve water by hotels by nudging patrons to reuse towels. Again, perhaps you participated in this field experiment. Goldstein et al. (2008) found that a message that communicated the descriptive norm that a "majority of people reused their towels" led to more towel reuse than traditional messages about why reusing towels was beneficial. The messages appeared to be even more effective when they used language that indicated that the behavior was exhibited by people who were particularly similar to them, such as people who had stayed in that room.

Some conservation programs have already begun to use social comparisons to induce greater conservation activity. For instance, Minnesota's Agricultural Water Quality Certification Program awards lawn signs to farmers once their adherence to a set of practices deemed to reduce water pollution has been verified. Likewise, several voluntary programs in the Pacific Northwest are using public signs and certifications to reward landowners for "Fish Friendly Farming" or for following management practices deemed "Salmon Safe." As these programs grow and additional landowners are certified, conservation groups may be able to use social comparison as a way of encouraging other landowners to participate in the programs.

Defaults and Anchoring

Particularly when pressed for time, people facing decisions are susceptible to choosing whatever default option is presented to them. Hence the practice in restaurants, for example, of suggesting a percentage for the gratuity and calculating the amount for you. However, the same thing can occur even with potentially life-altering decisions, such as the amount of money to save from a regular paycheck for retirement. Behavioral economists and psychologists have long noted that the inertia associated with the default option influences people's decision-making, a tendency referred to as status quo bias (Samuelson and Zeckhauser, 1988), and various studies have shown that people disproportionally stick with status quo decisions.

In a well-known study, Johnson and Goldstein (2003) showed that rates of organ donation around the world varied by whether the decision to be an organ donor was "opt in" or "opt out." For instance, in the United States, a person must act to become a donor upon their death (an opt-in decision). However, in some countries in Europe, people are treated as agreeing to be organ donors unless they act to opt out. Interestingly, some European countries that have similar traditions and cultures have very different rates of enrollment based on whether they use opt-in or opt-out structures. This simple difference has led to opt-out countries having roughly twice the organ-donor rate as opt-out countries.

Strategically incorporating the power of defaults can be a cost-effective nudge in conservation programs. As an example of how this idea could be used to promote environment-friendly behavior, a study by Kent and his colleagues showed that changing the framing of a charitable donation decision from opt in to opt out increased donations to a land trust by 25 percentage points (Zarghamee et al., 2017). The simple act of asking potential sellers or contributors to have to opt out of participating can be an effective way to increase their participation.

The difficulty in using defaults is that they can require an agency to completely revamp its process. Conservation occurs mostly in the opt-in world where people are asked to agree to adopt new behaviors. One potential way to harness the power of defaults would be to modify the sign-up process for large government programs such as the CRP, which spent nearly $35 billion between 1995 and 2014 (Environmental Working Group, 2017). In CRP's current enrollment process, landowners compete against each other to be enrolled based on an Environmental Benefits Index (EBI) score that is calculated using the owner's bid and the number and type of conservation practices the landowner promises to implement if accepted into the program. The current default in the EBI score is that the owner implements basic conservation practices but can improve the score by agreeing to implement one or more practices that have greater environmental benefits. Given what we know about human behavior, perhaps the CRP should change the default to selection of the most environmentally beneficial practices and require farmers to choose practices they *do not* want to implement (which would lower their EBI scores). Note that in both scenarios the program is voluntary, and with modern computer interfaces, the decision to add or subtract conservation practices can be done easily in a matter of seconds.

An emerging area of research concerns the idea that defaults can be self-selected by people through "active choice" – the idea that by providing people an initial option, they will select a choice that sets up a default that will then influence their behavior long after the original choice is made. Nonprofits and businesses often use active choice as a way of getting people to sign up voluntarily for services or donations that occur automatically each month until the person acts to stop paying. Examples include gym memberships and services such as Netflix; consumers sign up for the payments on their credit cards and the companies hope they will continue to choose the now default decision to continue to participate. Nonprofit organizations such as National Public Radio actively encourage donors to become "sustaining members" whose monthly donations are automatically charged to their bank accounts or credit cards. Kent and his colleagues tested this approach and found that people who signed up for recurring donations to a nonprofit organization routinely gave more than members who had no recurring donation option even though they were reminded monthly that they could stop the donations with one easy action (Zarghamee et al., 2017). It makes sense, then, for conservation groups to employ an active choice approach when fund-raising is possible.

Other Ideas Worth Considering

The field of behavioral economics continues to grow and there are many creative ways to use nudges in conservation. We are particularly interested in how the power of group behavior and invoking of democratic processes can accomplish greater conservation. For instance, experimental research has consistently shown that group communication can lead to greater support for projects that benefit the public. Furthermore, a voting referendum used in the conjunction with public discussions appears to be a promising approach since laboratory settings have shown that such combinations can lead to sustained contributions to the public good over time (Messer et al., 2007a, 2008, 2013).

Another promising mechanism to explore is framing of conservation efforts as threshold goods so that the conservation objective (e.g., preservation of a watershed) occurs only when a certain amount of money is raised. Economists have referred to these types of fund-raising efforts as "provision points" since the project is provided only if a certain level – a point – of donations is achieved. If the threshold is not achieved, the project does not happen and the donations are returned. While conservationists may be reluctant to enact this sort of "money back guarantee" after working hard to raise funds, laboratory research suggests that this type of approach motivates people more than traditional fund-raising approaches that retain the funds regardless of whether they are sufficient to purchase the full project (Messer et al., 2007b).

Economists have only begun to explore the power of behavioral nudges. Much remains to be learned about how people make decisions and how those decisions are affected by the structure of the choices presented, the messenger who presents them, and the emotional and psychological undertones attached to the presentation. Some of these ideas cost next to nothing to adopt. Others could require conservation organizations to restructure parts of their programs – changes which would probably pay for themselves many times over. Regardless of the specific nudges used, we hope we have given you reason to pay close attention to the messages you deliver and who delivers them as part of your strategic conservation efforts.

10 Putting It All Together: A Short Story

Now that we have explained the eight core principles of strategic conservation and provided you with a variety of tools to help you protect more with less, we conclude by telling a short story about how the various elements we have discussed work together to make conservation happen. The story is fictitious, but based on our experience with conservation projects we have worked on. Recall that at the beginning of the book we asked you earlier to imagine what would happen if you were a conservation planner and someone walked into your office and asked you to prepare a conservation plan for your community. Now that you are versed in the core principles of strategic conservation, let's imagine how you can respond when that day comes.

You are sitting in your office in downtown Optimal, USA, when Judy from Acme Pipeline walks in the door carrying a bunch of maps and files. "I need help!" she says as she dumps the papers onto the lobby table. "Can you help me figure out which of these projects we should fund?"

"Sure!" you say, rising from your desk and walking over to the pile of papers on the table. "What kind of projects?"

"We are an infrastructure development company, and we are building a new pipeline across a community where we already have a lot of pipelines. So, while we don't have a lot of compensatory mitigation to do, we feel that we should be good environmental stewards and good neighbors by investing in community projects above and beyond what's required," Judy explains.

"What environmental benefits are you trying to achieve?"

"Well, the new pipeline has quite a few stream crossings. And we have a great avoidance and minimization program to avoid most impacts to streams using our directional drilling techniques, but we

224

would really like to invest our environmental stewardship funds in stream restoration projects since that is what the community has told us is their highest priority. We convened some focus groups of local stakeholders and public agencies with help from your colleagues, and they agreed that these types of stream restoration projects would make the most sense."

"Great! So, your goal is stream restoration and you would like to figure out how to get the best bang for your buck with these potential stream restoration projects?" you ask, as you point at a file marked "Project A-1 – Rivers and Streams Conservancy – $509,301."

"Yes, but there's a problem," Judy says forlornly.

"What's that?" you ask, sensing what was likely to come next.

"Well, we have a budget of about $1.7 million to spend on these projects but received about $3 million in project proposals. We don't want to disappoint people, but we need a fair and scientifically valid way to decide how to select the projects. They all look good to me."

"Ah, you have definitely come to the right place," you say, smiling. You and Judy sit down at the table and start sorting through the project proposals.

"Nice! Your application collected really good information on project benefits, such as the length of stream to be restored, the acreage of riparian area that will be improved, useful information on the quality of the stream quality and condition of the watershed," you begin.

"And each of the proposals is very clear on how much the project will cost and documents any leverage funding they are receiving from other sources to complete it. Beyond these conservation benefits that we can calculate, are there any other selection criteria or mandatory requirements we should consider?"

"Well," Judy says, "everyone wants to make sure that the projects we select are good, definitely above average, in terms of all of the applications we received, and we also definitely want to restore as much stream and riparian area as possible with the money we have.

Table 10.1 *Attribute tree for Acme Pipeline stream restoration projects*

11 <u>Mandatory Requirements</u>
111 Stream length restored
112 Riparian area restored
113 Watershed/stream segment condition
12 <u>Desired Characteristics</u>
121 Project location
1211 Adjacent to protected lands
1212 Green infrastructure network
1213 Adopted plan priority
122 Project site characteristics
1221 Stream segment quality
1222 Resource designations
1223 Pollution/land-use change risk

But we also should consider what the science tells us about the stream conditions and watersheds. So, all things equal, let's try to restore areas that need it most. And, also, if the restoration could be adjacent to land with existing high-quality habitat and/or already protected land, making bigger blocks of land, that would be great too," Judy explains, waving her hands across the map of the area's green infrastructure and stream network.

"Excellent. I think that's enough information to get us started," you tell Judy as you walk over to your desk to retrieve your laptop running the LSP.NT and Optimization Decision-Support Tool software.

You continue the conversation with Judy, initially creating a clear, concrete, concise, and compelling vision of "healthy streams, healthy fish, healthy people" with a primary goal of maximizing restoration of streamside riparian vegetation and a primary objective of investing in areas with the greatest potential for improved stream conditions. You assemble the LSP attribute tree shown in Table 10.1 and then establish selection criteria for the attributes that make sense based on the information provided in the applications.

"This helps me visualize what an ideal project would look like," says Judy, appearing relieved. "All of the projects looked worthy to me, but some are clearly better for the environment than others, especially given our limited budget!"

Encouraged by Judy's response, you add that this process can do more than maximize benefits considered mandatory – that the criteria can reward projects that meet the mandatory requirements *plus* are adjacent to parcels that are already protected and have been identified as important green infrastructure assets. You note further that "It also lets you tell a nice story about the projects. For instance, some are located in areas that multiple existing land-use and watershed plans have identified as high priorities for investment."

You then work with Judy to organize the information needed to describe the criteria for the nine attributes using the example shown in Table 10.2.

You next use these narrative descriptions to create the elementary criteria by converting the nominal data into consistently scaled ratio data. The proposed projects will be compared to each criterion, generating a set of nine attribute scores for each project. Table 10.3 presents the completed attribute table for 113, watershed/stream segment condition.

While looking over the criteria, Judy notes that she "did not know what a TMDL (total maximum daily load) was before I started working on this project, but now I better understand why it makes sense to focus our investments in specific areas for this initiative. As you mentioned earlier, it probably makes sense to focus our compensatory mitigation in those TMDL watersheds since they have specific performance metrics that our regulatory projects often need."

"That's right, but if you find out later that you would rather prioritize watersheds that have a TMDL instead, it is easy to adjust the attribute tree and scores in LSP.NT and re-run the optimization."

You then examine the project folders, assign attribute scores to the projects using the nine criteria in the attribute tree, and enter those scores into the LSP.NT software. The LSP.NT software weighs

Table 10.2 *Example of criteria for the watershed/stream segment condition – attribute 113*

Goal	Restore riparian corridors with designated impaired streams
Objective	Give high priority for restoration along streams classified by the state and/or federal government as impaired and streams that lack an existing regulatory program (e.g., an EPA total maximum daily load (TMDL) or a state's use-supporting ratings)
Rationale	The marginal value to restore lands in already degraded areas is high; since this is intended as an environmental stewardship project and not a compensatory mitigation program, favoring investment in impaired watersheds and streams not already subject to specific regulations preferred
Approach	Highest value assigned to impaired streams that lack an existing regulatory program – Total Maximum Daily Load
	Medium value assigned to impaired streams that include an existing regulatory program
	Low value assigned to streams that are not impaired
	Streams are not suitable if they are located in a pristine watershed or designated as a high-quality intact stream segment
Data sources	Watershed GIS layers with information on TMDLs, use-support ratings, and other designations
Process steps	Assign projects a value based on their location

the relative values of the attributes with their scores and generates an overall score for each project. The LSP system then normalizes those scores, assigning a score of 100 to the top project, A-02. The resulting normalized scores and the cost of each project are presented in Table 10.4.

Judy looks at the scores and is surprised to find that project A-14, which looked good to her, received a score of 0.

Table 10.3 *Elementary criterion for attribute 113, watershed/ stream segment condition*

113		Watershed/Stream Segment Condition
Value	%	
0	0	Highest satisfaction for impaired streams without an existing regulatory program
1	30	Medium satisfaction for impaired streams with an existing regulatory program
2	70	Low satisfaction if not impaired
3	100	Not suitable if located in a pristine watershed or designated as a high-quality, intact stream segment 3 = Impaired without a TMDL 2 = Impaired with a TMDL and a use-support rating of "Nonsupporting" 1 = Not impaired but with a use-support rating of "Supported-threatened" 0 = No impairment and use-support rating of "Supporting"

"I can explain that," you say. "Remember the criteria we worked on? You want to avoid investing in projects in streams that are already in good shape, and it turns out that A-14 is in a watershed with an outstanding resource designation for water quality. Had the project been located in a different watershed, it looks like it would have scored well. But since we decided it was mandatory for projects to be in impaired or threatened watersheds, A-14's good water quality zeroed out the rest of the criteria."

You then remind Judy that she can adjust the logic aggregation to penalize projects in watersheds with good water quality rather than reducing their scores to 0. "It looks to me like A-14 can be in the mix if you change the logic structure. But, while the project has merit and is affordable, I think it would be easier to justify the location of the other projects based on your goals."

Table 10.4 *Overall project benefit (suitability) scores for the proposed projects calculated using LSP and their associated costs*

Project ID	LSP Score (%)	Cost
A-01	82.8	$509,301
A-02	100.0	$32,200
A-03	76.4	$40,000
A-04	62.5	$314,950
A-05	87.6	$290,500
A-06	73.0	$50,000
A-07	35.6	$23,770
A-08	83.2	$990,000
A-09	89.6	$296,800
A-10	81.6	$351,200
A-11	66.3	$16,360
A-12	86.7	$115,476
A-13	83.0	$50,000
A-14	0	$85,000

Note: Total cost of all projects: $3.08 million; available budget: $1.70 million; average project LSP score: 77.6.

"Ah," Judy replies, "that makes sense. Let's leave it as is for now."

After you and Judy discuss the rationales behind several other criteria and agree that the criteria are appropriate, you import the LSP overall project scores and the projects' costs into the ODST and run a BLP optimization that compares all the projects' benefits and costs simultaneously so you can see what an optimized portfolio will look like given a budget of $1.7 million. Table 10.5 presents the portfolio of eight projects selected by the optimization program.

"Wow," Judy exclaims, "that project A-08 is a huge budget sponge! You told me that might happen. We can invest in four alternative projects for about the same price and restore many more miles of stream by not selecting A-08!"

Table 10.5 *Projects selected with $1.7 million budget constraint and Binary Linear Programming listed in order by LSP score*

Project	LSP Score (%)	Cost	Optimal Selection
A-02	100.0	$32,200	Selected
A-09	89.6	$296,800	Selected
A-05	87.6	$290,500	Selected
A-12	86.7	$115,476	Selected
A-08	83.2	$990,000	
A-13	83.0	$50,000	Selected
A-01	82.8	$509,301	Selected
A-10	81.6	$351,200	Selected
A-03	76.4	$40,000	Selected
A-06	73.0	$50,000	
A-11	66.3	$16,360	
A-04	62.5	$314,950	
A-07	35.6	$23,770	
A-14	0.0	$85,000	

Note: Total cost of all projects: $3.08 million; available budget: $1.70 million; allocated funds: $1.685 million.

"Yes, that's right," you concur. "Project A-08 obviously has some good aspects based on its high score, but it is expensive relative to the others. Based on the application, the problem seems to be associated with the project's topography, the restoration techniques that must be used, and the existing condition of the stream. It may still be an important project to complete, but you can see the trade-offs – the opportunity costs – that come with investing in it. If you want to select that project and then optimize selection of the rest of the projects using the remaining budget, we can use the hybrid programming features of ODST to see which projects will be selected in that case."

"Wow," Judy exclaims, "this has been very helpful. When I walked in the door I had 14 file folders of projects to sort through, and now I can go back to the project managers and tell a great story about the projects and explain the transparent, science-based process we can use for making our selections, a process that I feel like the community will understand."

"That's great, Judy. Stop by anytime!" you say as you help roll up the maps and stack the folders into a pile, knowing that thanks to the core principles of strategic conservation you have helped Judy and her organization protect more with less.

11 Do It! Exercises Using the Optimization Decision Support Tool

You have read enough about optimization. Now it is time for you to do it! In this chapter, we will walk you step by step through two different exercises with the online Optimization Decision-Support Tool.[1] The first exercise is for the fictional Pangaea Conservancy. The second exercise is from the Maryland State Highway Administration's project to expand HWY 301 south of Washington, DC, that was discussed in Chapter 7.

Note that the exercises are designed to go from simple to more complex. Plus, to help you out, the answers are provided in the back of this chapter.

MAXIMIZING CONSERVATION IN PANGAEA

Imagine that you are the executive director of a nonprofit conservation group named The Pangaea Conservancy, which has a budget of $10 million to purchase land from private landowners so that these lands can be permanently protected. The six parcels available for purchase are shown in light gray in Figure 11.1, labeled A–F. Pangaea already has two protected national parks, which are shown in this figure as dark gray areas. Ecologists and conservation professionals from The Pangaea Conservancy have evaluated each of the available parcels and assigned each with a parcel-specific ecological benefit score, as shown in Table 11.1, where a higher score indicates a higher ecological benefit. As the executive director, which parcels would you recommend that The Pangaea Conservancy acquire? Why?

---

[1] These exercises build upon course materials (Messer, 2011) and trainings (Messer and Fooks, 2013) related to optimization.

Table 11.1 *Pangaea data*

Parcel ID	Ecological Score	Cost ($m)	Parcel Selected
A	2	$6	
B	5	$3	
C	4	$2	
D	6	$6	
E	2	$3	
F	9	$4	

Exercise 1

As described earlier in this book, most conservation organizations and government agencies in the United States and throughout the world use what is called "Benefit Targeting" (also referred to as "Rank-Based Models") to select which parcels to acquire for conservation. With benefit targeting, the organization prioritizes the parcels based solely on the parcels' benefits – in this case the ecological score – and then acquires the highest-ranked parcel first, the second highest parcel second, and so forth, until the budget is exhausted.

Assume that The Pangaea Conservancy uses the Benefit-Targeting approach to solving the problem. Which parcels would it

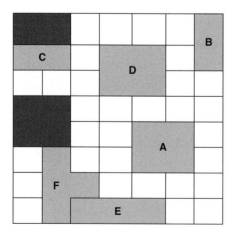

FIGURE 11.1 Map of Pangaea.

select? Comment on whether these parcels are similar to or different than the selections you recommended in the problem. In your comparison of the selected parcels evaluate a number of criteria including the total ecological score achieved, the total cost, the average values of the selected parcels, and the spatial location of the parcels.

Exercise 2

Proponents of strategic conservation have raised concerns about the use of benefit targeting, as this method does not take into account the costs of the selected parcels except when determining whether there remain sufficient funds. As an alternative, economists often have recommended that the selection be done based on benefit–cost ratios, where the parcel with the highest ratios should be acquired first, the parcel with the second highest ratio should be acquired second, and so forth, until the budget is exhausted. This technique is frequently referred to as Cost-Effectiveness Analysis (also referred to as Benefit–Cost Targeting). A parcel's benefit–cost ratio is calculated by simply dividing its benefit score by its costs. For example, Parcel A would be assigned the value of 0.33, as its ecological score of 2 is divided by its cost of $6 million.[2]

Given the same information that you used in the primary problem and Exercise 1, which parcels would The Pangaea Conservancy select if it used Cost-Effectiveness Analysis? Comment on whether these parcels are similar or different than the selections you recommended in the primary problem and the parcels selected by benefit targeting in Exercise 1. In your comparison of the selected parcels, evaluate a number of criteria including the total ecological scores, the total cost, the average values of the selected parcels, and parcels' spatial location.

Given the results, what method of selection would you suggest that The Pangaea Conservancy use? Why?

---

[2] To facilitate interpretation, the ratio is often multiplied by a large number, such as a thousand. As long as the same large number is used for each parcel, then this multiplication does not change the overall results.

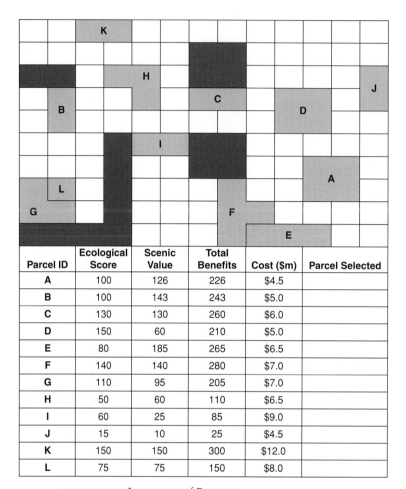

Parcel ID	Ecological Score	Scenic Value	Total Benefits	Cost ($m)	Parcel Selected
A	100	126	226	$4.5	
B	100	143	243	$5.0	
C	130	130	260	$6.0	
D	150	60	210	$5.0	
E	80	185	265	$6.5	
F	140	140	280	$7.0	
G	110	95	205	$7.0	
H	50	60	110	$6.5	
I	60	25	85	$9.0	
J	15	10	25	$4.5	
K	150	150	300	$12.0	
L	75	75	150	$8.0	

FIGURE 11.2 Larger map of Pangaea.

Exercise 3

Now look at another area The Pangaea Conservancy is considering protecting. This area already has four protected areas, shown in Figure 11.2 in dark gray.[3] In this area, The Pangaea Conservancy has budgeted $25 million to purchase land from private landowners so that it can permanently protect these areas. The 12 parcels available for purchase by The Pangaea Conservancy are lettered from A-L below and are shown in light gray. The Pangaea Conservancy has

---

[3] Data for this example are from Messer (2006).

used a new and improved benefit assessment technique which calculates two benefit scores as shown below. For both of these measures, the higher the score signifies the higher the quality.

Assuming that The Pangaea Conservancy considers the ecological score and the scenic value to be of equal importance, which parcels would you recommend that it acquire if it wants to use benefit targeting? Describe the selected parcels.

Exercise 4

Given the information provided above, identify the parcels that The Pangaea Conservancy would select if it used Cost-Effectiveness Analysis. (Note that a calculator can be helpful.) Discuss these results in comparison to the results of Exercise 3.

Exercise 5

Given the information provided above, identify the parcels that The Pangaea Conservancy would select if it used Binary Linear Programming. The binary variables should be either 0 (not selected) or 1 (selected), and can be multiplied to the original environmental benefits scores to calculate the overall benefits of the selected parcels. For example, if Parcel A is selected then by multiplying the total benefits score of 226 by 1 the entire amount can be added into the aggregate total benefits calculated for the selected parcels. If Parcel A is not selected, then by multiplying the total benefits score by 0, makes the resulting value zero. Discuss these results in comparison to the results of Exercises 3 and 4.

Step-by-Step Instructions

Starting the Optimization Decision Support Tool

1 Go to http://odstweb.conservationgis.com, where you will find a description about how to login and how to access the datasets described in this chapter.

2 Click **Register for a Free Demo Account**.

Uploading the Data

3 Click on the **New Project** button to start developing a new analysis. Name the project by typing "Pangaea" in the **Title** field.

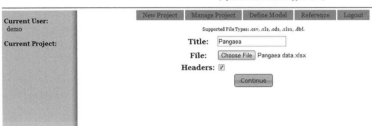

FIGURE 11.3 Screenshot 1.

4 Click the **Choose File** button. Open the Pangaea data file by navigating to the Desktop (or wherever you stored the data file) and selecting the file named "Pangaea data."

5 Make sure that the **Headers** box is checked. Click the **Continue** button.
   • You screen should look like Figure 11.3.

6 In the **Select Worksheet** box, click on the drop-down box, select "Question 4–7" and click the **Continue** button.

7 Verify that all of the data types (**Types**) are correct for all six **Variables**. All **Variables** should be checked as **Active** and their types should all be **Integer** except for **Parcel ID**, which should be **Text**, and **Cost**, which should be **Decimal** (Figure 11.4). Click the **Continue** button.

8 Once the data are uploaded and the project created, the message **"Project "Pangaea" Loaded from file:Pangaea data.xlsx"** will be displayed.

Setting Up the Model

9 Click on the **Define Model** button (middle button on top menu). Create a new model by typing "Question_6" into the **Title** box and click **Set Up**.

10 Change the optimization engine to Binary Linear Programming. To do this open the **Solver Options** pane and change the **Optimization Engine** from **Cost Effectiveness** to **Binary Linear Programming** (Figure 11.5). Then click the **Update** button.
   • All of the default options should be automatically set correctly.

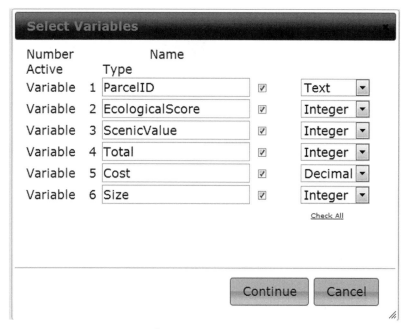

FIGURE 11.4 Screenshot 2.

Defining the Benefits

11 Click the **Define Model** tab (Figure 11.6).

12 Under the category **Objectives**, set the variable for total benefits (**total**) as the first benefit to maximize by clicking on *Click to Add*. Select **total** from the pull-down menu and click the **OK** button.

   - The **Weight** of 1 will be automatically set for this variable.

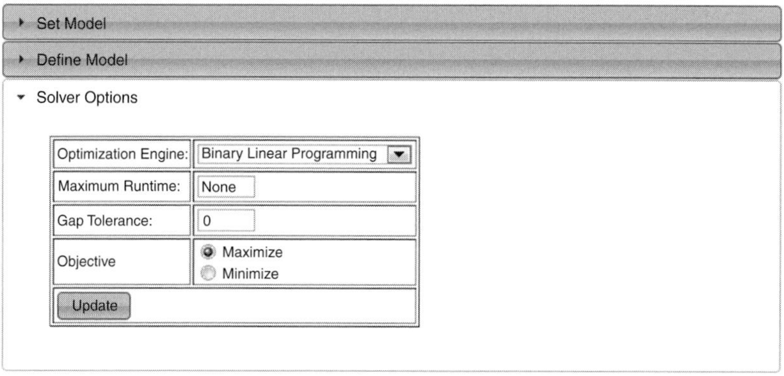

FIGURE 11.5 Screenshot 3.

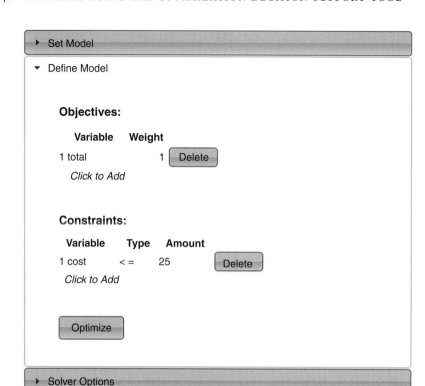

FIGURE 11.6 Screenshot 4.

Defining the Constraints

13 Define the project cost by clicking on *Click to Add* under **Constraints**. Select **cost** from the pull-down menu and click the **OK** button. Click on the **0** under the word "**Amount**," type in the total budget of "**25**" (for $25 million), and press Enter on the keyboard.

Optimizing

14 To answer this question, click on the **Optimize** button to calculate the optimal solution. This will bring up a page that lists the selected projects (B, C, E, and F) that achieves a total score of 1,048 at a total cost of $24,500,000 (Figure 11.7).[4]

---

[4] Note that you can compare the results of this exercise to the results of Exercise 5 (Cost-Effectiveness Analysis/Benefit-Cost Targeting). In Exercise 5, the selected projects were A, B, C, D, and J, which resulted in a total score of 964 at a total cost of $25,000,000. Thus, in this case, using Binary Linear Programming enabled The Pangaea Conservation to both achieve higher total benefits and save money.

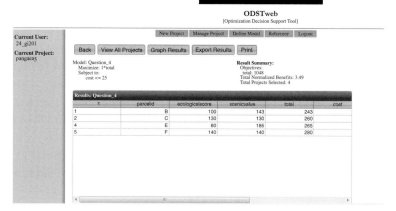

FIGURE 11.7 Screenshot 5.

- To see all of this information, you may need to scroll down to see both the individual projects selected and summary statistics for the group of selected projects.

Exercise 6

The Board of Directors for the Pangaea Conservancy are concerned that the aggregate ecological scores are lower in the analysis than desired. They would like to see that the selected parcels achieve a minimum value of 500 for the ecological score. Which method – benefit targeting, Cost-Effective Analysis (Benefit-Cost Targeting) or Binary Linear Programming – is best able to solve this problem? Using your preferred technique, identify a solution that addresses this concern while continuing to maximize the weighted total of the ecological score and scenic values given a budget of $25 million. Discuss the advantages and disadvantages of adding this type of minimum value threshold.

Step-by-Step Instructions

15 Click on the **Back** button to return to the **Define Model** pane.

Setting Up and Defining the Model

16 Click on **Set Model** and type "Question_6" in the **New Model** title box, and click the **Set Up** button.

17 Set the optimization engine as **Binary Linear Programming** (as described in Step 10).

18 Under Objectives, set **total** as the benefit (as described in Step 12).

19 Under Constraints, set **cost** less than or equal to **25** ($25 million) (as described in Step 13).

20 Add an additional constraint on ecological score by clicking *Click to Add* underneath the budget constraint (**cost**). Select **ecologicalscore** and change the **Type** of the constraint from less than or equal ($< =$) to greater than or equal ($> =$). Change the value of this constraint from **0** to **500** and press Enter.

21 Click on the **Optimize** button to calculate the solution. This will bring up a screen that lists the selected projects (C, D, E, and F) that achieves a total score of 1,015 at a cost of $24,500,000 (Figure 11.8).

- To see all of this information, you may need to scroll down to see both the individual projects selected and summary statistics for the group of selected projects.

- Note that by adding this additional constraint on ecological score that the total score of the selected projects declines. This is not necessarily a bad thing as this should ultimately better reflect The Pangaea Conservancy's preferences for ensuring a minimum quality in all selected projects.

Exercise 7

The Board of Directors for the Pangaea Conservancy has received some additional funds, so now have a budget of $35 million. They

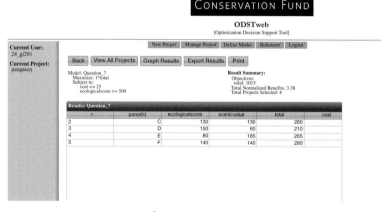

FIGURE 11.8 Screenshot 6.

would like to use Binary Linear Programming (BLP), but would also like to make sure they purchase the three highest-rated parcels as "signature" projects for the organization. Compare the BLP solution from Question 7 to the one they would get under a Hybrid Linear Programming (HLP) approach, were the organization purchases the three parcels with the highest scores and then use BLP to select parcels using the remainder of the budget. What are the advantages and disadvantages of this hybrid approach?

Step-by-Step Instructions

22 Click on the **Back** button to return to the **Define Model** pane.
23 Click on **Set Model** and type "Question_7" in the **New Model** title box, and click **Set Up**.
24 Select the **Solver Options** pane and change the **Optimization Engine** to **Hybrid Linear Programming**. Enter "**3**" in the **Always Select Top #** field (Figure 11.9) and click the **Update** button.
25 Define the model as in Question 6 (see steps 18, 19 and 20), except with a total **cost** constraint of **35** instead of **25**.
26 Click **Optimize** to use Hybrid Linear Programming to solve this problem.
27 The solution to this problem is Projects A, B, E, F, K. Note that the three highest scoring projects (K, F, and E) are now selected and with the rest of the budget the selection is optimized (Figure 11.10).

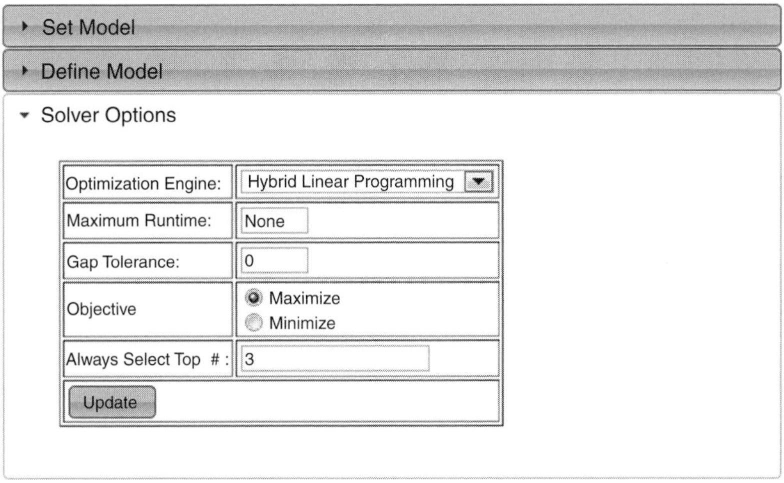

FIGURE 11.9 Screenshot 7.

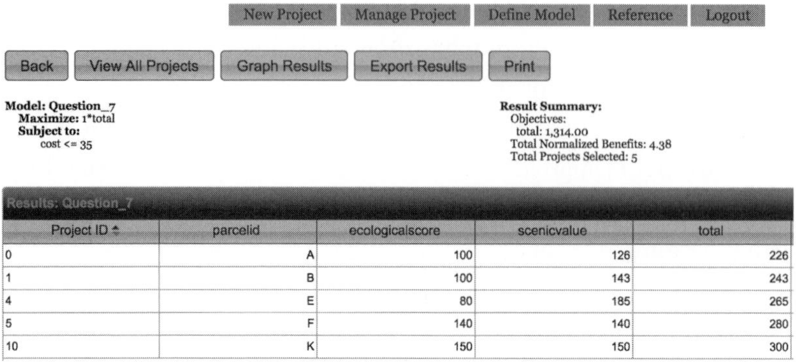

| New Project | Manage Project | Define Model | Reference | Logout |

| Back | View All Projects | Graph Results | Export Results | Print |

Model: Question_7
Maximize: 1*total
Subject to:
   cost <= 35

Result Summary:
Objectives:
   total: 1,314.00
Total Normalized Benefits: 4.38
Total Projects Selected: 5

Results: Question_7

Project ID ⬍	parcelid	ecologicalscore	scenicvalue	total
0	A	100	126	226
1	B	100	143	243
4	E	80	185	265
5	F	140	140	280
10	K	150	150	300

FIGURE 11.10 Screenshot 8.

Maryland Highway 301 Example

The following is a more sophisticated example that builds upon data related to a potential highway upgrade and expansion project in Maryland, south of Washington, DC. Recall from Chapter 7, that the Maryland State Highway Administration sought to ensure that environmental quality in the area *improved* as a result of this highway expansion. In other words, it was going above and beyond the mitigation requirements as established by the National Environmental Policy Act (Weber and Allen, 2010). This example was originally developed for the Maryland State Highway Administration and goes through a variety of scenarios that they were under consideration. For this book, these data are not intended to represent any specific projects, but instead enable further the skill development on optimization.

Step-by-Step Instructions

Starting ODST

28 Go to http://odstweb.conservationgis.com.

29 Click **Login** and enter your **User Name** and **Password**.

Upload the Data

30 Click on the **New Project** button to start developing a new analysis. Name the project by typing "Highway 301" in the **Title** field.

31 Click the **Choose File** button.

32 Open the Maryland Highway 301 data file by navigating to the Desktop (or wherever you stored the data file) and selecting the file named "301Parcels_top_tier."

33 In the **Select Worksheet** box make sure that "CH_properties_top_tier_gt_20ac" is selected and click the **Continue** button.

34 Verify that all of the **Types** are correct all 11 **Variables**. All **Variables** should be checked as **Active** and their types should all be **Integer** except for Variable 11 (**PER_AC**), which should be a decimal. Click the **Continue** button.

35 Once the data are uploaded and the project created, the message **Project "hwy_301" Loaded from file:301Parcels_top_tier 2.18.13.xlsx** will be displayed.

Variable Transformations

36 Click on the **Manage Project** button. The **Variables** pane will open automatically.

37 The first transformation that we will perform is an inversion. For example, since the variable "Proximity to Protected Parcels" (**PROT_PROX**) is measured in distances, and we want parcels with small proximity scores.

   a Click on **Invert** and in the **New Variable Name** box, enter "prot_prox_inv."

   b From the **Variable to Invert** box, use the pull-down menu to replace **oid_** (project ID#) and select **prot_prox**, and click the **Invert** button.

   c A popup box will open advising you that the variable has been inverted. Click **OK**.

38 The second transformation that we will perform is scaling-by-size. For example, since the variable "Ecological Score" (**ECO_SCORE**) is measured on a per-acre basis, it should be scaled by "Total Parcel Acreage" (**PROP_AC**) to get the total parcel benefits.

   a Click on **Scale** and in the **New Variable Name** box, enter "eco_scoreXprop_ac."

   b From the **Variable to Scale** box, use the pull-down menu replace **oid_** (project ID#) and select **eco_score**.

   c In the **Variable to Scale By** box, use the pull-down menu to select **prop_ac**.

d Click the **Multiply** button. A popup box will open advising you that the variable has been scaled. Click **OK**.

Scenario 1: $5 Million Budget with Equal Benefit Importance Weighing

This scenario does the classic comparison between the results of a rank-based model and an optimization model using Cost-Effectiveness Analysis.

Setting Up the Model

39 Click on the **Define Model** button. Create a new model by typing "Scenario 1" into the **Title** box and click **Set Up**. (Click on the **Define Model** pane if it does not open automatically.)

Defining Benefits

40 Set the variable for Green Infrastructure Acreage (**gi_ac**) as the first benefit to maximize by clicking on *Click to Add* under the word **Objective**s. Select **gi_ac** from the pull-down menu and click the **OK** button. The **Weight** of 1 will be automatically set for this variable. Follow similar procedures to add the second benefit variable for Scaled Ecological Score (**eco_scoreXprop_ac**) and the third benefit variable for Inverted Proximity Score (**prot_prox_inv**) (Figure 11.11).

FIGURE 11.11 Screenshot 9.

Setting Constraints

41 Set the variable for Appraised Land Value (**nfmlndvl**) as the project cost by clicking on ***Click to Add*** under **Constraints**. Select land value (**nfmlndvl**) from the pull-down menu and click the **OK** button. Click on the **0** to the right of the **< =** sign, type in the total budget of "5,000,000," and press enter.

42 Now the model is fully defined, your screen should look like the image to the right:

Rank-Based Analysis

43 Click on the **Rank Based** button to calculate the Scenario 1 rank-based solution. This will bring up the results sheet. Check these results against the Maryland Highway 301 Scenario Results tables that are the last page of this document. Note that you can scroll through the **Results: Scenario_1** box to look at parcel-specific results and along with total results.

Optimization

44 Click on the **Back** button to return to the **Define Model** pane.

45 This time, click on the **Optimize** button to calculate the Scenario 1 Cost-Effectiveness Analysis solution. This will bring up the results sheet. Again, check these results against the Maryland Highway 301 Scenario Results tables (Tables 11.2, 11.3, and 11.4).

Scenario 2: $10 Million Budget with Equal Benefit Importance Weighing

This scenario again compares the results from a rank-based model and an optimization model, but this time uses a budget of $10,000,000.

46 Click on the **Back** button to return to the **Define Model** pane.

47 Click on **Set Model** and type "Scenario 2" in the **New Model** title box, and click the **Set Up** button.

48 In the **Define Model** pane, set the variables Green Infrastructure Acreage (**gi_ac**), Scaled Ecological Score (**eco_scoreXprop_ac**) and the Inverted Proximity Score (**prot_prox_inv**) as benefits, each with a **Weight** of 1, as discussed above in Step 13.

49 Set the budget variable as **nfmlndvl** and define the **Amount** as "10,000,000" (instead of $5,000,000 as was used previously).

50 Click on the **Rank Based** button to calculate the Scenario 2 Rank Based solution. Check these results against the Maryland Highway 301 Scenario Results sheet.

51 Click on the **Back** button to return to the **Define Model** pane.

52 Click on the **Optimize** button to calculate the Scenario 2 Cost-Effectiveness Analysis solution. This will bring up the results sheet. Check these results against the Maryland Highway 301 Scenario Results sheet.

Scenario 3: $5 Million Budget with a Lower Proximity Importance Weighing and Minimum Size Constraint

This scenario uses a model that places a lower value on proximity to other protected areas and adds a minimum size constraint.

53 Click on the **Back** button to return to the **Define Model** pane.

54 Click on **Set Model** and type "Scenario 3" in the **New Model** title box, and click **Set Up**.

55 In this case, we will conduct the optimization analysis using Binary Linear Programming. To do this open the **Solver Options** pane and change the **Optimization Engine** from **Cost Effectiveness** to **Binary Linear Programming**. Then click on the **Update** button. (All of the default options should be automatically set correctly).

56 For benefits, set Green Infrastructure Acreage (**gi_ac**), Scaled Ecological Score (**eco_scoreXprop_ac**) and the Inverted Proximity Score (**prot_prox_inv**) as described above. In this case, set the weight for **prot_prox_inv** to "0.5" by click on the 1 in the **Weight** column and changing it to "0.5," and pressing enter.

57 Set the budget variable to **nfmlndvl**, and set the budget **Amount** to "5,000,000."

58 Add a second constraint on the minimum parcel size by clicking *Click to Add* under **Constraints**. Select **per_ac** from the drop-down and click **OK**. Change the constraint type by clicking on the > = by **per_ac**, and selecting **Minimum Value** from the drop-down menu and clicking **OK**. Set this new constraint as "100."

59 Click on the **Optimize** button to calculate the Scenario 3 solution. Check these results against the Maryland Highway 301 Scenario Results sheet.

Scenario 4: $5 Million Budget with a Minimum Size Constraint and Top Three Selected

This scenarios introduces use a Hybrid Linear Programming model where the top three parcels are selected and compares the results to Scenario 3.

60 Click on the **Back** button to return to the **Define Model** pane.

61 Click on **Set Model** and type "Scenario 4" in the **New Model** title box, and click **Set Up**.

62 Select the **Solver Options** pane and change the **Optimization Engine** to **Hybrid Linear Programming**. Enter "3" in the **Always Select Top #** field and click the **Update** button.

63 For benefits, set Green Infrastructure Acreage (**gi_ac**), Scaled Ecological Score (**eco_scoreXprop_ac**) and the Inverted Proximity Score (**prot_prox_inv**) as described above. Change the weight on **prot_prox_inv** to "0.5."

64 Set the budget variable to **nfmlndvl** and define this budget constraint as "5,000,000."

65 Add a second minimum value constraint on **per_ac** of 100 as described above in step 31.

66 Click on the **Optimize** button to calculate the Scenario 4 solution. Check these results against the Maryland Highway 301 Scenario Results sheet.

Scenario 5: $5 Million Budget with Goal Programming

This scenario uses the techniques of goal programming and seeks to maximize

67 Click on the **Back** button to return to the **Define Model** pane.

68 Click on **Set Model** and type "Scenario 5" in the **New Model** title box, and click **Set Up**.

69 In the **Solver Options** pane, change **Optimization Engine** to **Goal Programming** and click the **Update** button.

70 In the **Define Model** pane, set the **Objectives** of the goal-programming problem as the Green Infrastructure Acreage (**gi_ac**) and Scaled Ecological Score (**eco_scoreXprop_ac**). The **Goal** for each of these variables should automatically be set to **max**. Add **prot_prox** as an

objective and change its **weight** to "0.5." Then click on **max**, change it
to **min**, and click enter.

71 Define the budget variable as **nfmlnvl** and set it "5,000,000."

72 Click on the Optimize button to calculate the Scenario 5 solution.
Check these results against the Highway 301 Scenario Results sheet.

ANSWER KEY – PANGAEA

Answer 1

The goal of the first part of this problem is to get you thinking independently about the problem and potential solutions. Thus, there is
no "correct" answer to this problem. As using a Benefit-Targeting
approach and a $10 million budget, The Pangaea Conservancy would
select parcels D and F as shown in the hatched dark gray areas in
Figure 11.12. The total cost and ecological score are also shown in the
figure. The two selected parcels have the highest ecological scores
(6 and 9, respectively), but also have two of the three highest prices
$6 million and $4 million, respectively. The average value for the
ecological score of the parcels is 7.5 [= (6 + 9)/2] and the average cost
is $5 million [= ($6 + $4)/2].

Answer 2

Using Cost-Effectiveness Analysis and a $10 million budget, The Pan-
gaea Conservancy would select parcels B, C, and F as shown in the

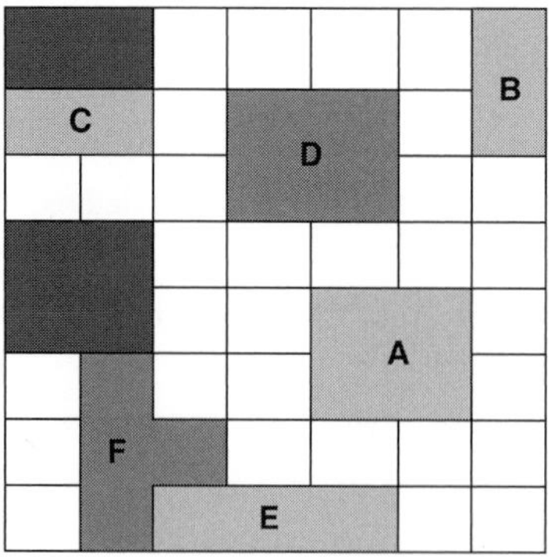

Parcel ID	Ecological Score	Cost ($m)	Parcel Selected
A	2	$6	
B	5	$3	
C	4	$2	
D	6	$6	Yes
E	2	$3	
F	9	$4	Yes
Total Selected:	15	$10	2 parcels

FIGURE 11.12 Answer 1.

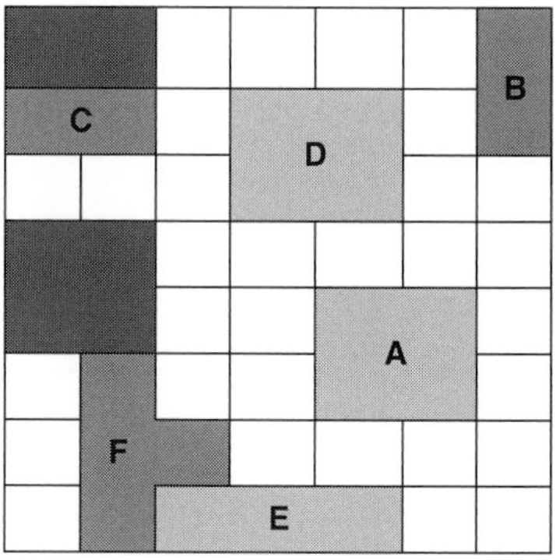

Parcel ID	Ecological Score	Cost ($m)	Parcel Selected
A	2	$6	
B	5	$3	Yes
C	4	$2	Yes
D	6	$6	
E	2	$3	
F	9	$4	Yes
Total Selected:	18	$9	3 parcels

FIGURE 11.13 Answer 2.

hatched dark gray areas in Figure 11.13. The total cost and ecological score are also shown in Figure 11.13. Note that parcel D is no longer selected as it was with benefit targeting, in large part because of its relative high cost. This type of project can be referred to as a "budget sponge" as it absorbs considerable financial resources that could be allocated to other projects.

The total ecological score from the three selected parcels is 18, which is 20 percent greater than the level of 15 achieved in Exercise 1. The total cost of these three parcels is also just $9 million instead of the $10 million in Exercise 1 (a 10 percent savings). Compared to benefit targeting, the average individual values for the ecological score of the selected parcels is lower (6.0) as is the average cost, $3 million (= $9/3). The lower individual values certainly are a disadvantage of being more cost-effective.

You might note some advantages of acquiring more parcels, which may be especially advantageous in certain political situations as more landowners are participating in conservation and receiving payments. Of course, the administrative burden of purchasing three parcels instead of two is higher. From a spatial analysis perspective, both the acquisition of parcel C and parcel F are adjacent to existing park land. This may be important from an ecological perspective as nonfragmented areas tend to provide better wildlife habitat and

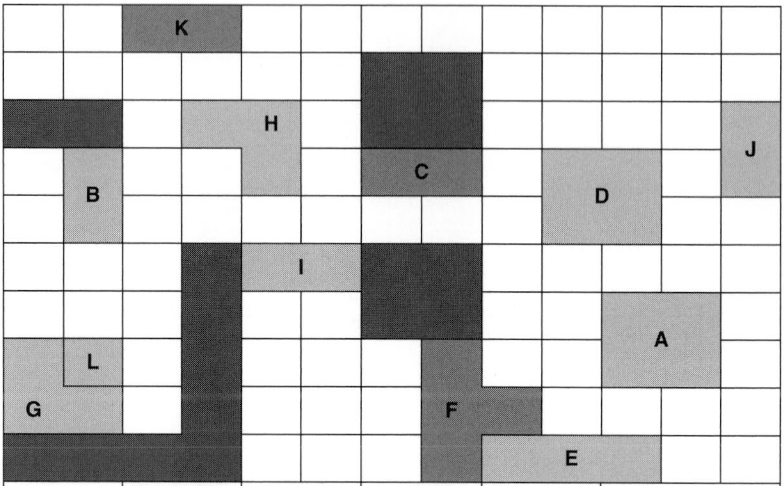

Parcel ID	Ecological Score	Scenic Value	Total Benefits	Cost ($m)	Parcel Selected
A	100	126	226	$4.5	
B	100	143	243	$5.0	
C	130	130	260	$6.0	Yes
D	150	60	210	$5.0	
E	80	185	265	$6.5	
F	140	140	280	$7.0	Yes
G	110	95	205	$7.0	
H	50	60	110	$6.5	
I	60	25	85	$9.0	
J	15	10	25	$4.5	
K	150	150	300	$12.0	Yes
L	75	75	150	$8.0	
	420	420	840	$25.0	

FIGURE 11.14 Answer 3, Benefit Targeting, where the last line is the total from the selected parcels.

connected areas are easier to manage. Of course, parcel B is quite isolated relative to the other protected areas.

Answer 3

The answer to Exercise 3 is shown in Figure 11.14. The average cost of the selected parcels is $8.33 ($25/3), the total benefit is 840, and the average benefit equals 280 (840/3).

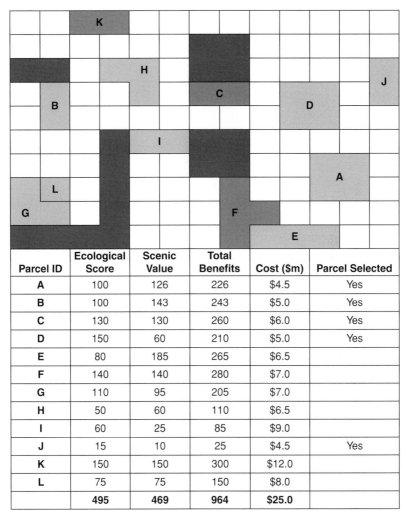

Parcel ID	Ecological Score	Scenic Value	Total Benefits	Cost ($m)	Parcel Selected
A	100	126	226	$4.5	Yes
B	100	143	243	$5.0	Yes
C	130	130	260	$6.0	Yes
D	150	60	210	$5.0	Yes
E	80	185	265	$6.5	
F	140	140	280	$7.0	
G	110	95	205	$7.0	
H	50	60	110	$6.5	
I	60	25	85	$9.0	
J	15	10	25	$4.5	Yes
K	150	150	300	$12.0	
L	75	75	150	$8.0	
	495	469	964	$25.0	

FIGURE 11.15 Answer 4, Cost-Effectiveness Analysis, where the last line is the total from the selected parcels.

Answer 4

The answer to Exercise 4 is shown in Figure 11.15. Note how Cost-Effective Analysis improves the overall environmental outcome compared to benefit targeting. The total benefit increases from 840 to 964.

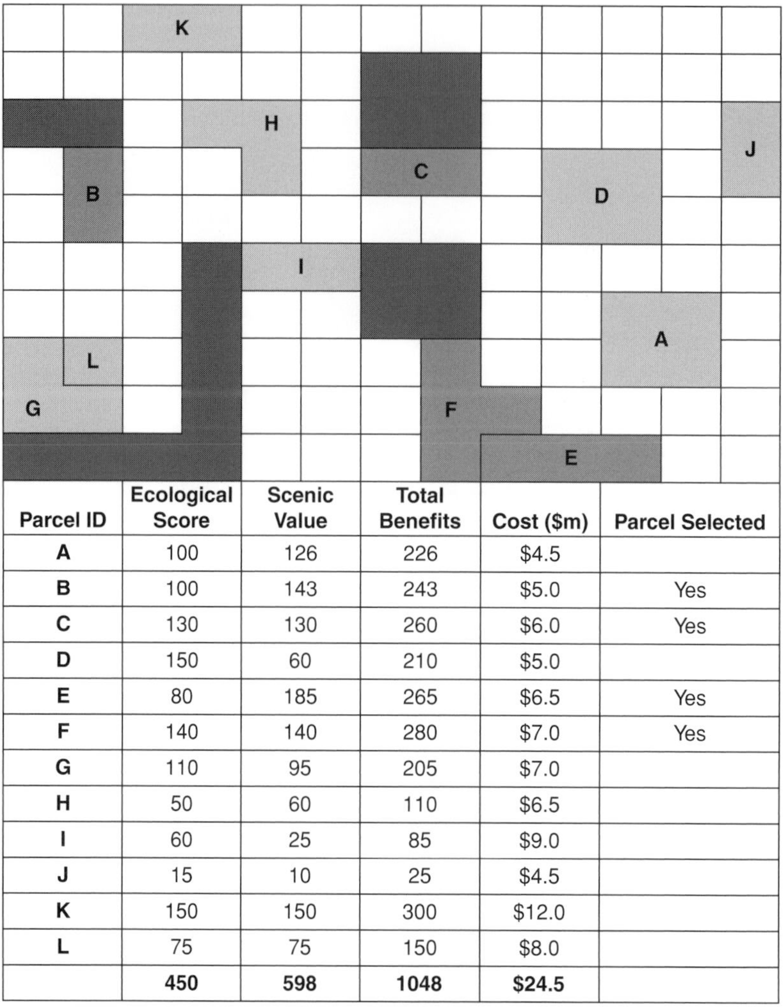

Parcel ID	Ecological Score	Scenic Value	Total Benefits	Cost ($m)	Parcel Selected
A	100	126	226	$4.5	
B	100	143	243	$5.0	Yes
C	130	130	260	$6.0	Yes
D	150	60	210	$5.0	
E	80	185	265	$6.5	Yes
F	140	140	280	$7.0	Yes
G	110	95	205	$7.0	
H	50	60	110	$6.5	
I	60	25	85	$9.0	
J	15	10	25	$4.5	
K	150	150	300	$12.0	
L	75	75	150	$8.0	
	450	598	1048	$24.5	

FIGURE 11.16 Answer 5, Binary Linear Programming, where the last line is the total from the selected parcels.

Answer 5

The answer to Exercise 5 is shown in Figure 11.16. Note Binary Linear Programming improves the overall environmental outcome compared to benefit targeting (a total benefit of 1048 compared to 840), and in this case, also provides an improvement compared to Cost-Effectiveness Analysis. This latter improvement is in large part due to

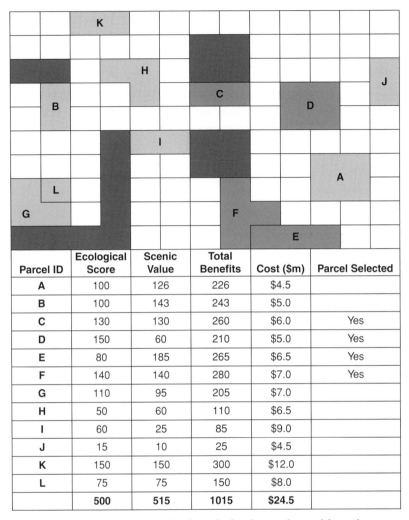

Parcel ID	Ecological Score	Scenic Value	Total Benefits	Cost ($m)	Parcel Selected
A	100	126	226	$4.5	
B	100	143	243	$5.0	
C	130	130	260	$6.0	Yes
D	150	60	210	$5.0	Yes
E	80	185	265	$6.5	Yes
F	140	140	280	$7.0	Yes
G	110	95	205	$7.0	
H	50	60	110	$6.5	
I	60	25	85	$9.0	
J	15	10	25	$4.5	
K	150	150	300	$12.0	
L	75	75	150	$8.0	
	500	515	1015	$24.5	

FIGURE 11.17 Answer 6, where the last line is the total from the selected parcels.

the fact that Binary Linear Programming does a better job at managing the overall budget and seeking the best opportunities that fit within the budget. In contrast, Cost-Effectiveness does a good job allocating the majority of the budget, but does not always lead to optimal results when allocating the last amounts of the budget, especially when the individual project costs are high.

Answer 6

Binary Linear Programming is the best method for solving this problem (Figure 11.17). Neither benefit targeting nor Cost-Effectiveness Analysis can solve this problem and meet the board of directors' minimum constraint on ecological score. Binary Linear Programming can readily handle this problem by simply adding a constraint that requires that the total value of the ecological score exceeds 500.

You should note that there is some trade-off with adding this constraint as the total benefits from the selection that accounts for this constraint is 1,015 instead of 1,048. However, this is only a 3.1 percent decrease, so perhaps the trade-off is not very large, especially if the board of directors believes that this constraint is important. After all, the goal is to set up a model that best represents the needs and preferences of The Pangaea Conservancy such that the end results help them achieve their goals in the best way possible.

ANSWER KEY – MARYLAND HIGHWAY 301 SCENARIO

Table 11.2 *Scenario 1: $5 million budget with equal benefit importance weighting*

	Rank Based	Optimization (CEA)	Difference	Percentage
Total number of projects	9	75	66	733.3%
Conservation value	12.2	66.5	54.3	445.1%
Total cost	$4,999,230	$4,957,428	$–41,802	–0.8%
Total acreage	4,255.0	5,434.0	1,179.0	27.7%
Total GI acreage	3,961.0	4,284.0	323.0	8.2%
Total ecological score	304,028.0	362,857.0	58,829.0	19.3%
Total proximity score	160.0	1,235.0	1,075.0	671.9%

Table 11.3 *Scenario 2: $10 million budget with equal benefit importance weighting*

	Rank Based	Optimization (CEA)	Difference	Percentage
Total number of projects	24	100	76	316.6%
Conservation value	28.9	86.2	57.3	198.3%
Total cost	$9,999,446	$9,966,541	$−32,905	−0.3%
Total acreage	6,207.0	7,208.0	1,001.0	16.1%
Total GI acreage	5,684.0	5,806.0	122.0	2.1%
Total ecological score	432,380.0	492,725.0	60,345.0	14.0%
Total proximity score	460.0	1,595.0	1,135.0	246.7%

Table 11.4 *Scenarios 3, 4, and 5: advanced engines*

	Scenario 3 (BLP)	Scenario 4 (HLP)	Scenario 5 (GP)
Total number of projects	72	36	49
Conservation value	36.0	19.5	NA
Total cost	$4,998,602	$4,998,570	$4,991,240
Total acreage	6,620.0	5,187.0	7,944.0
Total GI acreage	6,341.0	4,605.0	6,649.0
Total ecological score	514,523.0	372,413.0	533,374.0
Total proximity score	1165.0	580.0	850.0

12 Do It! Exercises Using the Logic Scoring of Preference Method

This chapter takes you through the process of using LSP (described in detail in Chapter 7) to make project selections using LSP.NT, a web-based application designed for evaluating and comparing complex systems. The exercise project is protection of Indiana bat summer habitat. In this process, you will:

1 Develop evaluation criteria that are compatible with observed human reasoning.
2 Use the criteria to assign overall suitability scores (a "competitive system" in LSP.NT) to a set of potential projects that reflect the degree to which each project satisfies your requirements.
3 Perform a cost/preference analysis that will generate a score for each project, allowing them to be ranked.

The highest-ranking projects identified using this system will be the ones that meet a large share of the suitability criteria you established *and* are highly affordable.

The first step in the process is to set up an LSP.NT account.

- Visit www.seas.com.
- Click on **LSP.NT** to go to the login page.
- Click **Register for a Free Demo Account**.
- Enter your email address in order to receive a temporary password. You will then be directed to the web page: www.seas.com/LSPNT/login.php.
- Enter the user name and password provided in the email from trial@seas.com to log in. The demo account provides full LSP functionality for 30 days for up to 12 attributes. If, after using the demo account, you would like to establish a professional account, use the **Contact Us** button on the www.seas.com main page.

REVIEW THE INDIANA BAT EXAMPLE IN LSP.NT

1 *Initial setup*
   - At the initial screen after login, click **Project** at the top.
   - Select **Indiana_Bat** from available projects and click **Copy Project**.
   - Rename this project so that you can experiment with it: e.g., IBAT_[Lastname].
   - Select IBAT_* from available projects and click **Select Project**.

2 *Review model documentation*
   Click on each of the documentation links to get a basic overview of the Indiana bat LSP attribute tree.
   - Attribute tree
   - Input attribute list
   - Attribute criteria
   - Aggregator list
   - Aggregators
     Return to the LSP.NT tab in your browser to return to the main attribute tree menu.

3 *Inspect the detailed logic structure of the attribute tree by examining the nodes*
   Note in Figure 12.1 that this project is set up for "medium precision uniform aggregators – UGCD 15." We will discuss aggregator options later, but note for now that this structure offers options for mandatory, sufficient, and optional logic relationships between criteria.
   a In the **Select node id** box, type node ID **1** and click **Edit node**.
     Note that it is set up with the logic aggregator CPA (conjunctive partial absorption), which allows selection of mandatory and nonmandatory nodes and of penalty and reward percentages for the values of nonmandatory factors.
     The type of aggregator can be changed to GCD (generalized conjunction/disjunction) or DPA (disjunctive partial absorption). These options are described later.
   b For now, click **Cancel** and leave it as is.
   c In the **Select node id** box, type node ID **11** and click **Edit node**.
     This node shows you the weights assigned to the three mandatory requirements. You can adjust these weights if you would like as long as they sum to 100.

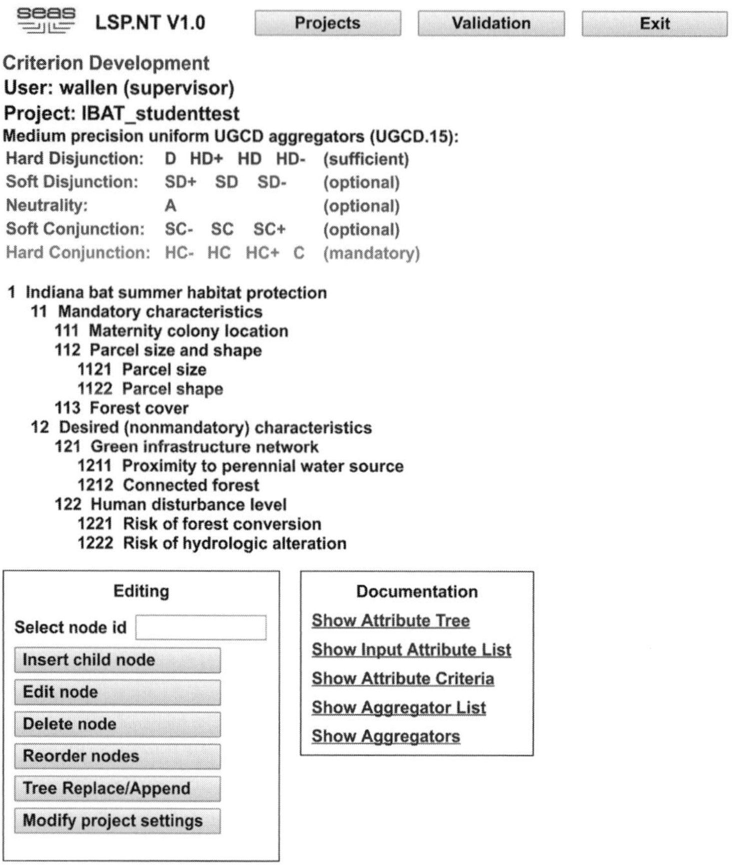

seas **LSP.NT V1.0** | Projects | | Validation | | Exit |

Criterion Development
User: wallen (supervisor)
Project: IBAT_studenttest
Medium precision uniform UGCD aggregators (UGCD.15):
Hard Disjunction:	D HD+ HD HD-	(sufficient)
Soft Disjunction:	SD+ SD SD-	(optional)
Neutrality:	A	(optional)
Soft Conjunction:	SC- SC SC+	(optional)
Hard Conjunction:	HC- HC HC+ C	(mandatory)

```
1 Indiana bat summer habitat protection
   11  Mandatory characteristics
      111  Maternity colony location
      112  Parcel size and shape
         1121  Parcel size
         1122  Parcel shape
      113  Forest cover
   12  Desired (nonmandatory) characteristics
      121  Green infrastructure network
         1211  Proximity to perennial water source
         1212  Connected forest
      122  Human disturbance level
         1221  Risk of forest conversion
         1222  Risk of hydrologic alteration
```

Editing	Documentation
Select node id [ ]	**Show Attribute Tree**
Insert child node	**Show Input Attribute List**
Edit node	**Show Attribute Criteria**
Delete node	**Show Aggregator List**
Reorder nodes	**Show Aggregators**
Tree Replace/Append	
Modify project settings	

FIGURE 12.1 Indiana bat summer habitat protection project in LSP.NT.

You also can adjust the **current aggregator**. It is set up initially as **HC+**, which is a "hard conjunction" and requires nonzero values for each input being weighted. A zero value for any of the attributes makes the entire project score zero.

d Make your desired changes and click **Save**. Or click **Cancel** if you do not want to make any changes.

e In the **Select node id** box, type node ID **12** and click **Edit node**. This node shows you the weights assigned to the two nonmandatory requirements. You can adjust these weights if you would like as long as they sum to 100.

You also can adjust the **current aggregator**. It is set up initially as **A** (arithmetic mean) – each criterion score (%) is simply multiplied by the weight to derive a percent satisfaction for that branch of the tree.

f Make your desired changes and click **Save**. Or click **Cancel** if you do not want to make any changes.

4 *Inspect the detailed elementary criteria of the attribute tree*

a In the **Select node id** box, type node ID **111** and click **Edit node**. For assigning values to elementary criteria, there always must be a *score of zero* and a *score of 100* and the *values* corresponding to the scores must have logical consistency (i.e., other breakpoints should be between 0 and 100).

In this node, the *value* is the distance from the center of the location of a maternity bat colony measured in miles.

If the project is 2.5 miles or more from the center, its score is 0 percent. If it is in the center (zero miles), its score is 100 percent. Therefore, the score is interpolated based on a linear function between 0 and 2.5 miles (similar to Figure A.2 in Appendix A).

You can adjust the *breakpoints* that weight projects that are relatively close to the center.

In this project, a distance of 1.25 miles from the center has been set as 50 percent satisfaction. If you feel that proximity to the center is particularly important, you can, for example, set a distance of 1.25 miles to represent 80 percent satisfaction and reduce a distance of 2.0 miles from 20 percent satisfaction to 10 percent. Figure 12.2 shows this revised set of elementary criteria. Scores would then interpolate based on these breakpoints. For example, a distance of 1.0 miles would be 60 percent based on the default values but would be a little over 86 percent with the new breakpoints.

b Make your desired changes and click **Save**. Or click **Cancel** if you do not want to make any changes.

c To look at additional examples of branches of the attribute tree that apply weights to subbranches and to select aggregators, type node IDs **112, 121,** and/or **122** in the **Select node id** box and click **Edit node** (see Table A.5 in Appendix A for a list of logic relationships available in LSP.NT).

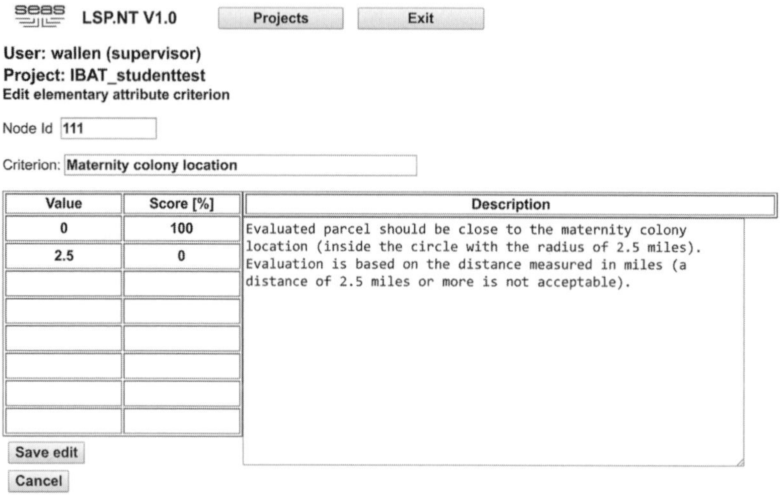

FIGURE 12.2 Elementary criterion for Node 111 in LSP.NT.

Node 112 uses default aggregator HC: (simultaneity + hard conjunction [medium "andness"]), where simultaneous satisfaction of inputs is mandatory, otherwise the evaluated choice is rejected

Node 121 uses default aggregator SD– (substitutability + soft disjunction [low "orness"]), where for full satisfaction of requirements, all inputs must be fully satisfied

Node 122 uses default aggregator SC– (simultaneity + soft conjunction [low "andness"]), where some requirements can not be satisfied but won't reject the choice entirely

- Make your desired changes and click **Save**. Or click **Cancel** if you don't want to make any changes.

d To look at additional elementary criteria for which you can adjust values and scores, enter node IDs **1121**, **1122**, **113**, **1211**, **1212**, **1221**, and/or **1222** in the **Select node id** box and click **Edit node**

Remember: You need values for when the scores are 0 percent and 100 percent and that you can set any breakpoints you want as long as the values are logically and mathematically consistent.

1121: Allows you to change the various size thresholds for the project. It is currently set to 46 acres based on habitat analysis performed by the US Fish and Wildlife Service. This breakpoint can be adjusted to accommodate newer or more geographically precise data. The 5-acre breakpoint is based on a regulatory requirement that no single project should be smaller than 5 acres since forest blocks that small would provide insufficient habitat.

113: Uses ratio data for the percent of forest cover within the 2.5-mile maternity colony circle. Since they are ratio data, you could just use the percent forest cover as your Score, but the default here has breakpoints set up to "reward" a higher percent forest cover than what the direct ratio data would offer between 30 and 80 percent.

1221: Uses nominal data for risk of forest conversion (None, Low, Medium, High, and Very High). Percentages can be adjusted as desired since they are subjective.

- Make your desired changes and click **Save**. Or click **Cancel** if you don't want to make any changes.

Now that we have reviewed the attribute tree, let's look at the potential parcels that are scored using this tree.

5 *Examine the project scores*

a Click **Validation** at the top to confirm that the elementary criteria in your attribute tree and the logic aggregators are all valid and can be used to evaluate the projects.

Once you have validated the criteria and aggregators, a screen will display the criterion file describing all of the attribute tree node numbers and the threshold values and scores.

b Click **Evaluation** to view the sample parcels.

From this main screen, which is shown in Figure 12.3, you can do many things. First, let's look at all of the parcels.

In each screen, click on **Evaluation** to return to the *main menu*.

> **Show evaluation results** – All five parcels with percent satisfactions for each criterion and aggregate LSP scores.
>
> **Show all competitive systems** – Raw elementary criteria scores and cost values of each parcel.
>
> **Attribute and suitability tables** – Another way to show the raw criteria values for all five parcels.
>
> **Evaluate selected system** – Select one of the five parcels to view the raw scores and percent satisfaction for each criteria.
>
> **View/edit selected system attributes** – Allows you to adjust raw elementary criteria values for each of the five parcels.

Have your elementary criteria handy if you want to make any adjustments.

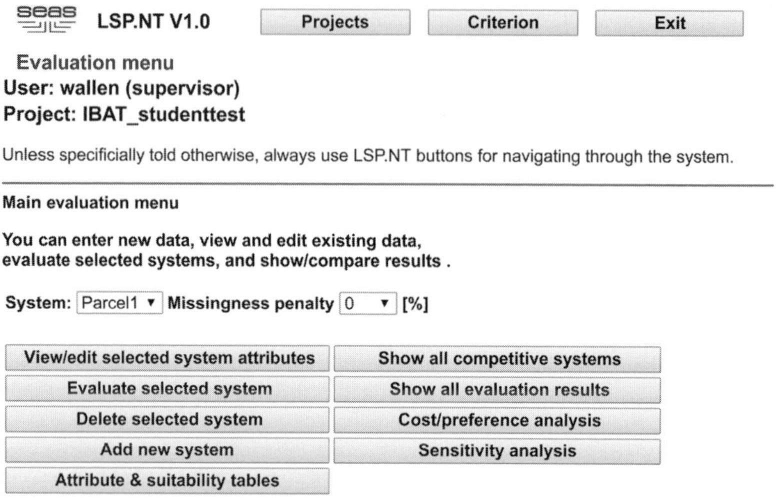

FIGURE 12.3 Evaluation menu for Parcel 1 in LSP.NT.

c Click **Save Data** if you make any changes. Otherwise, click on **Evaluation** to return to main menu.

You also can add and delete example parcels (e.g., Parcel 6) and experiment with other elementary criteria values. See what happens, for example, when you set one of the mandatory criteria to 0 percent satisfaction.

> **Cost/preference analysis** – Shows which parcels would be selected based on different weights for costs and scores.
>
> You can see how the preferred parcel changes as the relative importance of the suitability score increases.
>
> **Sensitivity analysis** – Provides additional functionality to evaluate the relative importance of criteria impacting the final LSP suitability score when you change the percent satisfaction.

d Click the **Criterion** button at the top to return to the *main menu for the attribute tree.*

e Click the **Validation** button if you want to return to the *systems.*

f Click **Projects** to return to the *main menu.*

SET UP A NEW ATTRIBUTE TREE IN LSP.NT

We next take you through the steps involved in setting up your own attribute tree.

1 *Initial set up to create a new attribute tree in LSP.NT*

   a Log in using your user name and password for your demo account.

   b Click **Create new project**

   c Enter a **project name** (e.g., farmland) and then click **Save project name**
You then get the option to keep settings or change settings for your aggregators.

    We recommend keeping the default initially as you become more familiar with LSP. The default is a Uniform GCD aggregator with Medium precision, which gives you 15 options for aggregation.

    But you do have a choice of GCD aggregators (see Table A.5 for information on the default Uniform Graded Conjunction/Disjunction (UGCD.15) as well as the LSP.NT user manual for additional details).

        Uniform GCD aggregators (UGCD) are the default. They offer all basic forms of soft and hard partial conjunction and disjunction and are used in majority of LSP evaluation projects. The threshold andness and orness are fixed, and the aggregators offer three levels of precision (Low/7, Medium/15, High/23). The numbers refer to the number of available aggregators with each choice.

        Generalized (nonuniform) GCD aggregators (GGCD) are used by professional evaluators and offer the greatest degree of flexibility because they have adjustable threshold andness. They also offer three levels of precision (Low/9, Medium/17, High/25).

        Weighted power means are the oldest type of aggregator and were used in most legacy LSP projects. They have low threshold andness, and the partial disjunction aggregators are always soft. Precision is fixed at medium/17.

2 *Build the attribute tree*

The tree starts by default with branch 1, which uses the name of your project. To build your tree, you need to insert and save **child nodes**. Set up two primary child nodes that each have three child notes.

   a In the **Select node id** box, type node ID **1** and click **Insert child node**.
Type in a name for *child node 11* (e.g., *Mandatory*) and click **Save**.

   b In the **Select node id** box, type node ID **1** and click **Insert child node**.
Type in a name for *child node 12* (e.g., *Desired*) and click **Save**.
Next, set up child nodes for branches 11 and 12.

   c In the **Select node id** box, type node ID **11** and click **Insert child node**.

Type in a name for *child node 111* (e.g., *Development Rights*) and click **Save**.

d In the **Select node id** box, type node ID **11** and click **Insert child node**. Type in a name for *child node 112* (e.g., *Soil Suitability*) and click **Save**.

e In the **Select node id** box, type node ID **11** and click **Insert child node**. Type in a name for *child node 113* (e.g., *Parcel Size*) and Click **Save**.

f In the **Select node id** box, type node ID **12** and click **Insert child node**. Type in a name for *child node 121* (e.g., *Agricultural Easements*) and click **Save**.

g In the **Select node id** box, type node ID **12** and click **Insert child node**. Type in a name for *child node 122* (e.g., *Green Infrastructure*) and click **Save**.

h In the **Select node id** box, type node ID **12** and click **Insert child node**. Type in a name for *child node 123* (e.g., *Public Benefits*) and click **Save**.

3 *Select aggregators*

a In the **Select node id** box, type node ID **1** and click **Edit node**.

b You will be asked to select an aggregator type. For this example, select **CPA – conjunctive partial absorption [mandatory/optional]** and click **Next**.

> *GCD – graded conjunction/disjunction*, as discussed earlier, is an aggregator that combines simultaneity and substitutability in a proportion that is selected by the decision-maker.
>
> *CPA – conjunctive partial absorption [mandatory/optional]* is an aggregator in which the mandatory input "absorbs" the impact of the optional input. The relative level of absorption is based on the percentage of penalty and reward you set for having low or high values for optional inputs.
>
> *DPA – disjunctive partial absorption [sufficient/optional]* is a combination of the arithmetic mean and a hard disjunction (HD) in which both the sufficient input and the optional input are desirable but their logic impact is different and is based on the specific values of the inputs as described in greater detail in Appendix A.

c At the next screen, which is shown in Figure 12.4.

- Enter a description of the desired objective in assessing suitability.
- Set the mandatory node of the attribute tree.
- Set values for the penalty and reward.

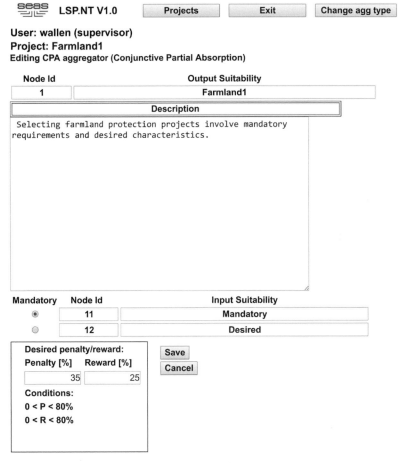

FIGURE 12.4 Editing the aggregator for Node 1 in LSP.NT.

The screen capture provides an example of how to fill out these values.

- Click **Save**.
    d The next screen provides mathematical details of your selected aggregator. Click **Continue**.
    e In the **Select node id** box, type node ID **11** and click **Edit node**. Enter a *description* of the desired objective in assessing suitability for the mandatory criteria (see Figure 12.5).
- Set the **weights** for nodes 111, 112, and 113 so that they sum to 100.
- Select one of the 15 aggregator options and click **Save**.

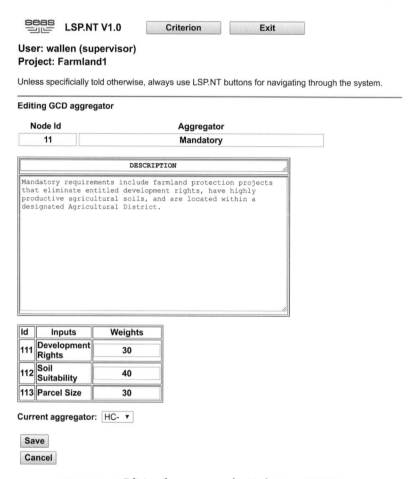

FIGURE 12.5 Editing the aggregator for Node 11 in LSP.NT.

The default is the arithmetic mean (A); however, based on a review of Table A.4, a good choice here would be **HC–** in which all of the mandatory requirements must be at least partially satisfied.

f In the **Select node id** box, type node ID **12** and click **Edit node**. Enter a *description* of the desired objective in assessing suitability for the desired criteria.

g Set the **weights** for nodes 121, 122, and 123 so that they sum to 100.

h Select one of the 15 aggregator options and click **Save**. A good choice here would be **SD–**. This is a substitutability called soft partial conjunction in which all inputs are desirable but not

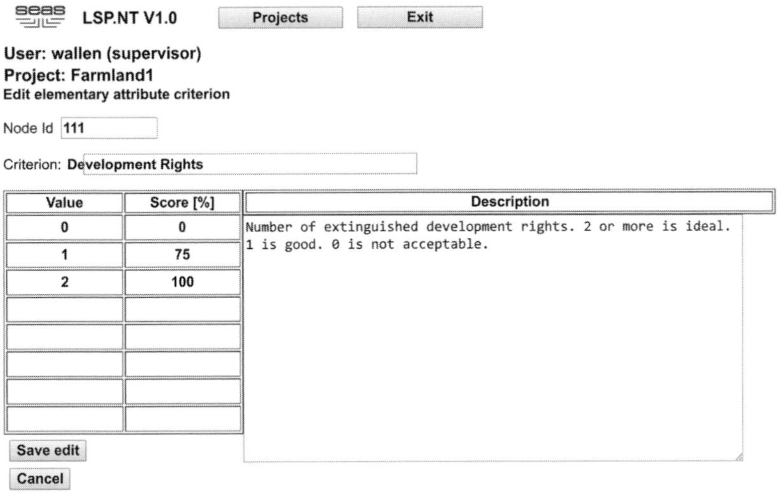

FIGURE 12.6 Editing the elementary criterion for Node 111 in LSP.NT.

sufficient. Had we chosen hard disjunction, a single fully satisfied input would satisfy the entire branch's requirements.

4 *Set elementary criteria*

a In the **Select node id** box, type node ID **111** and click **Edit node**. Enter a *description* of the desired objective in assessing suitability for the criterion and set the *Values* and *Scores* for the criterion (see Figure 12.6).

Remember that there always has to be a score of zero and a score of 100. You can add breakpoints as well but make sure the values are logically consistent.

b Repeat the same operation for node ID **112**, **113**, **121**, **122**, and **123** using your best expert judgment of how to structure the criteria.

112 – **Soil suitability** can be nominal data when soils are designated "prime agricultural" versus other types of soils. Sometimes there are nominal classes (e.g., I, II, III), and these would need to be entered as numeric values since LSP.NT does not accept nonnumeric values, e.g., Roman numerals. It can also be set as ratio data if a suitability model has been developed or if the percentage of the parcel with prime soils has been calculated.

113 – **Parcel size** would be a function of a specific location, but a minimum size can be set to a low percent satisfaction (e.g.,

 **LSP.NT V1.0**

Attribute tree for project: Farmland1

1 **Farmland1**
  11 **Mandatory**
    111 Development Rights
    112 Soil Suitability
    113 Parcel Size
  12 **Desired**
    121 Agricultural Easements
    122 Green Infrastructure
    123 Public Benefits

FIGURE 12.7 Attribute for farmland protection example in LSP.NT.

10 percent) and then zero can be set just below that. The ideal size can be set to 100 percent, and any parcels larger than that would also be 100 percent. Another option is to normalize based on the largest size, which would convert the size data (measured in acres or hectares) to ratio data.

121 – Close proximity to existing **agricultural easements** can be considered more suitable, and the distance thresholds and breakpoints can be set using your preferred unit of measure (e.g., meters, feet, miles). Make sure you specify this factor in the unit of your choice. Also, unlike other criteria that perhaps have been developed thus far (i.e., where a value of zero means a score of 0 percent satisfaction), a value of zero for this criterion may translate into a score of 100 percent since that would be a parcel that is directly adjacent to an easement property.

122 – The value of the parcel's **green infrastructure** can be set as nominal, interval, or ratio based on the data used.

123 – **Public benefits** can include characteristics such as cultural/historic significance, scenic value (a subjective but valid measure if you can develop an appropriate nominal data scale), and whether agricultural land provides community benefits, e.g., farmstand sales or U-pick opportunities. You can establish a nominal data scale based on the number of conditions the parcel meets.

This would be a good time to print the attribute tree or open a new browser window to display your new LSP attribute tree so that you can easily input suitability values for each potential parcel (see Figure 12.7).

c Click **Show Attribute Criteria** under Documentation so that you know what the appropriate values for each branch of the tree will be.

seas   **LSP.NT V1.0**   [**Criterion**]   [**Evaluation**]   [**Exit**]

User: wallen (supervisor)
Project: Farmland1

Unless specificially told otherwise, always use LSP.NT buttons for navigating through the system.

System: Parcel1   Cost: 350000   [**Save data**]

Id	Attribute	Value
111	Development Rights	1
112	Soil Suitability	70
113	Parcel Size	45
121	Agricultural Easements	0
122	Green Infrastructure	40
123	Public Benefits	2

FIGURE 12.8 Elementary criteria values for farmland protection example for Parcel 1 in LSP.NT.

  d Click **Validation** at the top to confirm your logic and elementary criteria are formatted correctly to allow you to start entering potential parcels.

  If you have no errors, the criterion file will be displayed.

  e Click **Evaluation**.

5 *Create competitive systems*

  When you validate your attribute tree for the first time, you will have no parcels to compare.

  a Click **Add new system**.

  b Enter the **System** name (e.g., the farm or landowner name), the **Cost** of the parcel, and the attribute **Values** for each elementary criterion (see Figure 12.8) and then click **Save data**.

  c Enter additional systems as desired.

  d Once you have enough systems to make useful comparisons, click **Show all competitive systems** (see Figure 12.9).

  This will summarize all of the suitability values that you entered.

  e Click **Evaluation** at the top to return to the systems menu.

  You can copy and paste your output table from the process completed in Figure 12.9 into the spreadsheet program of your choice to use your LSP.NT results in the ODST online tool described in Chapter 10.

  f Click **Show all evaluation results** to see the LSP scores for each of the parcels you entered.

seas LSP.NT V1.0 | Show reports | Criterion | Evaluation | Exit

User: wallen (supervisor)
Project: Farmland1

Unless specificially told otherwise, always use LSP.NT buttons for navigating through the system.

Evaluation results (all values expressed as percentages)
Missingness penalty: 0 %

Id	Attribute	Parcel1	Parcel2	Parcel3	Parcel4	Parcel5
1	Farmland1	67.61	64.35	86.09	77.89	0.00
11	Mandatory	58.80	76.96	87.29	72.94	0.00
12	Desired	87.14	39.26	83.57	88.57	85.71
123	Public Benefits	85.00	60.00	100.00	100.00	60.00
122	Green Infrastructure	40.00	35.00	60.00	20.00	80.00
121	Agricultural Easements	100.00	16.67	62.50	100.00	100.00
113	Parcel Size	41.67	91.67	100.00	100.00	41.67
112	Soil Suitability	70.00	60.00	90.00	60.00	95.00
111	Development Rights	75.00	100.00	75.00	75.00	0.00

FIGURE 12.9 Summary of evaluation results for farmland protection parcels in LSP.NT.

In the example in the screen capture, you can see that one of the parcels scored a zero because one of the mandatory criteria had 0 percent satisfaction.

g If you are happy with the results, you can click **Show reports** at the top to generate detailed results on the LSP scoring in a new browser window.

h You can return to the systems menu by clicking **Evaluation**.

i From here, you can experiment with **Cost/preference analysis** or **Sensitivity analysis** to see how the selected parcels might change based on changes in suitability values or in the weight you assign to cost relative to benefits.

From your demo account, you can review the project **Farmland 1**, which is a completed version of the project you just created from scratch in this exercise.

This chapter only scratches the surface on the possibilities available from LSP.NT to help you evaluate project choices. Appendix A provides more information about the mathematical foundations of the LSP method, and Chapter 10 demonstrates how you can use output from LSP.NT in the ODST.

A   Mathematical Foundations of the Logic Scoring of Preference Method

OVERVIEW OF THE LSP DECISION METHOD

For the reader with a strong interest in getting a better understanding of the process of the Logic Scoring of Preference (LSP) method, this section provides a detailed description of the LSP method for evaluation, comparison, and selection of alternatives. We will focus on fundamental concepts of the LSP method and techniques for development and use of LSP criteria for making professional evaluation and selection decisions. Readers interested in mathematical details can find them in specialized literature (Dujmović and Nagashima, 2006; Dujmović and Larsen, 2007; Dujmović, 2007, 2018), and LSP software exists to apply the method without having to develop your own software. Chapter 12 provides an opportunity to use LSP.NT, an online software platform based in the LSP method.

The main goal of the LSP method is to provide a quantitative methodology for making evaluation decisions using criteria that correctly reflect stakeholder goals and requirements. The main features of the LSP method can be summarized as follows:

- LSP method is based on observable properties of human evaluation reasoning.
- The LSP evaluation process is performed in small steps that evaluators can easily understand and control.
- Suitability evaluation can include any number of systematically derived relevant suitability attributes. Criteria with up to several hundred suitability attributes have been successfully used in professional practice.
- Suitability attributes are individually evaluated using precise and easily defined elementary attribute criteria that precisely reflect stakeholder's interests.
- The process of suitability aggregation uses soft computing evaluation logic functions that support all logic patterns encountered in human evaluation reasoning.
- The LSP criteria are sophisticated nonlinear logic decision models suitable for professional decision-making.
- LSP models of total value of evaluated objects are based on logic combinations of suitability and affordability with adjustable degrees of importance.

- All operations of the LSP method are supported by corresponding software tools. Supported are the development and editing of LSP criteria, combination of multiple evaluation projects, evaluation and comparison of alternatives, production of project documentation, sensitivity analysis, optimization, and reliability analysis of final results.

Based on the above properties, LSP criteria can be used in a variety of applications where you need precise and justifiable professional decision models. Main applications areas where the LSP method has been used so far include ecology, selection of computer equipment, suitability maps, agriculture, medical evaluations, real estate, software evaluation, and others.

The basic concept of the LSP method is that evaluation is a human mental activity and consequently professional quantitative evaluation methods must be fully compatible with human intuitive evaluation and selection processes. Indeed, it is not possible to trust any decision methodology that is not compatible with observable properties of human decision-making. Human intuitive evaluation process is observable and consists of the following four main steps:

- Selection of suitability attributes
- Development of attribute criteria
- Aggregation of attribute suitability degrees
- Cost/suitability analysis for determining the overall value

All these steps are visible in intuitive evaluation processes and the LSP method follows these steps in a well-organized, quantitative way. Through this example, we will be using the purchase of a car as an illustration of the LSP method. For example, a car buyer typically analyzes car suitability attributes such as power of engine, acceleration, number of doors, number of passengers, available space, or color. Each suitability attribute is separately evaluated. The car buyer knows what power of engine would be insufficient and unacceptable and what power of engine would be sufficient and fully acceptable. Therefore, each specific power of engine causes a perception of satisfaction which can vary in the range from the lowest satisfaction to the highest satisfaction.

In a systematic way, a car buyer sequentially creates attribute criteria and uses them for evaluating all relevant suitability attributes. For each of them the buyer assigns a degree of satisfaction. At the end of the process of individual evaluation of attributes the evaluator has a set of attribute suitability degrees. The goal of evaluation is to determine the overall suitability degree of each evaluated object.

Unsurprisingly, the degrees of importance of all attributes can be very different. In the next step, the car buyer intuitively aggregates all attribute suitability degrees and establishes an overall suitability degree of each analyzed car. As we initially observed, each attribute contributes to the overall degree of satisfaction in its specific way, both logically and semantically. Semantics is present in the form of the meaning, role, and contribution of each suitability attribute to the perception of overall satisfaction. Some attributes contribute more, some attributes contribute less, and the degree of contribution is usually interpreted as the degree of importance and in quantitative models expressed as weight.

Logic is present in the aggregation process in various ways. Some attributes must be simultaneously satisfied, while some other attributes can substitute for each other. Some attributes are mandatory, in the sense that their dissatisfaction yields unconditional rejection of an evaluated criterion, while other attributes are desirable but not mandatory and consequently their dissatisfaction does not automatically disqualify the evaluated criterion. Some attributes can be sufficient in the sense that their satisfaction can create the perception of full satisfaction regardless of the degrees of satisfaction of other attributes. The human logic aggregation process includes various combinations of simultaneity requirements and substitutability requirements and such aggregators are available in the LSP suitability aggregation process.

At the end of the suitability aggregation process, a typical car buyer creates an overall perception of satisfaction of the car buyer's requirements. This perception reflects the overall car buyer's benefits. However, the decision about the overall value of each car also depends on the overall cost that the buyer must pay. The cost usually has multiple components, such as down payment, cost of financing, and costs of registration, insurance, maintenance and operation. The overall cost indicator can also be reduced by subtracting the anticipated price when selling the car after the period of ownership. Obviously, the overall cost indicator is expected to balance the overall suitability indicator. In other words we do not suggest considering cost components as car attributes. The cost is what the buyer gives, and the overall suitability is what the buyer gets for the money. The overall value of a car can be defined as a simultaneous combination of good suitability and good affordability. The overall value is the overall buyer's perception of the quality of the deal after both financial and nonfinancial considerations are aggregated together.

The overall value is computed in the final phase of the LSP evaluation process. This phase is called the cost/suitability analysis. The cost/suitability analysis generates the final aggregated value indicators that reflect the overall values of each alternative. Consequently, the ranking of cars (or other objects/alternatives) is simply based on decreasing overall value indicators. The highest value is used to select the most suitable alternative.

SELECTION OF SUITABILITY ATTRIBUTES

In many professional evaluation projects, evaluated alternatives can have a large number of suitability attributes. All attributes are not necessarily suitability attributes. Suitability attributes are only those attributes that justifiably contribute to the overall suitability of an evaluated alternative. For example, height and weight are obvious human attributes, but they do not affect the suitability of a candidate to serve as a judge on the Supreme Court. In the area of evaluation, we are interested only in suitability attributes and the term "attribute" always means only the suitability attribute.

Precise and justifiable evaluations can include from about a dozen to a few hundred attributes. The attributes should not be selected randomly and out of order. We need a systematic process of selecting suitability attributes, and the LSP method uses a hierarchical decomposition process that generates an attribute tree. We first identify a few basic groups of nonredundant attributes at the first level of decomposition. At each decomposition step the number of components should be limited, and we suggest using from 2 to 5 components. If the number of groups is greater than 5, then it is difficult to reliably identify their relative importance (Miller, 1956).

The process of developing a suitability attribute tree is illustrated in Table A.1 for a family car evaluation, which includes 27 elementary attributes most car buyers take into account when deciding about purchasing a car. In this example, the hierarchical decomposition process begins by identifying four basic groups of attributes: (1) driving experience, (2) functionality and equipment, (3) comfort and aesthetics, and (4) manufacturer and maintenance. These four groups include the majority of relevant suitability attributes.

The next step is to focus on components of each group of attributes. For example, in the first group (driving experience) we can identify performance, safety, and handling. The decomposition continues with each new group. For example, the car performance group can be decomposed generating three new attributes: the power of engine, acceleration, and the maximum speed. Obviously, the power of engine is a single fixed value and cannot be further decomposed. Consequently, the power of engine can be used as one of 29 elementary suitability attributes. A similar conclusion holds for acceleration, maximum speed, and all other suitability attributes generated using the systematic hierarchical decomposition method shown in Figure A.1. In all cases, the decomposition process terminates when we generate sufficiently simple suitability attributes which can be individually evaluated.

Table A.1 does not include cost components. It only includes attributes which affect the benefits that the car buyer expects from using a car. In

Table A.1 *Decomposition of suitability attributes for a family car suitability evaluation*

1 Car	Input Attributes
11 Driving experience	
111 Performance	
1111 Power of engine	1. Power of engine
1112 Acceleration	2. Acceleration
1113 Maximum speed	3. Maximum speed
112 Safety	4. Brakes
1121 Basic safety	5. Airbags
11211 Brakes	6. Collision avoidance system
11212 Airbags	7. Visibility
1123 Collision avoidance system	8. Steering
113 Handling	9. Cruise control
1131 Visibility	10. Front wheel drive
1132 Steering	11. Rear wheel drive
1133 Cruise control	12. Number of passengers
1134 Drive	13. Number of doors
11341 Front wheel drive	14. Size of trunk
11342 Rear wheel drive	15. Maximum useful load
12 Functionality and equipment	16. Instruments and displays
121 Functional characteristics	17. Audio equipment
1211 Number of passengers	18. Navigation equipment
1212 Number of doors	19. Available passenger space
1213 Size of trunk	20. Seat material and comfort
1214 Maximum useful load	21. Suspension
122 Electronic equipment	22. Noise isolation
1221 Instruments and displays	23. Heating
1222 Audio equipment	24. Cooling
1223 Navigation equipment	25. Exterior design
13 Comfort and aesthetics	26. Interior design
131 Space and comfort	27. Colors
1311 Available passenger space	28. Consumer report ratings
1312 Seat material and comfort	29. Local automobile repair shop
1313 Suspension	
1314 Noise isolation	

(cont.)

Table A.1 *(cont.)*

1 Car	Input Attributes
132 Air conditioning	
1321 Heating	
1322 Cooling	
133 Aesthetics	
1331 Design	
13311 Exterior design	
13312 Interior design	
1332 Colors	
14 Manufacturer and maintenance	
141 Consumer report ratings	
142 Local automobile repair	

addition, elementary attributes should generally be independent and nonredundant. For example, the car acceleration is independent of audio equipment. If there are related (and statistically correlated) attributes (as the power of engine, acceleration and the maximum speed), such attributes should be kept in the same group (performance). If related attributes are scattered all over the attribute tree, then it is not possible to precisely control their impact. If they are inside the same group, then it is possible to precisely control the impact of the group.

The suitability attribute tree in Table A.1 does not include all possible attributes. In all cases, there are attributes that are insignificant and deliberately not included in the evaluation process. For example, the car attributes shown in Table A.1 do not include the transmission type (manual or automatic). That can be done unintentionally or intentionally. The reasons for omitting the transmission type attribute can be that the assumed transmission type is automatic and can be omitted because it is expected to satisfy the average quality criteria. Another reason can be that the car buyer has equal experience in driving cars with manual and automatic transmission and has no preference between them, so that it is justified to omit transmission as a relevant suitability attribute. Of course, omitting relevant suitability attributes is a frequent error that should be detected and avoided in the process of development of the attribute tree.

The car buyer example in Table A.1 includes only the most obvious suitability evaluation attributes. Even in that case the number of attributes is 29, and it would be very difficult to generate and process all of them intuitively without

Table A.2 *The general structure of an elementary criterion table and the criterion table rules*

Suitability Attribute a	Suitability x (%)	Criterion Table Rules
$A_1 = A_{min}$	S_1	$A_{min} = A_1 < A_2 < A_3 < A_4 < A_5 = A_{max}$
A_2	S_2	if $a \geq A_{min}$ then $x = S_1$
A_3	S_3	if $a \geq A_{max}$ then $x = S_k$
$\cdots$	$\cdots$	if $A_i \leq a \leq A_{i+1}$ then $x = S_i + (a - A_i)\dfrac{S_{i+1} - S_i}{A_{i+1} - A_i}$
$A_k = A_{max}$	S_k	

using a systematic procedure which solves the evaluation problem in small and easily controllable steps. That is the basic concept of the LSP method and the remaining phases of the LSP evaluation process are also organized in small and simple steps.

DEVELOPMENT OF ATTRIBUTE CRITERIA

For each suitability attribute it is necessary to develop an attribute criterion that reflects user needs and requirements. Each attribute criterion is a mapping of the value of the attribute into the corresponding suitability degree. The suitability degree is expressed in the range from 0 to 100 percent (or equivalently, from 0 to 1). The simplest way to define an attribute criterion is in the form of the elementary criterion table presented in Table A.2. The first column of the suitability attribute table contains the values of attribute a in the range from the minimum value A_{min} to the maximum value A_{max}. If $a \leq A_{min}$ we assume that the suitability is $x = S_1$ and if $a \geq A_{max}$ we assume that the suitability is $x = S_k$. For all other values of a, the value of suitability is computed using linear interpolation as shown in Table A.1. For example if $a = pA_i + (1 - p)A_{i+1}$, $0 \leq p \leq 1$, then the corresponding suitability is $x = pS_i + (1 - p)S_{i+1}$.

The criterion table definition of an elementary attribute criterion can have any form defined by the distribution of break points $(A_1, S_1), \ldots, (A_k, S_k)$, $k > 1$. Not surprisingly, some forms of attribute criteria are more frequent than other forms and four most frequently used types of criteria are shown in Figures A.1–A.4.

The first very frequently used attribute criterion form is shown in Figure A.1. It corresponds to situations where preferred are large values of the attribute a. The presented example assumes that the car buyer needs the trunk

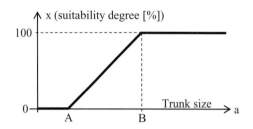

Suitability attribute (a) Trunk size	Suitability S [%]
A	0
B	100

FIGURE A.1 Preferred large values: graph notation and criterion table notation.

size that is unacceptable if it is less than or equal to A. On the other hand, the car buyer is completely satisfied if the trunk volume is greater than or equal to B. For trunk sizes between A and B we use linear interpolation (e.g., if $a = (A + B)/2$ then the corresponding suitability is 50 percent). The basic shape shown in Figure A.1 can be further refined if we can provide more justified breakpoints in the interval $A < a < B$.

A similar frequently used attribute criterion form is shown in Figure A.2. It corresponds to situations where preferred are small values of the attribute a. The presented example assumes that the car buyer prefers cars that can be repaired

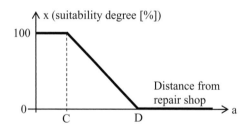

Suitability attribute (a) Repair shop distance	Suitability S [%]
C	100
D	0

FIGURE A.2 Preferred small values: graph notation and criterion table notation.

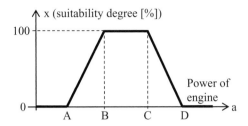

Suitability attribute (**a**) Power of engine	Suitability **S** [%]
A	0
B	100
C	100
D	0

FIGURE A.3 Preferred range of values: graph notation and criterion table notation.

and maintained in shops close to home. So, it is unacceptable if the distance to shop is greater than or equal to D. On the other hand, the car buyer is completely satisfied if the distance is less than or equal to C. For distances between C and D we use linear interpolation (e.g., if $a = (C + D)/2$ then the corresponding suitability is 50 percent). Similar to the previous example, the basic shape shown in Figure A.2 can be further refined if we can provide more justified breakpoints in the interval $C < a < D$.

In some situations, preferred is the range of values. Such an attribute criterion is shown in Figure A.3. In this example the car buyer considers unacceptable cars that have an insufficient power of engine that is less than or equal to A. The ideal case are powers of engine in the range $B \leq a \leq C$. However, the car buyer is not interested in excessive powers of engine that would significantly increase fuel consumption and weight of car without providing significant benefits. If the power of engine is greater than or equal to D, then such engine is again unacceptable.

In many cases we have to deal with attributes that cannot be objectively measured and easily quantified. In the car buyer example such criteria are noise isolation, exterior design, interior design, color suitability and others. In such cases, the attribute criterion can use rating scales.

An example of a rating scale is shown in Figure A.4. The presented rating scale has five levels identified using linguistic labels:

$$unacceptable < poor < fair < good < excellent$$

Table A.3 *A discrete multilevel attribute criterion*

Suitability Attribute (a) Audio Equipment	Suitability x (%)
0 = No audio equipment	0
1 = Car radio only	50
2 = Car radio and a single CD player	85
3 = Car radio and a multiple CD player	100

The evaluator is now forced to subjectively evaluate the engine noise suppression in analyzed (nonelectric) cars and express the degree of satisfaction by selecting the most appropriate among the five selected labels.

Several discrete values of attributes can be numerically coded yielding criteria similar to rating scales. An example is shown in Table A.3, where various versions of audio equipment are numerically coded as $a = 0, 1, 2, 3$ and then assigned appropriate degrees of suitability. A frequent criterion in this category is a binary criterion exemplified in Table A.4. Binary criteria are used to evaluate the presence or absence of a desirable feature.

Elementary attribute criteria can have other forms, different from those studied above. An example are relative criteria where we compare several objects

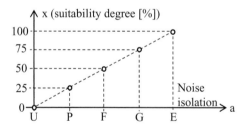

Suitability attribute (a) Noise isolation	Suitability S [%]
U (unacceptable)	0
P (poor)	25
F (fair)	50
G (good)	75
E (excellent)	100

FIGURE A.4 Rating scale criterion: graph notation and criterion table notation.

Table A.4 *A sample binary attribute criterion*

Suitability Attribute (a) Sunroof	Suitability x (%)
0 = Sunroof not available	0
1 = Sunroof available	100

so that the best object is assigned the maximum suitability (100 percent) and other objects have suitability $x = 100a/a_{max}$. Of course, in such cases it is important to make sure that $a = a_{max}$ really deserves the full satisfaction, e.g., it is possible that we evaluate two objects that have equal values of a specific attribute. In such a case the relative criterion will assign maximum satisfaction to these alternatives regardless of the value of such an attribute.

AGGREGATION OF ATTRIBUTE SUITABILITY DEGREES

For each evaluated alternative, elementary attribute criteria create corresponding suitability degrees. In the car evaluation example, each car is characterized using 29 suitability degrees, $x_1, \ldots, x_{29}$ some of them good and some of them bad. Obviously, the decision cannot be made using 29 different numbers; we need an overall suitability degree that reflects the perception of overall suitability of each evaluated car. The overall suitability is a quantitative indicator of expected benefits if we decide to use the evaluated object (e.g., if we decide to buy a specific car).

At this point we are faced with the problem of aggregation of attribute suitability degrees. It is easy to see that this is a logic problem. We might be tempted to simply compute the simple mean value of all attribute suitability degrees $x = (x_1 + \cdots + x_{29})/29$, but in such a case we can be sure that we will make the following serious errors:

- All attributes are not equally important. Some attributes contribute to the overall suitability more than other attributes. For example, in the car evaluation case the power of engine is usually more important than the internal noise level.
- Some attributes are so important that their satisfaction is mandatory. In such cases if $x_i = 0$ we expect $x = 0$ but the simple mean value is not giving such a result. For example if the power of engine is insufficient, we may want to reject such a car and the suitability aggregation method must reflect such a requirement.

- Some attributes in a group of attributes can be so important that their full satisfaction is sufficient to satisfy the evaluator regardless of the values of other attributes in the group. For example some evaluators may want to be fully satisfied with the car performance if the power of engine (or the resulting acceleration) is sufficiently high, and in such case the other performance attributes can be considered negligible. This property cannot be expressed using the simple arithmetic mean.
- Some attributes are optional, and if they are not satisfied we are still ready to accept such a car. For example, the absence of cruise control will be acceptable for most city drivers. Unfortunately, the arithmetic mean criterion makes *all* attributes optional, and that is not acceptable.

LSP method offers all aggregation methods that are observable in human reasoning. There are nine such basic patterns. That gives the opportunity to create aggregation structures that are fully justifiable because they are the model of human expert reasoning. Creating suitability aggregation structures step by step, following the structure of the attribute decomposition tree (Table A.1) reduces the complexity of aggregation and provides a way to create evaluation criteria in small easy steps. This gives the possibility to systematically expand human reasoning far beyond the limitations of intuitive reasoning which is limited to very small number of suitability attributes.

In most evaluation criteria, decision-makers require simultaneity in satisfaction of multiple requirements. A careful observation of human evaluation reasoning shows that simultaneity can have different grades of strength. The degree of simultaneity is called *andness* and its minimum value is 0 and the maximum value is 100 percent. The maximum andness (100 percent) denotes the highest degree of simultaneity where absolutely all inputs must be satisfied. The logic behind the highest andness is "the strength of the chain is defined by its weakest link." In other words, if for simplicity we aggregate two degrees of suitability x and y, and we want the highest degree of their simultaneity, then in the case where $x < y$ the resulting suitability is $z = \min(x, y) = x$. Obviously, the need for simultaneous satisfaction is so high that the lack of sufficient satisfaction expressed by the lowest value (x) is so significant that it cannot be compensated by increasing the value of y. Consequently, if the andness is 100 percent then the case $x = 40\%, y = 60\%$ and a different and seemingly better case $x = 40\%, y = 90\%$ yield the same result $z = \min(40, 60) = \min(40, 90) = 40\%$. Of course, that is an extreme standpoint because it claims that the impact of the lowest suitability is so high that it cannot be compensated even with the highest values of other components in a group.

The highest andness (100 percent) denotes the extreme simultaneity. As a counterpart of the highest andness we have the other extreme standpoint denoted by the lowest andness (0). In this case the simultaneity is completely needless (i.e., absent). In such an extreme case any input is sufficient to completely satisfy a compound criterion. In other words, all inputs are fully substitutable. So, substitutability is a complementary counterpart of simultaneity. Minimum simultaneity means maximum substitutability, and maximum simultaneity means minimum substitutability. Obviously, substitutability also has different grades of strength and the degree of substitutability is called *orness*. The andness and orness are complementary: for each logic model of simultaneity or substitutability we have *andness* + *orness* = 100 percent.

In human logic reasoning, we frequently combine a specific degree of simultaneity and a specific degree of substitutability, i.e., 0 < *andness* < 100 percent and 0 < *orness* < 100 percent. If *andness* > *orness* then such an aggregator is "conjunctively polarized" and called *partial (or graded) conjunction*. In linguistic interpretation, conjunction denotes an AND connective. It is called "partial" because the full conjunction is the term reserved for the extreme case of maximum andness. It is graded because its strength can be adjusted by selecting an appropriate value of andness. If *orness* > *andness*, than such an aggregator is "disjunctively polarized" and called *partial (or graded) disjunction*. In linguistic interpretation, disjunction denotes an OR connective. It is called "partial" because the full disjunction is the term reserved for the extreme case of maximum orness. It is graded because its strength can be adjusted by selecting an appropriate value of orness.

If *andness* = *orness* = 50 percent, then we call this case the *logic neutrality*, and its model is a simple arithmetic mean $z = (x + y)/2$. The meaning of neutrality is clearly visible in cases where it is used for computing the Grade Point Average (GPA) of students in schools. All schools prefer students who are capable to simultaneously have highest grades in all courses that are used for computing GPA. So this is the simultaneity requirement. At the same time, schools offer to all students the possibility to compensate any bad grade with any other good grade. This is a substitutability requirement, and it is equally present and equally significant as the simultaneity requirement. The result is logic neutrality, i.e., an aggregator that is 50 percent conjunctive and 50 percent disjunctive.

The most frequent property of human intuitive evaluation is compensativeness, i.e., the possibility that the shortfall of suitability of any input can be partially compensated by the excess of suitability of any other input. This property can be achieved using an appropriate combination of simultaneity and substitutability, achieved by selecting the right ratio of andness and orness, different from extreme cases. Properties of adjustable simultaneity and substitutability aggregators are

Table A.5 *Uniform Graded Conjunction/Disjunction (UGCD.15) and its special cases*

Logic Relationship	Modeled Property	Type	Level	Symbol	Orness	Andness
Substitutability (full or partial disjunction)	Sufficient requirements (each fully satisfied input can fully satisfy the group requirements)	Hard disjunction	Highest	D	100%	0
			High	HD+	92.9	7.1
			Medium	HD	85.7	14.3
			Low	HD–	78.6	21.4
	Soft partial disjunction (inputs are desirable but not sufficient)	Soft disjunction	High	SD+	71.4	28.6
			Medium	SD	64.3	35.7
			Low	SD–	57.1	42.9
Logic neutrality: perfect balance of simultaneity and substitutability				A	50	50
Simultaneity (full or partial conjunction)	Soft partial conjunction (inputs are simultaneously desirable but not mandatory)	Soft conjunction	Low	SC–	42.9	57.1
			Medium	SC	35.7	64.3
			High	SC+	28.6	71.4
	Mandatory requirements (all inputs must be at lest partially satisfied, zero satisfaction is unacceptable)	Hard conjunction	Low	HC–	21.4	78.6
			Medium	HC	14.3	85.7
			High	HC+	7.1	92.9
			Highest	C	0	100%

provided in Table A.5, and their use in creating compound logic aggregation structures is discussed next.

Basic human aggregation patterns include four patterns of simultaneity (graded logical AND function), four patterns of substitutability (graded logical OR function) and neutrality (a balanced combination of simultaneity and substitutability). Below we present these models using the aggregation function called Uniform Graded Conjunction/Disjunction (UGCD) presented in Table A.5. This function is usually classified as UGCD.15 because it is uniform (providing the same area for each soft and hard group of aggregators) and it offers 15 levels of andness and orness. GCD aggregators can also be nonuniform and have more or less levels of andness/orness. We are going to use UGCD.15 because it is a balanced aggregator that offers the best combination of precision, versatility, and simplicity of use.

Each version of the GCD function provides a model of graded simultaneity and substitutability (graded AND and graded OR operators). In a general case of n input suitability degrees GCD provides adjustable continuous transition from the pure conjunction (logical AND modeled as $x = \min(x_1, \ldots, x_n)$) to the pure disjunction (logical OR modeled as $x = \max(x_1, \ldots, x_n)$). Consequently, it is possible to interpret andness as a degree of similarity between the selected form of GCD and the pure conjunction (the maximum similarity is 100 percent). Similarly, orness can be interpreted as a degree of similarity between a specific form of GCD and the pure disjunction.

Table A.5 suggests that human reasoning combines requests for simultaneity and substitutability of suitability degrees. Each suitability degree reflects the level of satisfaction of specific requirements. The request for simultaneous satisfaction of multiple requirements means that the decision-maker wants to penalize cases where any of two or more requirements is insufficiently satisfied. In other words, if the andness is high, the ability of compensating low values of some input suitability degrees by increasing the suitability degrees of other inputs in a group is rather low; the impact of unsuitable components is higher than the impact of suitable components. The compensative properties (that reflect substitutability) still exist showing that decision-makers combine simultaneity and substitutability, but adjust their balance at any step in the aggregation process.

In the case of criteria that support substitutability, the compensative properties are desirable and present. The compensation of low input suitability degrees becomes easy and can be achieved using any subset of high suitability degrees in a group. Of course, even if the compensation of low inputs is possible and relatively easy we still like to have all requirements simultaneously satisfied. So, disjunctive properties can be predominant, but in real life they are always combined with some desired conjunctive properties.

The GCD function is an aggregator that combines simultaneity and substitutability in proportion that is freely selected by the decision-maker. The desired properties are adjusted by selecting the appropriate ratio of andness and orness. If andness is greater than orness, then the GCD is a model of simultaneity. If orness is greater than andness, then the GCD is a model of substitutability. By combining various version of the GCD function we can create sophisticated aggregation structures that precisely reflect justifiable requirements of decision-makers and systematically expand the decision models far beyond the limits of intuitive reasoning.

Mathematical details of various implementations of GCD are beyond the scope of this book. Fortunately, GCD is an aggregator that is "andness-directed" or "orness-directed," i.e., its properties (summarized in Table A.5) can be understood and correctly selected by specifying desired degrees of andness and orness. At the beginning of aggregator selection process the evaluator must decide whether the aggregator describes neutrality, or simultaneity, or substitutability. The next step is to select one of characteristic forms of these aggregators, and to adjust degrees of relative importance of inputs.

MODELING LOGIC NEUTRALITY

Logic neutrality provides a perfect balance between simultaneity and substitutability requirements. It is modeled as the weighted arithmetic mean $x = W_1 x_1 + \cdots + W_n x_n$ where normalized weights $0 < W_i < 1, \quad W_1 + \cdots + W_n = 1$ denote the degrees of relative importance of suitability degrees $x_1, \ldots, x_n$. Unsurprisingly, only exceptionally all inputs have the same degree of importance. In a general case, the weights $W_1, \ldots, W_n$ reflect the level of impact that inputs $x_1, \ldots, x_n$ have on supporting the stakeholder's goals and requirements. The adjustment of weights is based on understanding the role of each input in a given evaluation project. In addition to adjusting weights (as semantic components of decision criterion), evaluators independently adjust andness/orness (as formal logic components of decision criterion). As Table A.5 suggests, aggregation operators are complementary combinations of simultaneity and substitutability. In some cases simultaneity is a dominant feature (in which case andness is greater than orness) and in other cases substitutability is a dominant feature (and in such cases orness is greater than andness).

In the case of neutrality, both andness and orness are equal to 50 percent suggesting that the neutrality operator provides a balanced mix of simultaneity and substitutability. An example of neutrality aggregator is presented in Figure A.5. In this example, the car buyer specifies that the audio equipment is the most

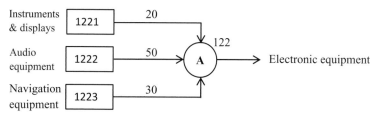

FIGURE A.5 Sample neutrality aggregator.

important component of car electronics (50 percent), navigation equipment is less important (30 percent), and standard instruments/displays are the least important (20 percent). Of course, the evaluator would like to have all inputs simultaneously satisfied (good audio, instruments, and navigation). At the same time, the evaluator believes that any electronic component can partially compensate other components. In an extreme case, the car buyer is ready to accept cases where some of these inputs are completely not satisfied, provided that other inputs are very good. For example, by specifying the aggregator shown in Figure A.5 the evaluator asserts the readiness to accept a car without navigation equipment provided that other attributes are sufficiently satisfied. The justification for this criterion can be that audio equipment is regularly used for entertainment and informing, navigation equipment is not important for drivers who repeatedly use the same roads, and basic instruments are standard and available in all modern cars. Of course, if the evaluator's standpoint is different, than the aggregator type and parameters should be changed in a way that supports a different evaluation standpoint.

MODELING SIMULTANEITY REQUIREMENTS

Simultaneity requirements are the most frequent logic aggregation form in evaluation practice. It is in human nature to try to simultaneously satisfy all desirable requirements. In the car buyer example, most people would like to simultaneously have sufficiently satisfied all 29 individual requirements specified by the attribute criteria.

Simultaneity criteria can have various properties, and we differentiate three fundamental forms of simultaneity derived from observing human intuitive reasoning:

- *Soft simultaneity* (optional simultaneous requirements)
- *Hard simultaneity* (mandatory simultaneous requirements)
- *Asymmetric simultaneity* (mandatory/optional requirements)

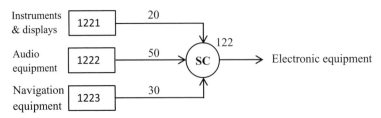

FIGURE A.6 A soft partial conjunction aggregator.

These three types of aggregators support different forms of simultaneity: optional, mandatory, and combined optional/mandatory. The first two are modeled using GCD, and the asymmetric form is combined using two GCD aggregators.

Soft Simultaneity

In many cases we want simultaneous satisfaction of several optional requirements. The meaning of optional requirement is that we are ready to tolerate some (but not all) zero inputs without producing the zero output. The main properties of such aggregators are the following:

1 Soft simultaneity is used as a model of moderate simultaneity of inputs that penalizes small inputs more than the neutrality aggregators.
2 The degree of penalizing low inputs is adjustable and in the case of UGCD.15 (Table A.5) we use three levels: low (SC-), medium (SC), and high (SC+).
3 Zero output suitability is produced only in cases where all input suitability degrees are zero. If at least one of inputs is to some extent satisfied, the output will be positive.

Soft simultaneity is a conjunctive aggregator and its technical name is the soft partial conjunction (SPC), where the partial conjunction refers to the possibility to adjust the degree of simultaneity (andness). According to Table A.5, in the case of UGCD.15, the range of SPC andness 11 is from 57.1 percent to 71.4 percent.

In the case where a car buyer wants simultaneously good instruments, audio and navigation equipment, the criterion shown in Figure A.5 can be modified as shown in Figure A.6. The relative importance indicators (weights) remain unchanged but the degree of andness is increased from 50 percent to 64.3 percent, providing more penalties for cars that have electronic equipment weaknesses. For example, according to neutrality criterion in Figure A.5, if Instruments = 60 percent, Audio = 80 percent, and Navigation = 30 percent, then Electronics = 61 percent. In the case of the SC aggregator in Figure A.6, the resulting suitability degree is Electronics = 56.1 percent. If we want more penalizing we can use SC+ aggregator and the corresponding suitability degree would be Electronics = 53.65 percent.

Hard Simultaneity

Hard simultaneity provides logic models of mandatory requirements. We use such aggregators if we want strict simultaneous satisfaction of several requirements and we do not want to tolerate any zero input suitability. All inputs must be to some extent satisfied. The main properties of such aggregators are the following:

1 Hard simultaneity aggregators are used as models of strong simultaneity of inputs that penalizes small inputs more than the soft simultaneity aggregators.
2 The degree of penalizing low inputs is adjustable, and in the case of UGCD.15 (Table A.5) we use four levels: low (HC-), medium (HC), high (HC+), and the highest (C).
3 Zero output suitability is produced if any input suitability degree is zero. Consequently, in order to avoid zero output suitability, all inputs must be simultaneously satisfied, creating a model of mandatory requirements.

All hard simultaneity aggregators except the pure conjunction C are called the hard partial conjunction (HPC). The partial conjunction refers to the possibility to adjust the degree of simultaneity (andness). According to Table A.5, in the case of UGCD.15, the range of HPC andness is from 78.6 percent to 100 percent. In the extreme case of the highest andness we have the pure conjunction (C) where the output suitability is equal to the minimum input suitability. Consequently, in this case the lowest suitability degree cannot be compensated by increasing other inputs. This is an extreme behavior that is rather infrequently used in soft computing logic. For all HPC aggregators different than C we can have compensatory properties which are generally desirable in evaluation.

Hard simultaneity is regularly used at the levels close to the root of the suitability attribute tree. In the case of the family car evaluation example, the root of the attribute tree is presented in Figure A.7. This aggregator shows that all four inputs are mandatory and must be satisfied. If any of four inputs is rated unsuitable (zero suitability) the whole car will be assigned the zero overall suitability and rejected.

All inputs in Figure A.7 represent groups of attributes. If the previous aggregators along the path from the leaves to the root of the aggregation tree are HPC, then some of the input attributes are mandatory and can cause the zero overall suitability and the car rejection. So, some attributes in Table A.1 can be selected to be mandatory and others are desirable, but logically optional.

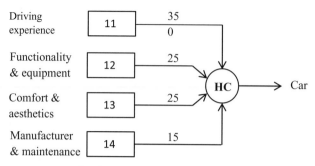

FIGURE A.7 A hard partial conjunction aggregator.

Asymmetric Simultaneity

Both soft simultaneity and hard simultaneity aggregators are symmetric in the sense that the logic impact of all inputs is the same. In the case of soft simultaneity all inputs are mandatory and in the case of hard simultaneity all inputs are mandatory.

In many applications, however, we need asymmetric aggregators where we aggregate a mandatory (or primary) input and an optional (or secondary) input. The asymmetric structure of CPA is shown in Figure A.8. It is a combination of the arithmetic mean (neutrality) and a hard conjunction (HC). Both the mandatory input x and the optional input y are desirable but their logic impact is different as follows:

1 If the mandatory input x is zero, then the output suitability degree is zero regardless the value of the optional input y: $z(0,y) = 0$.
2 If the mandatory input is not zero $(x>0)$ and the optional input y is zero, then the output suitability is equal to the input suitability decreased by an adjustable penalty degree: $0<z(x,0)<x$.
3 If the mandatory input x is less than 100 percent and the optional input is perfectly satisfied $(y = 100 \text{ percent})$, then the output suitability is equal to the input suitability increased by an adjustable reward degree: $x<(x,100)<100$.

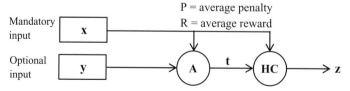

FIGURE A.8 The structure of asymmetric simultaneity (conjunctive partial absorption).

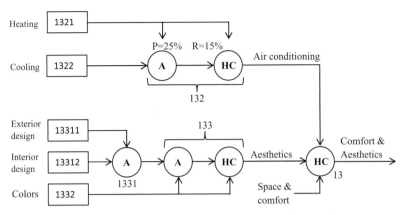

FIGURE A.9 CPA criteria for air conditioning and car aesthetics.

4 The degrees of penalty and reward depend on the values of mandatory and optional inputs (x, y). The mean values of penalty (P) and reward (R) are selected by evaluators to adjust the desired behavior of the asymmetric simultaneity aggregator.

The mandatory input x is applied as an input of the output HC aggregator and if x = 0 then the output z will be 0 regardless the value of y (and the intermediate value t). On the other hand, if x is to some extent satisfactory (0 < x < 100), then the high value of y (i.e., any y > x) will first increase the intermediate suitability t, and subsequently improve the output suitability z. Similarly, if y is not satisfied, then the zero suitability y will first decrease the intermediate suitability t, and then the output suitability z.

The asymmetric simultaneity aggregator is a generalization of the logic absorption theorem. In the classic Boolean logic the mandatory input completely absorbs the impact of the optional input; in our case the absorption is partial and adjustable. This gives the name conjunctive partial absorption (CPA) to this aggregator.[1]

Two combined examples of asymmetric simultaneity are shown in Figure A.9. In the first example of air conditioning, we assume that the evaluated car will be operated in very cold areas where good heating is mandatory and must be available. As opposed to that, cooling is optional and might be used only a few times per year. The mandatory input (heating) is applied as an input of the output HC aggregator; consequently, if heating is not acceptable (score 0), then the air conditioning suitability will be 0 regardless the quality of cooling system. On

---

[1] Mathematical details of partial absorption functions are available in the literature (Dujmović, 2014).

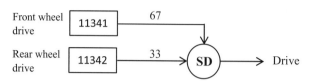

FIGURE A.10 A soft partial disjunction aggregator.

the other hand, if the heating is satisfactory, then the high-quality cooling will improve the output suitability. Similarly, if the cooling does not exist, then the zero cooling suitability will decrease the output suitability. In the air conditioning example shown in Figure A.9 both the average penalty P and the average reward R are selected to be small (25 percent and 15 percent). For example, if the heating is average (50 percent) then the absence of cooling would decrease the output suitability of air conditioning to 37.5 percent and the perfect cooling would increase it to 59.6 percent. So, in this example the cooling system can affect the air conditioning score in the range [37.5 percent, 59.6 percent]. Similarly, if the heating suitability is 80 percent, then the cooling system would affect the output suitability of air conditioning in the range [60 percent, 84.2 percent]. Let us again note that selected P and R represent *average values* and not constants that reflect a specific example.

The second example in Figure A.9 illustrates the situation where the evaluator wants to eliminate cars which have an unacceptable color. So, if the color is unacceptable (scored 0 percent) then the output suitability for car aesthetics would be 0 regardless of design quality. The color and heating in Figure A.9 are defined as mandatory requirements; their zero values would propagate to the output aggregator 13, and from there (according to Figure A.7) these values would cause zero output value of the evaluated car. Therefore, in Figure A.10, the attributes 1321 and 1332 are mandatory (they must be at least partially satisfied), while the remaining attributes (1322, 13311, 13312) are optional and their nonsatisfaction would not automatically disqualify the evaluated car. This example illustrates the situation where the optional inputs (exterior and interior design) are connected directly to the input neutrality aggregator.

MODELING SUBSTITUTABILITY REQUIREMENTS

Substitutability requirements are used in cases where there are independent alternative ways to satisfy stakeholder's requirements. Substitutability is a logic condition fully symmetrical to simultaneity. Substitutability criteria can have various properties, and we differentiate three fundamental forms of substitutability derived from observing human intuitive reasoning:

- *Soft substitutability* (optional substitutable requirements)
- *Hard substitutability* (sufficient substitutable requirements)
- *Asymmetric substitutability* (sufficient/optional requirements)

These three types of aggregators support different forms of substitutability: optional, sufficient, and combined optional/sufficient. The first two are modeled using GCD, and the asymmetric form is combined using two GCD aggregators, similarly as in the case of asymmetric simultaneity.

Soft Substitutability

In some cases, input attributes can substitute each other. Such situations regularly occur when we evaluate inconvenient attributes. In such cases, we frequently consider that the overall result is inconvenient if any of inconvenient inputs is sufficiently present. Substitutable attributes can also be desirable. In such cases, we are ready to tolerate some zero inputs without significant negative consequences. The main properties of such aggregators are the following:

1 Soft substitutability is used as a model of moderate substitutability of inputs where inputs are substitutable by none of them is sufficient to completely satisfy requirements.
2 The degree of rewarding high inputs is adjustable and in the case of UGCD.15 (Table A.5) we use three levels: low (SD-), medium (SD), and high (SD+).
3 Zero output suitability is produced only in cases where all input suitability degrees are zero. If at least one of inputs is to some extent satisfied, the output will be positive.

Soft substitutability is a disjunctive aggregator and its technical name is the soft partial disjunction (SPD), where the partial disjunction refers to the possibility to adjust the degree of substitutability (orness). According to Table A.5, in the case of UGCD.15, the range of SPD orness is from 57.1 percent to 71.4 percent. An example of soft substitutability is shown in Figure A.10. The intention of this criterion is to accept either the front wheel drive or the rear wheel drive. However, the front wheel drive is preferred and the all-wheel drive is considered the ideal solution.

The behavior of this criterion in the case of the neutrality aggregator and three levels of soft simultaneity is shown in Table A.6. Obviously, by increasing the degree of substitutability, the drive suitability increases for both the front wheel drive and the rear wheel drive, and the front/rear difference decreases. If the evaluator knows what desirable results are, the parameters of the SPD aggregator can be appropriately adjusted.

Table A.6 *Sample criterion for drive evaluation*

Drive Suitability (%)		Aggregator			
		A	SD−	SD	SD+
Type of drive	Front wheel drive	67	76.43	85.86	95.29
	Rear wheel drive	33	52.14	71.29	90.43
	All-wheel drive	100	100	100	100

Hard Substitutability

Hard substitutability provides logic models of sufficient requirements. Such aggregators are used if an LSP criterion must be fully satisfied whenever any of the inputs are fully satisfied. The main properties of such aggregators are the following:

1 Hard substitutability aggregators are used as logic models of strong substitutability of inputs that reward large inputs more than the soft substitutability aggregators.

2 The degree of rewarding large inputs is adjustable, and in the case of UGCD.15 (Table A.5) we use four levels: low (HD-), medium (HD), high (HD+), and the highest (D).

3 Zero output suitability is produced only if all input suitability degrees are zero. Maximum output suitability (100 percent) is achieved if any of inputs is fully satisfied.

All hard substitutability aggregators except the pure disjunction D are called the hard partial disjunction (HPD). The partial disjunction refers to the possibility to adjust the degree of substitutability (orness). According to Table A.5, in the case of UGCD.15, the range of HPD orness is from 78.6 percent to 100 percent. In the extreme case of the highest orness we have the pure disjunction (D) where the output suitability is equal to the maximum input suitability. Consequently, in this case the highest suitability degree cannot be reduced by decreasing other inputs. This is an extreme behavior that is not frequently used in evaluation models based on soft computing logic. For all HPD aggregators different than D, we can have compensatory properties which are generally desirable in evaluation. All UGCD aggregators except C and D are "partial," i.e., they provide flexible and adjustable combinations of simultaneity and substitutability.

In the example shown in Figure A.9 we aggregated exterior design and interior design using the neutrality operator. In such a case we offer modest compensatory properties expecting that both exterior and interior design should

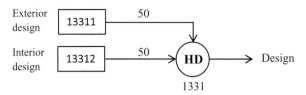

FIGURE A.11 A hard partial disjunction aggregator.

be to an average extent simultaneously satisfied. That requirement could be some-times relaxed to the extent shown in Figure A.11. In this example each highly sat-isfied design component is sufficient to provide high overall design suitability. In an extreme case, if either exterior or interior design criteria are perfectly satisfied, the car buyer would be completely satisfied with the quality of design, regardless that the remaining input can be far from ideal. Consequently, the use of HPD pro-vides strong compensatory properties that are sometimes useful in LSP criteria. It is useful to note that both high simultaneity and high substitutability contribute to the human perception of high importance of input attributes.

Asymmetric Substitutability

Both the soft substitutability and the hard substitutability aggregators are symmet-ric in the sense that the logic impact of all inputs is the same. In the case of soft substitutability, all inputs are desirable but not sufficient and in the case of hard substitutability all inputs are sufficient.

In some applications, however, we need asymmetric aggregators where we aggregate a sufficient (or primary) input and an optional (or secondary) input. Such aggregators provide an asymmetric form of disjunction. They are also called dis-junctive partial absorption (DPA). The asymmetric structure of DPA is shown in Figure A.12. It is a combination of the arithmetic mean (neutrality, A) and a hard disjunction (HD). Both the sufficient input x and the optional input y are desirable but their logic impact is different as follows:

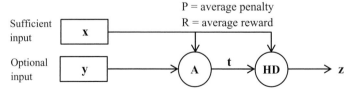

FIGURE A.12 The structure of asymmetric substitutability (disjunctive partial absorption).

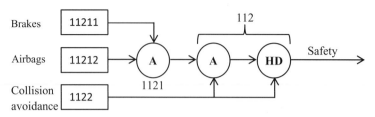

FIGURE A.13 DPA criterion for car safety.

1 If the sufficient input x is 100 percent (fully satisfied), then the output suitability degree is 100 percent regardless the value of the optional input y: $z(100,y) = 100$.

2 If the sufficient input is not fully satisfied ($0<x<100$ percent) and the optional input y is zero, then the output suitability is equal to the input suitability decreased by an adjustable penalty degree: $0<z(x,0)<x$.

3 If the sufficient input x is less than 100 percent and the optional input is perfectly satisfied ($y = 100$ percent), then the output suitability will be equal to the input suitability increased by an adjustable reward degree: $x<z(x,100)<100$ percent.

4 The degrees of penalty and reward depend on the values of sufficient and optional inputs (x, y). The mean values of penalty (P) and reward (R) are used by evaluators to adjust the desired behavior of the asymmetric substitutability aggregator.

The sufficient input x is applied as an input of the output hard HD aggregator and if $x = 100$ percent then the output z will be 100 percent regardless the value of y (and the intermediate value t). On the other hand, if x is to some extent satisfactory ($0<x<100$ percent), then the high value of y (i.e., any $y>x$) will first increase the intermediate suitability t, and subsequently improve ("reward") the output suitability z. Similarly, if y is not satisfied, then the zero suitability y will first decrease the intermediate suitability t, and then decrease ("penalize") the output suitability z.

Similarly to the case of asymmetric simultaneity, the asymmetric substitutability aggregator is a generalization of the logic absorption theorem. In the classic Boolean logic the sufficient input completely absorbs the impact of the optional input; in our case the absorption is partial and adjustable. This gives the name disjunctive partial absorption (DPA) to this aggregator.

An example of DPA aggregator is presented in Figure A.13. In this case brakes and airbags are used as basic safety components. The collision avoidance system (which is currently not available in most cars) is considered an advanced safety feature. So, if the collision avoidance system is available, that can be currently considered the ultimate contribution to car safety, sufficient to fully satisfy the safety criterion. Standard brakes and airbags are not sufficient to fully satisfy safety requirements if the collision avoidance system is not available. This logic reasoning yields the DPA-based aggregation structure shown in Figure A.13.

COST/SUITABILITY ANALYSIS AND THE OVERALL VALUE

The suitability attributes exemplified in Table A.1 do not include cost components. Consequently, the overall suitability computed using logic aggregation of all attribute suitability degrees reflects only the expected benefits of the stakeholder. The overall suitability is an indicator of the degree of satisfaction of stakeholder's goals. Unsurprisingly, the overall suitability is not sufficient to make the decision about selecting the best among several alternatives, because all rational evaluators must also take into account the total cost.

The LSP method considers the total cost (C) to be a counterpart of the overall suitability (X). Consequently, the total cost must include all relevant cost components and in some evaluation projects, the cost analysis is a significant effort. Even in the simple example of car evaluation there are multiple cost components. The total car cost calculation must include the purchasing cost (car price, cost of financing, taxes and registration), the cost of ownership and use for an expected number of years (fuel, tires, maintenance, repairs, insurance, inspection, registration, tolls, parking, washing, and traffic tickets), and the resale value at the end of ownership.

Generally, the *total value* of an evaluated object (V) should be defined as a function of C and X. Of course, all stakeholders are interested in maximizing X and minimizing C. In addition, we assume that all competitors must satisfy two mandatory conditions. First, the overall suitability must be higher than the threshold value X_t (typically $67\% \leq X_t \leq 75\%$); no stakeholder wants a solution that insufficiently satisfies justifiable requirements. Second, the total cost must be less than the threshold value C_t; this value denotes funding that is available and/or approved for acquiring the evaluated object. Therefore, we initially reject all competitors that satisfy $X < X_t$ or $C > C_t$. The remaining acceptable competitors are then ranked according to the decreasing total value.

The simplest way to define the total value is $V = X/C$. In such a case the ranking of competitive objects is performed using a decreasing sequence of V values, and the best competitor is selected as one that has the highest total value.

Note that in this case the overall suitability and the total cost are assumed to have the same importance for the stakeholder.

In a general case, the overall suitability can be more important or less important than the total cost. The logic condition that the suitability and affordability must satisfy is a hard simultaneity: generally, we simultaneously want high suitability and high affordability of competitive objects.

Let X_{max} denote the overall suitability of the most suitable competitor, and let C_{min} denote the total cost of the least expensive competitor. Then X/X_{max} denotes the relative suitability of a given object and C_{min}/C denotes the relative affordability of the same object. Obviously, $X/X_{max} \leq 1$ and $C_{min}/C \leq 1$. If W denotes the relative importance of high suitability and $1 - W$ denotes the relative importance of high affordability $(0 < W < 1)$ then the total value which is a hard partial conjunction of relative suitability and relative affordability can be defined using a simple weighted geometric mean (which is one of hard partial conjunction aggregators) as follows:

$$V = 100 \left(\frac{X}{X_{max}} \right)^{W} \left(\frac{C_{min}}{C} \right)^{1-W}.$$

The resulting total value V depends on the relative importance W. Thus, V can be computed either for the most appropriate value of weight or (more frequently) for all weight values in the range $0 < W < 1$ (to find whether the ranking of competitors significantly depends on the weights). In the car buyer example, there are buyers who are primarily interested in inexpensive cars and for them the appropriate weight is $0 < W < 0.5$. On the other hand, wealthy buyers would be primarily interested in the car's quality, and for them $0.5 < W < 1$. The majority of car buyers regularly use $W \approx 0.5$.

For any value of W the largest value of V denotes the winner of the competition and the most appropriate selection for the stakeholder. If the winner can keep the first position in a wide range of weights, then that proves the strength of its dominance and validates the result of the evaluation.

References

CHAPTER I

Allen, W. L., O. M. Amundsen, J. Dujmović, and K. D. Messer. 2011. Identifying and selecting strategic mitigation opportunities: criteria design and project evaluation using Logic Scoring of Preference and optimization. *Journal of Conservation Planning* 7: 61–68.

Armsworth, P. R., B. E. Kendall, and F. W. Davis. 2004. An introduction to biodiversity concepts for environmental economists. *Resource and Energy Economics* 26: 115–136.

Banzhaf, H. S. 2010. Economics at the fringe: non-market valuation studies and their role in land use plans in the United States. *Journal of Environmental Management* 91: 592–602.

Diamond, H. L., and P. F. Noonan. 1996. *Land Use in America.* Washington, DC: Island Press.

Duke, J. M., S. J. Dundas, and K. D. Messer. 2013. Cost-effective conservation planning: Lessons from economics. *Journal of Environmental Management* 125: 126–133.

Dujmović, J. 2018. *Soft Computing Evaluation Logic: The LSP Decision Method and Its Applications.* Hoboken, NJ: John Wiley.

Ehrlich, P. R. 1968. *The Population Bomb.* New York: Ballantine Books.

Eurostat. 2017. Environmental protection expenditure accounts. http://ec.europa.eu/eurostat/statistics-explained/index.php/Environmental_protection_expenditure_accounts#Main_statistical_findings, accessed May 1, 2017.

Ferraro, P. J., and S. K. Pattanayak. 2006. Money for nothing? A call for empirical evaluation of biodiversity conservation investments. *PLoS Biology* 4(4): e105.

Grand, L., K. D. Messer, and W. Allen. 2017. Understanding and overcoming the barriers for cost-effective conservation. *Ecological Economics* 138: 139–144.

Kreuter, M. W., C. De Rosa, E. H. Howze, and G. T. Baldwin. 2004. Understanding wicked problems: A key to advancing environmental health promotion. *Health Education & Behavior* 31(4): 441–454.

Lewis, M. 2004. *Moneyball: The Art of Winning an Unfair Game.* New York: W. W. Norton.

McCarthy, D. P., P. F. Donald, J. P. Scharlemann, G. M. Buchanan, A. Balmford, J. M. Green, L. A. Bennun, N. D. Burgess, L. D. Fishpool, S. T. Garnett, and D. L. Leonard. 2012. Financial costs of meeting global biodiversity conservation targets: current spending and unmet needs. *Science* 338(6109): 946–949.

McHarg, I. 1969. *Design with Nature*. Garden City, NY: Natural History Press.

Messer, K. D. 2006. The conservation benefits of land acquisition: a case study in Maryland. *Journal of Environmental Management* 79: 305–315.

Messer, K. D., and W. L. Allen. 2010. Applying optimization and the analytic hierarchy process to enhance agricultural preservation strategies in the state of Delaware. *Agricultural and Resource Economics Review* 39(3): 442–456.

Messer, K. D., W. Allen, M. Kecinski, and C. Chen. 2016. Agricultural preservation professionals' perception and attitudes about cost-effective land selection methods. *Journal of Soil and Water Conservation* 71(2): 148–155.

National Commission on the Environment. 1993. *Choosing a Sustainable Future*. Washington, DC: Island Press.

Prendergast, J. R., R. M. Quinn, and J. H. Lawton. 1999. The gaps between theory and practice in selecting nature reserves. *Conservation Biology* 13: 484–492.

Redford, K. H., W. Adams, and G. M. Mace. 2013. Synthetic biology and conservation of nature: wicked problems and wicked solutions. *PLoS Biology* 11(4): e1001530.

US Environmental Protection Agency. 2016. FY 2017 EPA budget in brief. www.epa.gov/sites/production/files/2016-02/documents/fy17-budget-in-brief.pdf, accessed May 2, 2017.

US Fish and Wildlife Services. 2014. Federal and state endangered and threatened species expenditures. www.fws.gov/endangered/esa-library/pdf/20160302_final_FY14_ExpRpt.pdf, accessed May 2, 2017.

CHAPTER 2

Aldrich, R., and J. Wyerman. 2006. *Land Trust Alliance 2005 Census*. Washington, DC: Land Trust Alliance.

American Farmland Trust. 2015. Status of State PACE Programs. www.farmlandinfo.org/sites/default/files/State_Purchase_of_Agricultural_Conservation_Easement_Programs_2015_AFT_FIC_0.pdf, accessed May 17, 2017.

Ando, A., J. Camm, S. Polasky, and A. Solow. 1998. Species distributions, land values, and efficient conservation. *Science* 279: 2126–2128.

Arnold, M., J. M. Duke, and K. D. Messer. 2013. Adverse selection in reverse auctions for environmental services. *Land Economics* 89(3): 387–412.

Babcock, B. A., P. G. Lakshminarayan, J. Wu, and D. Zilberman. 1997. Targeting tools for the purchase of environmental amenities. *Land Economics* 73(3): 325–339.

Duke, J. M., S. J. Dundas, R. J. Johnston, and K. D. Messer. 2014. Prioritizing payment for environmental services: using nonmarket benefits and costs for optimal selection. *Ecological Economics* 105: 319–329.

European Union Directorate-General for Agriculture and Rural Development. 2009. *Rural Development in the European Union: Statistical and Economic Information Report 2009*. Brussels: European Union.

Ferraro, P. J. 2003. Assigning priority to environmental policy interventions in a heterogeneous world. *Journal of Policy Analysis and Management* 22: 27–43.

Fooks, J. R., and K. D. Messer. 2012. Maximizing conservation and in-kind cost share: applying goal programming to forest protection. *Forest Economics* 18: 207–217.

Fooks, J. R., and K. D. Messer. 2013. Mathematical programming applications to land conservation and environmental quality. In *Computational Intelligent Data Analysis for Sustainable Development*. T. Yu, N. Chawla, and S. Simoff, editors. Boca Raton, FL: CRC/Taylor and Francis.

Gole, C., M. Burton, K. J. Williams, H. Clayton, D. P. Faith, B. White, A. Huggett, and C. Margules. 2005. *Auction for landscape recovery: final report*. Sydney: WWF-Australia.

Langpap, C., and J. Kerkvilet. 2010. Allocating conservation resources under the Endangered Species Act. *American Journal of Agricultural Economics* 92: 110–124.

Lerner, J., J. Mackey, and F. Casey. 2007. What's in Noah's wallet? Land conservation spending in the United States. *BioScience* 57(5): 419–423.

Messer, K. D., and W. L. Allen. 2010. Applying optimization and the analytic hierarchy process to enhance agricultural preservation strategies in the state of Delaware. *Agricultural and Resource Economics Review* 39(3): 442–456.

Messer, K. D., W. Allen, M. Kecinski, and C. Chen. 2016. Agricultural preservation professionals' perception and attitudes about cost-effective land selection methods. *Journal of Soil & Water Conservation* 71(2): 148–155. doi:10.2489/jswc.71.2.148.

Messer K. D., and A. Borchers. 2015. Choice for goods under threat of destruction. *Economic Letters* 135: 137–140. doi:10.1016/j.econlet.2015.07.026.

National Park Services. 2016. NPS Statistical Abstract. https://irma.nps.gov/Stats/Reports/AbstractsAndForecasts, accessed May 5, 2017.

National Sustainable Agriculture Coalition. 2016. Conservation Reserve Program: taking environmentally sensitive land out of production and establishing long-term ground cover. http://sustainableagriculture.net/publications/grassrootsguide/conservation-environment/conservation-reserve-program/, accessed on May 23, 2017.

Polasky, S., J. D. Camm, and B. Garber-Yonts. 2001. Selecting biological reserves cost-effectively: an application to terrestrial vertebrate conservation in Oregon. *Land Economics* 77: 68–78.

Ribaudo, M. O. 1986. Consideration of offsite impacts in targeting soil conservation programs. *Land Economics* 62(4): 402–411.

Stoneham, G., V. Chaudhri, A. Ha, and L. Strappazzon. 2003. Auctions for conservation contracts: an empirical examination of Victoria's BushTender trial. *Australian Journal of Agricultural and Resource Economics* 47(4): 477–500.

UNEP-WCMC. 2016. Global statistics from the World Database on Protected Areas (WDPA). www.protectedplanet.net/country/USA, accessed September 20, 2017.

US Department of Agriculture. 2009. Projected spending under the 2014 Farm Bill. www.ers.usda.gov/topics/farm-economy/farm-commodity-policy/projected-spending-under-the-2014-farm-bill/, accessed September 20, 2017.

Wiest, W. A., W. G. Shriver, and K. D. Messer. 2014. Incorporating climate change with conservation planning: A case study for tidal marsh bird conservation in Delaware, USA. *Journal of Conservation Planning* 10: 25–42.

Wilson, K. A., J. Carwardine, and H. P. Possingham. 2009. Setting conservation priorities. *The Year in Ecology and Conservation Biology* 1162: 237–264.

Wu, J. 2004. Using sciences to improve the economic efficiency of conservation policies. *Agricultural and Resource Economics Review* 33: 18–23.

Wu, J., D. Zilberman, and B. A. Babcock. 2001. Environmental and distributional impacts of conservation targeting strategies. *Journal of Environmental Economics and Management* 41: 333–350.

Xu, J., R. Tao, Z. Xu, and M. T. Bennett. 2010. China's sloping land conversion program: does expansion equal success? *Land Economics* 86(2): 219–244.

CHAPTER 3

Allen, W. L., and K. D. Messer. 2009. Optimizing project selection for the U.S. Army Compatible Use Buffer Program. Prepared for the US Army Environmental Center, Aberdeen Proving Ground, MD. McLean, VA: LMI Government Consulting.

Amundsen, O. M. 2004. Implementing strategic conservation: Establishing criteria. *Exchange* 25(3).

Ando, A., J. Camm, S. Polasky, and A. Solow. 1998. Species distributions, land values, and efficient conservation. *Science* 279: 2126–2128.

Arponen, A., M. Cabeza, J. Eklund, H. Kujala, and J. Lehtomaki. 2010. Costs of integrating economics and conservation planning. *Conservation Biology* 24: 1198–1204.

Azzaino, Z., J. M. Conrad, and P. J. Ferraro. 2002. Optimizing the riparian buffer: Harold Brook in the Skaneateles Lake Watershed, New York. *Land Economics* 78(4): 501–514.

Babcock, B. A., P. G. Lakshminarayan, J. Wu, and D. Zilberman. 1996. The economics of a public fund for environmental amenities: a study of CRP contracts. *American Journal of Agricultural Economics* 78: 961–971.

Babcock, B. A., P. G. Lakshminarayan, J. Wu, and D. Zilberman. 1997. Targeting tools for the purchase of environmental amenities. *Land Economics* 73: 325–339.

Cherry, A. 2016a. Farmers cry foul over New Castle County farmland deal. *WDEL*, August 2. www.wdel.com/news/farmers-cry-foul-over-new-castle-county-farmland-deal/article_eed7218d-fb3b-5fde-8d6d-0c874c86c571.html, accessed January 6, 2017.

Cherry, A. 2016b. Del. farmers alarmed at proposed farm preservation deal. *Lancaster Farming*, August 12. www.lancasterfarming.com/news/southern_edition/del-farmers-alarmed-at-proposed-farm-preservation-deal/article_fdc29944-b38b-50f9-8c48-140904dd3085.html, accessed January 6, 2017.

Cherry, A. 2017. A better deal for Delaware taxpayers: farmland preservation at a fraction of the cost. www.wdel.com/news/video-a-better-deal-for-delaware-taxpayers-farmland-preservation-at/article_44731214-4d55-11e7-9c33-63ba1a703573.html, accessed June 15, 2017.

Duke, J. M., S. J. Dundas, and K. D. Messer. 2013. Cost-effective conservation planning: lessons from economics. *Journal of Environmental Management* 125: 126–133.

Ferraro, P. J. 2003. Assigning priority to environmental policy interventions in a heterogeneous world. *Journal of Policy Analysis and Management* 22: 27–43.

Ferraro, P., K. D. Messer, and S. Wu. 2017. Applying behavioral insights to improve water security. *Choices* 32(4): 1–6.

Fooks, J. R., and K. D. Messer. 2013. Mathematical programming applications to land conservation and environmental quality. In *Computational Intelligent Data Analysis for Sustainable Development*. T. Yu, N. Chawla, and S. Simoff, editors. Boca Raton, FL: CRC/Taylor and Francis.

Gowdy, J., C. Hall, K. Klitgaard, and L. Krall. 2010. What every conservation biologist should know about economic theory. *Conservation Biology* 24: 1440–1447.

Grand, L., K. D. Messer, and W. Allen. 2017. Understanding and overcoming the barriers for cost-effective conservation. *Ecological Economics* 138: 139–144.

Messer, K. D. 2006. The conservation benefits of land acquisition: a case study in Maryland. *Journal of Environmental Management* 79: 305–315.

Messer, K. D., and W. L. Allen. 2010. Applying optimization and the analytic hierarchy process to enhance agricultural preservation strategies in the state of Delaware. *Agricultural and Resource Economics Review* 39(3): 442–456.

Messer, K. D., W. Allen, M. Kecinski, and C. Chen. 2016a. Agricultural preservation professionals' perception and attitudes about cost-effective land selection methods. *Journal of Soil and Water Conservation* 71(2): 148–155. doi:10.2489/jswc.71.2.148.

Naidoo, R., A. Balmford, P. J. Ferraro, S. Polasky, T. H. Ricketts, and M. Rouget. 2006. Integrating economic costs into conservation planning. *Trends in Ecology and Evolution* 21: 681–687.

Newburn, D., S. Reed, P. Berck, and A. Merenlender. 2005. Economics and land-use change in prioritizing private land conservation. *Conservation Biology* 19: 1411–1420.

Odling-Smee, L. 2005. Conservation: dollars and sense. *Nature* 437: 614–616.

Olmsted, F. L. 1868. Address to [the] Prospect Park Scientific Association [May 1868]. *The Papers of Frederick Law Olmsted, Supplementary Series* 1: 147–157.

Pease, J. R., and R. E. Coughlin. 1996. *Land Evaluation and Site Assessment: A Guidebook for Rating Agricultural Lands.* Ankeny, IA: Soil and Water Conservation Society.

Polasky, S., J. D. Camm, and B. Garber-Yonts. 2001. Selecting biological reserves cost-effectively: an application to terrestrial vertebrate conservation in Oregon. *Land Economics* 77: 68–78.

Ribaudo, M. O. 1986. Consideration of offsite impacts in targeting soil conservation programs. *Land Economics* 62(4): 402–411.

Smith, K. R. 2006. Public payments for environmental services from agriculture: precedents and possibilities. *American Journal of Agricultural Economics* 88: 1167–1173.

Szczygiel, B., and R. Hewitt. 2000. Nineteenth-century medical landscapes: John H. Rauch, Frederick Law Olmsted, and the search for salubrity. *Bulletin of the History of Medicine* 74(4): 708–734.

Wilson, K. A., M. F. McBride, M. Bode, and H. P. Possingham. 2006. Prioritizing global conservation efforts. *Nature* 440(7082): 337–340.

Wilson, X. 2017. NCCo farmland deal a departure from controversy. *The News Journal.* www.delawareonline.com/story/news/2017/05/30/county-preserves-farm-through-state-departure-previous-administration/355502001/, accessed June 6, 2017.

Wu, J., D. Zilberman, and B. A. Babcock. 2001. Environmental and distributional impacts of conservation targeting strategies. *Journal of Environmental Economics and Management* 41: 333–350.

CHAPTER 4

Ando, A., J. Camm, S. Polasky, and A. Solow. 1998. Species distributions, land values, and efficient conservation. *Science* 279: 2126–2128.

Arnold, M., J. M. Duke, and K. D. Messer. 2013. Adverse selection in reverse auctions for environmental services. *Land Economics* 89(3): 387–412.

Banerjee, S., F. P. De Vries, N. Hanley, and D. P. van Soest. 2014. The impact of information provision on agglomeration bonus performance: an experimental study on local networks. *American Journal of Agricultural Economics* 96(4): 1009–1029.

Banerjee, S., A. M. Kwasnica, and J. S. Shortle. 2012. Agglomeration bonus in small and large local networks: a laboratory examination of spatial coordination. *Ecological Economics* 84: 142–152.

Cattaneo, A., D. Hellerstein, C. Nickerson, and C. Myers. 2006. *Balancing the Multiple Objectives of Conservation Programs.* Publication no. 19. Washington, DC: USDA Economic Research Service.

Costello, C., and S. Polasky. 2004. Dynamic reserve site selection. *Resource and Energy Economics* 26: 157–174.

Drechsler, M., F. Watzold, K. Johst, and J. F. Shogren. 2010. An agglomeration payment for cost-effective biodiversity conservation in spatially structured landscapes. *Resource and Energy Economics* 32: 261–275.

Duke, J. D., S. J. Dundas, R. J. Johnston, and K. D. Messer. 2014. Prioritizing payment for environmental services: using nonmarket benefits for optimal selection. *Ecological Economics* 105: 319–329.

Duke, J. D., S. J. Dundas, R. J. Johnston, and K. D. Messer. 2015. The effect of spatial interdependencies on prioritization and payments for environmental services. *Land Use Policy* 48: 341–350.

Duke, J. M., S. J. Dundas, and K. D. Messer. 2013. Cost-effective conservation planning: lessons from economics. *Journal of Environmental Management* 125: 126–133.

Department of Agriculture's Bureau of Farmland Preservation. 2009. Farmland preservation in Pennsylvania. http://mapmaker2.millersville.edu/pamaps/FarmlandPreserv/#defs, accessed January 18, 2018.

Fooks, J. R., N. Higgins, K. D. Messer, J. M. Duke, D. Hellerstein, and L. Lynch. 2016. Conserving spatially explicit benefits in ecosystem service markets: experimental tests of network bonuses and spatial targeting. *American Journal of Agricultural Economics* 98(2): 468–488.

Fooks, J. R., and K. D. Messer. 2013. Mathematical programming applications to land conservation and environmental quality. In *Computational Intelligent Data Analysis for Sustainable Development*. T. Yu, N. Chawla, and S. Simoff, editors. Boca Raton, FL: CRC/Taylor and Francis.

Fooks, J., K. D. Messer, and J. Duke. 2015. Dynamic entry, reverse auctions, and the purchase of environmental services. *Land Economics* 91(1): 57–75.

Fooks, J., K. D. Messer, and M. Kecinski. 2017. A cautionary note on the use of benefit metrics for cost-effective conservation. *Environmental and Resource Economics*.

Gardner, B. D. 1977. The economics of agricultural land preservation. *American Journal of Agricultural Economics* 59: 1027–1036.

Grove, J. M., S. L. Harlan, J. P. Kaye, and A. K. Knapp. 2011. An integrated conceptual framework for long-term social–ecological research. *Frontiers in Ecology and the Environment* 9(6): 351–357.

Hajkowicz, S., K. Collins, and A. Cattaneo. 2009. Review of agri-environmental indexes and stewardship payments. *Environmental Management* 43: 221–236.

Jayachandra, S. 2017. Using the Airbnb model to protect the environment. New York Times, December 29.

Kaiser, H. M., and K. D. Messer. 2011. *Mathematical Programming for Agricultural, Environmental and Resource Economics*. Hoboken, NJ: John Wiley.

Kirwan, B., R. N. Lubowski, and M. J. Roberts. 2005. How cost-effective are land retirement auctions? Estimating the difference between payments and willingness to accept in the Conservation Reserve Program. *American Journal of Agricultural Economics* 87: 1239–1247.

LancasterOnline. 2017. Map: The price of farmland preservation in Pennsylvania, February, 2014. http://lancasteronline.com/news/local/map-the-price-of-farmland-preservation-in-pennsylvania/article_b20c60f8-9fea-11e3-8982-001a4bcf6878.html, accessed January 18, 2018.

Li, J., J. Michael, J. Duke, K. D. Messer, and J. Suter. 2014. Behavioral response to contamination risk information in a spatially explicit groundwater environment: experimental evidence. *Water Resources Research* 50: 6390–6405.

Lynch, L. 2006. Critical mass: does the number of productive farmland acres or of farms affect farmland loss? In *Economics and Contemporary Land Use Policy: Development and Conservation at the Rural-Urban Fringe.* Robert J. Johnson and Stephen K. Swallow, editors. Hoboken, NJ: John Wiley.

Messer, K. D. 2006. The conservation benefits of cost-effective land acquisition: a case study in Maryland. *Journal of Environmental Management* 79: 305–315.

Messer, K. D. 2007. Transferable development rights programs: an economic framework for success. *Journal of Conservation Planning* 3: 47–53.

Messer, K. D., and W. L. Allen. 2010. Applying optimization and the analytic hierarchy process to enhance agricultural preservation strategies in the state of Delaware. *Agricultural and Resource Economics Review* 39(3): 442–456.

Messer, K. D., and A. Borchers. 2015. Choice for goods under threat of destruction. *Economic Letters* 135: 137–140. doi:10.1016/j.econlet.2015.07.026.

Messer, K. D., M. Kecinski, X. Tang, and R. Hirsch. 2016. Applying multiple knapsack optimization to improve the cost effectiveness of land conservation. *Land Economics* 92(1): 117–130.

Newburn, D., S. Reed, P. Berck, and A. Merenlender. 2005. Economics and land-use change in prioritizing private land conservation. *Conservation Biology* 19: 1411–1420.

Parkhurst, G. M., and J. F. Shogren. 2007. Spatial incentives to coordinate contiguous habitat. *Ecological Economics* 63: 344–355.

Parkhurst, G. M., J. F. Shogren, C. Bastian, P. Kivi, J. Donner, and R. B. W. Smith. 2002. Agglomeration bonus: an incentive mechanism to reunite fragmented habitat for biodiversity conservation. *Ecological Economics* 41: 305–328.

Pruetz, R., and N. Standridge. 2008. What makes transfer of development rights work? Success factors from research and practice. *Journal of the American Planning Association* 75(1): 78–87.

Stoms, D. M., P. A. Jantz, F. W. Davis, and G. DeAngelo. 2009. Strategic targeting of agricultural conservation easements as a growth management tool. *Land Use Policy* 26(4), 1149–1161.

Sullivan, P., et al. 2004. *The Conservation Reserve Program: Economic Implications for Rural America.* Agricultural Economic Report no. 834. Washington, DC: Economic Research Service.

Wu, J. 2004. Using sciences to improve the economic efficiency of conservation policies. *Agricultural and Resource Economics Review* 33: 18–23.

Wu, J., R. M. Adams, and W. G. Boggess. 2000. Cumulative effects and optimal targeting of conservation efforts: steelhead trout habitat enhancement in Oregon. *American Journal of Agricultural Economics* 82: 400–413.

Wu, J., and B. A. Babcock. 1996. Contract design for the purchase of environmental goods from agriculture. *American Journal of Agricultural Economics* 78: 935–945.

Wu, J., and K. Skelton-Groth. 2002. Targeting conservation efforts in the presence of threshold effects and ecosystem linkages. *Ecological Economics* 42: 313–331.

CHAPTER 5

Allen, W. L., III. 2012. Advancing green infrastructure at all scales: from landscape to site. *Environmental Practice* 14(1): 17–25.

Allen, W. L., III. 2016. Strategic conservation planning really works: just ask Nashville. www.conservationfund.org/blog/1264-strategic-conservation-planning-really-works-just-ask-nashville, accessed February 20, 2017.

American Planning Association. 2016a. Greater Baltimore wilderness regional resilience green infrastructure local implementation toolkit. www.planning.org/nationalcenters/green/gbwc/, accessed February 20, 2017.

American Planning Association. 2016b. Supporting a regional green infrastructure network through local policy and action: best practices for using green infrastructure to enhance resilience to coastal storms and climate change. www.planning.org/nationalcenters/green/gbwc/, accessed February 20, 2017.

Benedict, M. A., and E. T. McMahon. 2006. *Green Infrastructure: Linking Landscapes and Communities*. Washington, DC: Island Press.

Center for Neighborhood Technology and American Rivers. 2010. *The Value of Green Infrastructure: A Guide to Recognizing Its Economic, Environmental and Social Benefits*. Washington, DC: American Rivers.

Conservation Fund. 2008. Cecil County green infrastructure plan. www.conservationfund.org/images/projects/files/Green-Infrastructure-Plan-Cecil-County-Maryland-The-Conservation-Fund.pdf, accessed February 21, 2017.

Conservation Fund. 2011. Nashville open space plan: creating, enhancing and preserving the places that matter. www.conservationfund.org/projects/open-space-plan-for-nashville, accessed February 20, 2017.

Conservation Fund. 2012. R Chicago Wilderness Green Infrastructure Vision 2.1. https://datahub.cmap.illinois.gov/dataset/green-infrastructure-vision-2-2-giv-refinement/resource/511ba9c9–803d-47e9–87f5-d4cf41f56058, accessed August 7, 2017.

Conservation Fund. 2013. Houston-Galveston green infrastructure and ecosystem services assessment. www.conservationfund.org/images/projects/files/Houston_Galveston_Report.pdf, accessed February 21, 2017.

Conservation Fund. 2014. Houston-Galveston: green infrastructure and ecosystem services assessment. www.conservationfund.org/projects/green-infrastructure-plans-for-houston-galveston, accessed February 20, 2017.

Conservation Fund. 2015. Chicago Wilderness Green Infrastructure Vision 2.3: ecosystem service valuation. https://datahub.cmap.illinois.gov/dataset/green-infrastructure-vision-2–3-ecosystem-valuation, accessed August 7, 2017.

Conservation Fund and Lake County Forest Preserve District. 2016. Lake County green infrastructure strategy. www.conservationfund.org/projects/lake-county-green-infrastructure-strategy, accessed February 21, 2017.

Corridor Design. 2013. GIS tools for connectivity, corridor, or habitat modeling www.corridordesign.org/designing_corridors/resources/gis_tools, accessed August 7, 2017.

Ehrlich, P. R., and H. A. Mooney. 1983. Extinction, substitution, and ecosystem services. *BioScience* 33(4): 248–254.

Farber, S. C., R. Costanza, and M. A. Wilson. 2002. Economic and ecological concepts for valuing ecosystem services. *Ecological Economics* 41: 375–392.

Firehock, K. 2015. *Strategic Green Infrastructure Planning: A Multi-Scale Approach*. Washington, DC: Island Press.

Forman, R. T. T., and M. Godron. 1986. *Landscape Ecology*. New York: John Wiley.

Galatowitsch, S., L. Frelich, and L. Philips-Mao. 2009. Regional climate change adaptation strategies for biodiversity conservation in a midcontinental region of North America. *Biological Conservation* 142: 2012–2022.

Johnston, R. J., K. J. Boyle, W. Adamowicz, J. Bennett, R. Brouwer, T. A. Cameron, W. M. Hanemann, N. Hanley, M. Ryan, R. Scarpa, R. Tourangeau, and C. A. Vossler. 2017. Contemporary guidance for stated preference studies. *Journal of the Association of Environmental and Resource Economists* 4(2): 319–405.

Kaiser, E. J., D. R. Godschalk, and F. S. Chapin Jr. 1995. *Urban Land Use Planning*. 4th ed. Chicago: University of Illinois Press.

Lerner, J., and W. L. Allen III. 2012. Landscape scale green infrastructure investments as a climate adaptation: a case example for the Midwest United States. *Environmental Practice* 14(1): 45–56.

Lindenmayer, D. B., and H. A. Nix. 1993. Ecological principles for the design of wildlife corridors. *Conservation Biology* 7(3): 627–630.

McDonald (King), L. A., W. L. Allen III, M. A. Benedict, and K. O'Connor. 2005. Green infrastructure plan evaluation frameworks. *Journal of Conservation Planning* 1: 6–25.

Millar C. I., N. L. Stephenson, and S. L. Stephens. 2007. Climate change and forest of the future: managing in the face of uncertainty. *Ecological Applications* 17(8): 2145–2151.

Natural Resources Conservation Service. N.d. LESA system design and uses. www.nrcs.usda.gov/wps/portal/nrcs/detail/national/technical/nra/nri/?cid=stelprdb1043786, accessed August 7, 2017.

Nature Conservancy. 2016. *Maryland Coastal Resiliency Assessment*. M. R. Canick, N. Carlozo, and D. Foster, editors. Bethesda, MD: Nature Conservancy. http://dnr.maryland.gov/ccs/Documents/MARCH-2016_MDCoastalResiliencyAssessment.pdf, accessed August 7, 2017.

Olander, L., S. Polasky, J. Kagan, R. J. Johnston, L. Wainger, D. Saah, L. Maguire, J. Boyd, and D. Yoskowitz. 2017. So you want your research to be relevant? Building the bridge between ecosystem services research and practice. *Ecosystem Services* 26(A): 170–182.

Schwab, J. C., ed. 2009. *Planning the Urban Forest: Ecology, Economy, and Community Development*. New York: Routledge.

Theobald, D. M., S. E. Reed, K. Fields, and M. Soulé. 2012. Connecting natural landscapes using a landscape permeability model to prioritize conservation activities in the United States. *Conservation Letters* 5: 123–133.

Weber, T., J. Wolf, and A. Sloan. 2006. Maryland's green infrastructure assessment: development of a comprehensive approach to land conservation. *Landscape and Urban Planning* 77: 94–110.

CHAPTER 6

Carr, M. H., and P. D. Zwick. 2007. Smart land-use analysis: The LUCIS model. Redlands, CA: Esri Press.

Duke, J. M., and R. A. Hyde. 2002. Identifying public preferences for land preservation using the analytic hierarchy process. *Ecological Economics* 42(1–2): 131–145.

Esri. 2017. The geoprocessing framework – Help | ArcGIS Desktop. http://desktop.arcgis.com/en/arcmap/latest/analyze/main/geoprocessing-framework.htm, accessed August 7, 2017.

Expert Choice. 2017. www.expertchoice.com, accessed August 7, 2017.

Hajkowicz, S. A., G. T. McDonald, and P. N. Smith. 2000. An evaluation of multiple objective decision support weighting techniques in natural resource management. *Journal of Environmental Planning and Management* 43(4): 505–518.

Homer, C. G., J. A. Dewitz, L. Yang, et al. 2015. Completion of the 2011 National Land Cover Database for the conterminous United States – representing a decade of land cover change information. *Photogrammetric Engineering and Remote Sensing* 81(5): 345–354.

Manning, W. H. 1923. National plan study brief. *Landscape Architecture* 13(4): 3.

McHarg, I. 1967. *Design with Nature*. Garden City, NY: Natural History Press.

Messer, K. D., and W. L. Allen III. 2010. Applying optimization and the analytic hierarchy process to enhance agricultural preservation strategies in the state of Delaware. *Agricultural and Resource Economics Review* 39(3): 442–456.

Nutt, P. C. 1980. Comparing methods for weighting decision criteria. *Omega* 8(2): 163–172.

Saaty, T. L. 1982. *Decision Making for Leaders: The Analytical Hierarchy Process for Decisions in a Complex World*. Pittsburgh, PA: Lifetime Learning Publications.

Springer, C. 2016. The Conservation Fund helps energy company fuel collaborative results. www.conservationfund.org/blog/1457-the-conservation-fund-helps-energy-company-fuel-collaborative-results, accessed August 7, 2017.

Stevens, S. S. 1946. On the theory of scales of measurement. *Science* 103(2684): 677–680.

Triantaphyllou, E. 2000. *Multi-Criteria Decision Making Methods: A Comparative Study*, Dordrecht, Netherlands: Springer.

Trust for Public Land. 2006. The Upper Neuse Clean Water Initiative Conservation Plan. www.ctnc.org/wp-content/uploads/2014/10/final-conservation-plan.pdf, accessed August 7, 2017.

Upper Neuse Clean Water Initiative. 2015. https://issuu.com/rebeccahankins/docs/2015-2045_conservation_strategy, accessed August 7, 2017.

Walters, D. 2007. *Designing Community, Charrettes, Master Plans and Form-Based Codes*. Oxford, UK: Taylor and Francis.

Weistroffer, H. R., C. H. Smith, and S. C. Narula. 2005. Multiple criteria decision support software. In *Multiple Criteria Decision Analysis: State of the Art Surveys Series*. J. Figueira, S. Greco, and M. Ehrgott, editors. New York: Springer.

Williams. 2017. Atlantic Sunrise – about the project – overview. http://atlanticsunriseexpansion.com/about-the-project/overview, accessed August 7, 2017.

CHAPTER 7

Allen, W. L., III, O. M. Amundsen, J. J. Dujmović et al. 2011. Identifying and selecting strategic mitigation opportunities: criteria design and project evaluation using Logic Scoring of Preference and optimization. *Journal of Conservation Planning* 7: 61–68.

Dujmović, J. J. 2007. Continuous preference logic for system evaluation. *IEEE Transactions on Fuzzy Systems* 15(6): 1082–1099.

Dujmović, J. J. 2014. An analysis of penalty and reward for partial absorption aggregators. In *Proceedings of the 2014 World Conference on Soft Computing*, Berkeley, CA.

Dujmović, J. J. 2018. *Soft Computing Evaluation Logic: The LSP Decision Method and Its Applications*. Hoboken, NJ: John Wiley.

Dujmović, J. J., and H. L. Larsen. 2007. Generalized conjunction/disjunction. *International Journal of Approximate Reasoning* 46: 423–446.

Dujmović, J. J., and H. Nagashima. 2006. LSP method and its use for evaluation of Java IDE's. *International Journal of Approximate Reasoning* 41(1): 3–22.

Dujmović, J. J., and D. Scheer. 2010. Logic aggregation of suitability maps. Paper presented at the IEEE International Conference on Fuzzy Systems, Barcelona.

Dujmović, J. J., G. D. Tré, and N. Van de Weghe. 2010. LSP suitability maps. *Soft Computing* 14: 421–434.

Gregory, R., L. Failing, M. Harstone, G. Long, T. McDaniels, and D. Ohlson. 2012. *Structured Decision Making: A Practical Guide to Environmental Management Choices*. Hoboken, NJ: John Wiley.

Hatch, K., S. Dragićević, and J. Dujmović. 2014. Logic Scoring of Preference and spatial multicriteria evaluation for urban residential land use analysis. In *International Conference on Geographic Information Science*. New York: Springer.

Klir, G. J., and B. Yuan. 1996. *Fuzzy Sets, Fuzzy Logic, and Fuzzy Systems: Selected Papers by Lotfi A. Zadeh*. Singapore: World Scientific.

Miller, G. A. 1956. The magical number seven, plus or minus two: some limits on our capacity for processing information. *Psychological Review* 63(2): 81–97.

US Fish and Wildlife Service. 2008. Structured decision making fact sheet. www.fws.gov/science/doc/structured_decision_making_factsheet.pdf, accessed August 7, 2017.

US Fish and Wildlife Service. 2014. Region 3 Indiana bat resource equivalency analysis model for wind energy projects. Version 4. Unpublished.

US Fish and Wildlife Service. 2017. Midwest wind multi-species habitat conservation plan. www.fws.gov/Midwest/endangered/permits/hcp/r3wind/index.html, accessed August 7, 2017.

Zadeh, L. A. 1965. Fuzzy sets. *Information and Control* 8(3): 338–353.

CHAPTER 8

Abbitt, R. J., J. M. Scott, and D. S. Wilcove. 2000. The geography of vulnerability: incorporating species geography and human development patterns into conservation planning. *Biological Conservation* 96(2): 169–175.

Allen, W. L., III, T. C. Weber, and K. A. Hoellen. 2010. Green infrastructure design and benefit-cost optimization in transportation planning: maximizing conservation and restoration opportunities in four southern Maryland watersheds. In

A Sustainable Chesapeake: Better Models for Conservation. D. G. Burke and J. E. Dunn, editors. Arlington, VA: The Conservation Fund.

Ando, A., J. Camm, S. Polasky, and A. Solow. 1998. Species distributions, land values, and efficient conservation. *Science* 279: 2126–2128.

Babcock, B. A., P. G. Lakshminarayan, J. Wu, and D. Zilberman. 1996. The economics of a public fund for environmental amenities: a study of CRP contracts. *American Journal of Agricultural Economics* 78: 961–971.

Ballestero, E., S. Alarcón, and A. García-Bernabeu. 2002. Establishing politically feasible water markets: a multi-criteria approach. *Journal of Environmental Management* 65(4): 411–429.

Balmford, A., K. J. Gaston, A. S. L. Rodrigues, and A. James. 2000. Integrating costs of conservation into international priority setting. *Conservation Biology* 14: 567–605.

Boice, L. P. 2014. Threatened and endangered species on DoD lands. www .dodnaturalresources.net/TES_fact_sheet_12-17-14.pdf, accessed July 2, 2017.

Center for Dirt and Gravel Road Studies. 2009. Better Roads, Cleaner Streams. www.dirtandgravel.psu.edu, accessed January 18, 2018.

Costello, C., and S. Polasky. 2004. Dynamic reserve site selection. *Resource and Energy Economics* 26: 157–174.

Douglas, B. C. 1991. Global sea level rise. *Journal of Geophysical Research* 96: 6981–6992.

Drynan, R. G., and F. Sandiford. 1985. Incorporating economic objectives in goal programs for fishery management. *Marine Resource Economics* 2(2): 175–195.

Duke, J. D., S. J. Dundas, R. J. Johnston, and K. D. Messer. 2014. Prioritizing payment for environmental services: using nonmarket benefits for optimal selection. *Ecological Economics* 105: 319–329.

Ferraro, P. J. 2003. Conservation contracting in heterogeneous landscapes: an application to watershed protection with threshold constraints. *Agricultural and Resource Economics Review* 32(1): 53–64.

Fooks, J. R., and K. D. Messer. 2012a. Maximizing conservation and in-kind cost share: applying goal programming to forest protection. *Forest Economics* 18: 207–217.

Fooks, J. R., and K. D. Messer. 2013. Mathematical programming applications to land conservation and environmental quality. In *Computational Intelligent Data Analysis for Sustainable Development*. T. Yu, N. Chawla, and S. Simoff, editors. Boca Raton, FL: CRC/Taylor and Francis.

Fooks, J., K. D. Messer, and J. Duke. 2015. Dynamic entry, reverse auctions, and the purchase of environmental services. *Land Economics* 91(1): 57–75.

Fooks, J., K. D. Messer, and M. Kecinski. 2017. A cautionary note on the use of benefit metrics for cost-effective conservation. *Environmental and Resource Economics.*

Gjerdrum, C., C. S. Elphick, and M. Rubega. 2005. Nest site selection and nesting success in saltmarsh breeding sparrows: the importance of nest habitat, timing, and study site differences. *The Condor* 107: 849–862.

Gjerdrum, C., K. Sullivan-Wiley, E. King, M. A. Rubega, and C. S. Elphick. 2008. Egg and chick fates during tidal flooding of saltmarsh sharp-tailed sparrow nests. *The Condor* 110: 579–584.

Greenburg, R. 2006. Tidal marshes: home for the few and the highly selected. In *Terrestrial Vertebrates of Tidal Marshes: Evolution, Ecology, and Conservation.* R. Greenburg, J. E. Maldonado, S. Droege, and M. V. McDonald, editors. Camarillo, CA: Cooper Ornithological Society.

Higgins, A. J., and S. Hajkowicz. 2008. A model for landscape planning under complex spatial conditions. *Environmental Modeling and Assessment* 13(4): 459–471.

Intergovernmental Panel on Climate Change. 2007. *Climate Change 2007 – the Physical Science Basis: Contribution of Working Group I to the Fourth Assessment Report of the IPCC.* Cambridge: Cambridge University Press.

Kaiser, H. M., and K. D. Messer. 2011. *Mathematical Programming for Agricultural, Environmental and Resource Economics.* Hoboken, NJ: John Wiley.

Lynch, L., and W. N. Musser. 2001. A relative efficiency analysis of farmland preservation programs. *Land Economics* 77(4): 577–594.

Machado, E. A., D. M. Stoms, F. W. Davis, and J. Kreitler. 2006. Prioritizing farmland preservation cost-effectively for multiple objectives. *Journal of Soil and Water Conservation* 61(5): 250–258.

Mallawaarachchi, T., and J. Quiggin. 2001. Modelling socially optimal land allocations for sugar cane growing in North Queensland: a linked mathematical programming and choice modelling study. *Australian Journal of Agricultural and Resource Economics* 45(3): 383–409.

Mardle, S., and S. Pascoe. 1999. A review of applications of multiple-criteria decision-making techniques to fisheries. *Marine Resource Economics* 14(1): 41–63.

Mardle, S., S. Pascoe, M. Tamiz, and D. Jones. 2000. Resource allocation in the North Sea demersal fisheries: a goal programming approach. *Annals of Operations Research* 94(1): 321–342.

Maryland Department of Planning. 2014a. *Demographic and Socio-economic Outlook.* Baltimore: Maryland Department of Planning. http://planning.maryland .gov/MSDC/County/stateMD.pdf, accessed March 20, 2014.

Maryland Department of Planning. 2014b. *Farms and Farmland*. Baltimore: Maryland Department of Planning. http://planning.maryland.gov/msdc/census_agriculture/Farm_Farmland/Table1_Farms2012.pdf, accessed May 6, 2014.

McSweeny, W. T., and R. A. Kramer. 1986. The integration of farm programs for achieving soil conservation and nonpoint pollution control objectives. *Land Economics* 62(2): 159–173.

Messer, K. D. 2006. The conservation benefits of cost-effective land acquisition: a case study in Maryland. *Journal of Environmental Management* 79: 305–315.

Messer, K. D. (ed.). 2010. *Achieving Cost Effective Conservation: ORES801 Case Studies of Applying Optimization to Wetland Mitigation from Highway Expansions in Maryland, Improving Water Quality from the Impact of Dirt and Gravel Roads in Pennsylvania, Increase Cost-Sharing for Forest Protection, and Preserving Agricultural Lands in Delaware and Baltimore County, Maryland*. Food and Resource Economics Research Report no. RR10-01. Newark: University of Delaware.

Messer, K. D., M. Kecinski, Z. Liu, M. A. Korch, and T. Bounds. 2016. Military readiness and environmental protection through cost-effective land conservation. *Land Economics* 92(3): 433–449.

Messer, K. D., M. Kecinski, X. Tang, and R. Hirsch. 2016. Applying multiple knapsack optimization to improve the cost effectiveness of land conservation. *Land Economics* 92(1): 117–130.

Neely, W. P., R. M. North, and J. C. Fortson. 1977. An operational approach to multiple objective decision making for public water resources projects using integer goal programming. *American Journal of Agricultural Economics* 59(1): 198–203.

Newburn, D., S. Reed, P. Berck, and A. Merenlender. 2005. Economics and land-use change in prioritizing private land conservation. *Conservation Biology* 19: 1411–1420.

Nijkamp, P. 1977. Theory and application of environmental economics. *Studies in Regional Science and Urban Economics*.

Önal, H. 1997. Trade-off between structural diversity and economic objectives in forest management. *American Journal of Agricultural Economics* 79(3): 1001–1012.

Rahmstorf, S. 2007. A semi-empirical approach to projecting future sea-level rise. *Science* 315: 368–370.

REPI. 2014. 8th annual report to Congress. www.repi.mil/Portals/44/Documents/Reports_to_Congress/2014REPI%20RTC_030414_Final.pdf, accessed February 3, 2015.

REPI. 2015. Readiness and environmental protection integration. www.repi.mil/AboutREPI.aspx, accessed February 23, 2015.

Sarkar, S., et al. 2006. Biodiversity conservation planning tools: present status and challenges for the future. *Annual Review of Environment and Resources* 31: 123–159.

Shriver, W. G., P. D. Vickery, T. P. Hodgman, and J. P. Gibbs. 2007. Flood tides affect breeding ecology of two sympatric sharp-tailed sparrows. *The Auk* 124: 552–560.

Silva, D., and T. Nakata. 2009. Multi-objective assessment of rural electrification in remote areas with poverty considerations. *Energy Policy* 37(8): 3096–3108.

Stein, B. A., C. Scott, and N. Benton. 2008. Federal lands and endangered species: the role of military and other federal lands in sustaining biodiversity. *AIBS Bulletin* 58(4): 339–347.

Underhill, L. G. 1994. Optimal and Suboptimal Reserve Selection Algorithms. *Biological Conservation* 70(1): 85–87.

US Department of Defense. 2015. *Base Structure Report, Fiscal Year 2015 Baseline*. Washington, DC: US Department of Defense. www.acq.osd.mil/eie/Downloads/BSI/Base%20Structure%20Report%20FY15.pdf, accessed July 2, 2017.

Weber, T. C., and W. L. Allen. 2010. Beyond on-site mitigation: an integrated, multi-scale approach to environmental mitigation and stewardship for transportation projects. *Landscape and Urban Planning* 96: 240–256.

Wiest, W., G. Shriver, and K. D. Messer. 2014. Incorporating climate change with conservation planning: a case study for tidal marsh bird conservation in Delaware, USA. *Journal of Conservation Planning* 10: 25–42.

Williams, J. C., and S. A. Snyder. 2005. Restoring habitat corridors in fragmented landscapes using optimization and percolation models. *Environmental Modeling and Assessment* 10(3): 239–250.

Wu, J. 2004. Using sciences to improve the economic efficiency of conservation policies. *Agricultural and Resource Economics Review* 33: 18–23.

Wu, J., D. Zilberman, and B. A. Babcock. 2001. Environmental and distributional impacts of conservation targeting strategies. *Journal of Environmental Economics and Management* 41: 333–350.

CHAPTER 9

Allcott, H. 2011. Social norms and energy conservation. *Journal of Public Economics* 95(9): 1082–1095.

Allcott, H., and S. Mullainathan. 2010. Behavior and energy policy. *Science* 327(5970): 1204–1205.

Allcott, H., and T. Rogers. 2014. The short-run and long-run effects of behavioral interventions: Experimental evidence from energy conservation. *The American Economic Review* 104(10): 3003–3037.

American Farmland Trust. 1997. *Farming on the Edge*. Washington, DC: AFT.

Arnold, M., J. M. Duke, and K. D. Messer. 2013. Adverse selection in reverse auctions for environmental services. *Land Economics* 89(3): 387–412.

Bajari, P., and A. Hortacsu. 2003. The winner's curse, reserve prices, and endogenous entry: empirical insights from eBay auctions. *RAND Journal of Economics* 34(2): 329–355.

Banerjee, S., J. S. Shortle, and A. M. Kwasnica. 2011. An iterative auction for spatially contiguous land management: an experimental analysis. Paper presented at the annual meeting of the Agricultural and Applied Economics Association, Pittsburgh, PA.

Bernedo, M., P. J. Ferraro, and M. Price. 2014. The persistent impacts of norm-based messaging and their implications for water conservation. *Journal of Consumer Policy* 37(3): 437–452.

Butler, J., J. Fooks, L. Palm-Forster, and K. Messer. 2017. How public information, mascots, and data graphics can help the environment: an experimental study related to nonpoint source pollution. Working paper.

Cason, T. N., and L. Gangadharan. 2004. Auction design for voluntary conservation programs. *American Journal of Agricultural Economics* 86(5): 1211–1217.

Cason, T. N., L. Gangadharan, and C. Duke. 2003. A laboratory study of auctions for reducing non-point source pollution. *Journal of Environmental Economics and Management* 46(3): 446–471.

Chestnut, L. G., and D. M. Mills. 2005. A fresh look at the benefits and costs of the US acid rain program. *Journal of Environmental Management* 77(3): 252–266.

Cialdini, R. B., C. A. Kallgren, and R. R. Reno. 1991. A focus theory of normative conduct: a theoretical refinement and reevaluation of the role of norms in human behavior. *Advances in Experimental Social Psychology* 24: 201–234.

CJC Consulting. 2004. Economic evaluation of the central Scotland forest and grampian challenge funds. Final report for Forest Commission Scotland.

Connor, J. D., J. R. Ward, and B. Bryan. 2008. Exploring the cost effectiveness of land conservation auctions and payment policies. *Australian Journal of Agricultural and Resource Economics* 52(3): 303–319.

Cowling, R. M. 2014. Let's get serious about human behavior and conservation. *Conservation Letters* 7(3): 147–148.

Cramton, P., Y. Shoham, and R. Steinberg. 2006. *Combinatorial Auctions*. Cambridge, MA: MIT Press.

Cummings, R. G., C. A. Holt, and S. K. Laury. 2004. Using laboratory experiments for policymaking: an example from the Georgia irrigation reduction auction. *Journal of Policy Analysis and Management* 23(2): 341–363.

Delaware Population Consortium. 2016. Annual population projections. http://stateplanning.delaware.gov/information/dpc/DPC2016v0.pdf, accessed on July 12, 2017.

Devetag, G. 2003. Coordination and information in critical mass games: an experimental study. *Experimental Economics* 6(1): 53–73.

Duffy, J., and N. Feltovich. 2002. Do actions speak louder than words? An experimental comparison of observation and cheap talk. *Games and Economic Behavior* 39(1): 1–27.

Duke, J., K. D. Messer, L. Lynch, and T. Li. 2017. The effect of information on discriminatory-price and uniform-price reverse auction efficiency: An experimental economics study of the purchase of ecosystem services. *Strategic Behavior and the Environment* 7(1–2): 41–71.

Environmental Protection Agency. 2006. Acid Rain Program, 2005 progress report. www.epa.gov/sites/production/files/2015-08/documents/2005report.pdf, accessed July 18, 2017.

Environmental Protection Agency. 2016. 2014 program progress – Clean Air Interstate Rule, Acid Rain Program, and former NO_x Budget Trading Program. www3.epa.gov/airmarkets/progress/reports/index.html, accessed July 18, 2017.

Environmental Working Group. 2017. Conservation Reserve Program payments in the United States totaled $34.9 billion from 1995–2014. https://farm.ewg.org/progdetail.php?fips=00000&progcode=total_cr, accessed September 26, 2017.

Ferraro, P. J. 2008. Asymmetric information and contract design for payments for environmental services. *Ecological Economics* 65(4): 810–821.

Ferraro, P., K. D. Messer, and S. Wu. 2017. Applying behavioral insights to improve water security. *Choices* 32(4): 1–6.

Ferraro, P. J., and M. K. Price. 2013. Using nonpecuniary strategies to influence behavior: evidence from a large-scale field experiment. *Review of Economics and Statistics* 95(1): 64–73.

Festinger, L. 1954. A theory of social comparison processes. *Human Relations* 7(2): 117–140.

Fooks, J. R., N. Higgins, K. D. Messer, J. M. Duke, D. Hellerstein, and L. Lynch. 2016. Conserving spatially explicit benefits in ecosystem service markets: experimental tests of network bonuses and spatial targeting. *American Journal of Agricultural Economics* 98(2): 468–488.

Fooks, J., K. D. Messer, and J. Duke. 2015. Dynamic entry, reverse auctions, and the purchase of environmental services. *Land Economics* 91(1): 57–75.

Garcia-Sierra, M., J. C. van den Bergh, and C. Miralles-Guasch. 2015. Behavioural economics, travel behaviour and environmental-transport policy. *Transportation Research Part D: Transport and Environment* 41: 288–305.

Glebe, T. W. 2013. Conservation auctions: should information about environmental benefits be made public? *American Journal of Agricultural Economics* 95(3): 590–605.

Goldstein, N. J., R. B. Cialdini, and V. Griskevicius. 2008. A room with a viewpoint: using social norms to motivate environmental conservation in hotels. *Journal of Consumer Research* 35(3): 472–482.

Gole, C., M. Burton, K. J. Williams, H. Clayton, D. P. Faith, B. White, A. Huggett, and C. Margules. 2005. *Auction for Landscape Recovery: Final Report*. Sydney: WWF-Australia.

Hackett, K. F., and K. D. Messer. 1998. Bilateral negotiations versus reverse auctions: cost effective water procurement in the Snake River basis. University of Michigan. Unpublished.

Hailu, A., and S. Schilizzi. 2004. Are auctions more efficient than fixed price schemes when bidders learn? *Australian Journal of Management* 29(2): 147–168.

Hanley, N., S. Banerjee, G. D. Lennox, and P. R. Armsworth. 2012. How should we incentivize private landowners to "produce" more biodiversity? *Oxford Review of Economic Policy* 28(1): 93–113.

Harrison, G. W., and J. A. List. 2004. Field experiments. *Journal of Economic Literature* 42(4): 1009–1055.

Haruvy, E., and E. Katok. 2013. Increasing revenue by decreasing information in procurement auctions. *Production and Operations Management* 22(1): 19–35.

Hellerstein, D., and N. Higgins. 2010. The effective use of limited information: do bid maximums reduce procurement cost in asymmetric auctions? *Agricultural and Resource Economics Review* 39(2): 288–304.

Horowitz, J. K., L. Lynch, and A. Stocking. 2009. Competition-based environmental policy: an analysis of farmland preservation in Maryland. *Land Economics* 85(4): 555–575.

Johnson, E. J., and D. Goldstein. 2003. Do defaults save lives? *Science* 302(5649): 1338–1340.

Kahneman, D., and A. Tversky (eds.). 2000. *Choices, Values, and Frames*. Cambridge: Cambridge University Press.

Klemperer, P. 2002. What really matters in auction design. *Journal of Economic Perspectives* 16(1): 169–189.

Krishna, V. 2010. *Auction Theory*. 2nd ed. New York: Academic Press.

Latacz-Lohmann, U., and S. Schilizzi. 2005. *Auctions for Conservation Contracts: A Review of the Theoretical and Empirical Literature*. Report to the Scottish Executive Environment and Rural Affairs Department, Project no. UKL/001/05.

Latacz-Lohmann, U., and C. Van der Hamsvoort. 1997. Auctioning conservation contracts: a theoretical analysis and an application. *American Journal of Agricultural Economics* 79(2): 407–418.

List, J. A., and M. K. Price. 2016. The use of field experiments in environmental and resource economics. *Review of Environmental Economics and Policy* 10(2): 206–225.

List, J. A., and J. F. Shogren. 1999. Price information and bidding behavior in repeated second-price auctions. *American Journal of Agricultural Economics* 81(4): 942–949.

Lynch, L., and W. N. Musser. 2001. A relative efficiency analysis of farmland preservation programs. *Land Economics* 77(4): 577–594.

Katkar, R., and D. H. Reiley. 2007. Public versus secret reserve prices in eBay auctions: results from a Pokémon field experiment. *BE Journal of Economic Analysis and Policy* 6(2).

Khanna, M., and A. W. Ando. 2009. Science, economics and the design of agriculture programs in the US. *Journal of Environmental Planning and Management* 52: 575–592.

Kirwan, B., R. N. Lubowski, and M. J. Roberts. 2005. How cost-effective are land retirement auctions? Estimating the difference between payments and willingness to accept in the Conservation Reserve Program. *American Journal of Agricultural Economics* 87: 1239–1247.

McAfee, R. P., and J. McMillan. 1987. Auctions and bidding. *Journal of Economic Literature* 25(2): 699–738.

Messer, K. D., and W. L. Allen. 2010. Applying optimization and the analytic hierarchy process to enhance agricultural preservation strategies in the state of Delaware. *Agricultural and Resource Economics Review* 39(3): 442–456.

Messer, K. D., J. Duke, and L. Lynch. 2014. Applying experimental economics to land economics: public information and auction efficiency in land preservation markets. In *Oxford Handbook of Land Economics*. J. Duke and J. Wu, editors. Oxford: Oxford University Press.

Messer, K. D., J. Duke, L. Lynch, and T. Li. 2017. When does public information undermine the effectiveness of reverse auctions for the purchase of ecosystem services? *Ecological Economics* 134: 212–226.

Messer, K. D., H. M. Kaiser, and G. L. Poe. 2007a. Voluntary funding for generic advertising using a provision point mechanism: an experimental analysis of option assurance. *Review of Agricultural Economics* 29(3): 612–631.

Messer, K. D., H. M. Kaiser, and W. D. Schulze. 2008. The problem of free riding in voluntary generic advertising: parallelism and possible solutions from the lab. *American Journal of Agricultural Economics* 90(2): 540–552.

Messer, K. D., J. Suter, and J. Yan. 2013. Context effects in a negatively framed social dilemma experiment. *Environmental and Resource Economics* 55(3): 397–405.

Messer, K. D., H. Zarghamee, H. M. Kaiser, and W. D. Schulze. 2007b. New hope for the voluntary contribution mechanism: the effects of context. *Journal of Public Economics* 91(9): 1783–1799.

Metcalfe, R., and P. Dolan. 2012. Behavioural economics and its implications for transport. *Journal of Transport Geography* 24: 503–511.

Rassenti, S. J., V. L. Smith, and B. J. Wilson. 2003. Discriminatory price auctions in electricity markets: low volatility at the expense of high price levels. *Journal of Regulatory Economics* 23(2): 109–123.

Ribaudo, M., L. Hansen, D. Hellerstein, and C. Greene. 2008. *The Use of Markets to Increase Private Investment in Environmental Stewardship*. Economic Research Report no. 64. Washington, DC: Economic Research Service, US Department of Agriculture.

Rolfe, J., J. Windle, and J. McCosker. 2009. Testing and implementing the use of multiple bidding rounds in conservation auctions: a case study application. *Canadian Journal of Agricultural Economics/Revue Canadienne d'Agroeconomie* 57(3): 287–303.

Schilizzi, S., and U. Latacz-Lohmann. 2007. Assessing the performance of conservation auctions: an experimental study. *Land Economics* 83(4): 497–515.

Schmidt, A., M. Kecinski, T. Li, K. D. Messer, and J. J. Parker. 2017. Measuring the impacts of different messengers on consumer preferences for products irrigated with recycled water: a field experiment. Paper presented at the Conference on Behavioral and Experimental Agri-Environmental Research: Methodological Advancements and Applications to Policy, Shepherdstown, WV.

Shawhan, D. L., K. D. Messer, W. D. Schulze, and R. E. Schuler. 2011. An experimental test of automatic mitigation of wholesale electricity prices. *International Journal of Industrial Organization* 29(1): 46–53.

Shoemaker, R. 1989. Agricultural land values and rents under the Conservation Reserve Program. *Land Economics* 65(2): 131–137.

Shogren, J. F. 2004. Incentive mechanism testbeds: discussion. *American Journal of Agricultural Economics* 86(5): 1218–1219.

Shogren, J. F., and L. O. Taylor. 2008. On behavioral-environmental economics. *Review of Environmental Economics and Policy* 2(1): 26–44.

Shortle, J. 2013. Economics and environmental markets: lessons from water-quality trading. *Agricultural and Resource Economics Review* 42(1): 57–74.

Smith, V. 1987. Experimental methods in economics. In *The New Palgrave: A Dictionary of Economics*. J. Eatwell, M. Milgate, and P. Newman, editors. New York: Palgrave.

Stoneham, G., V. Chaudhri, A. Ha, and L. Strappazzon. 2003. Auctions for conservation contracts: an empirical examination of Victoria's BushTender trial. *Australian Journal of Agricultural and Resource Economics* 47(4): 477–500.

Sunstein, C., and R. Thaler. 2008. *Nudge: The Politics of Libertarian Paternalism.* New Haven, CT: Yale University Press.

Tversky, A., and D. Kahneman. 1991. Loss aversion in riskless choice: a reference-dependent model. *Quarterly Journal of Economics* 106(4): 1039–1061.

US Department of Agriculture. 2012. Conservation Reserve Program, annual summary and enrollment statistics, FY 2012. www.fsa.usda.gov/Assets/USDA-FSA-Public/usdafiles/Conservation/PDF/summary12.pdf, accessed January 18, 2018.

US Department of Agriculture. 2016. State agriculture overview. www.nass.usda.gov/Quick_Stats/Ag_Overview/stateOverview.php?state=DELAWARE, accessed January 18, 2018.

US Department of Agriculture. 2017. Conservation Reserve Program, monthly summary, May 2017. www.fsa.usda.gov/Assets/USDA-FSA-Public/usdafiles/Conservation/PDF/MAY2017summary1.pdf, accessed January 18, 2018.

Vincent, D. R. 1995. Bidding off the wall: why reserve prices may be kept secret. *Journal of Economic Theory* 65(2): 575–584.

Vossler, C. A., T. D. Mount, R. J. Thomas, and R. D. Zimmerman. 2009. An experimental investigation of soft price caps in uniform price auction markets for wholesale electricity. *Journal of Regulatory Economics* 36(1): 44–59.

Vukina, T., X. Zheng, M. Marra, and A. Levy. 2008. Do farmers value the environment? Evidence from a Conservation Reserve Program auction. *International Journal of Industrial Organization* 26(6): 1323–1332.

Weigel, C., P. Ferraro, K. Messer, and T. Li. 2017. The influence of an identifiable victim in motivating household conservation actions. Unpublished.

Wu, J., and B. A. Babcock. 1996. Contract design for the purchase of environmental goods from agriculture. *American Journal of Agricultural Economics* 78: 935–945.

Wu, S., A. Zia, M. Ren, and K. D. Messer. 2017. Simulating heterogeneous farmer behaviors under different policy schemes: integrating economic experiments and agent-based modeling. *Journal on Policy and Complex Systems* 3(2): 164–195.

Zarghamee, H. S., K. D. Messer, J. R. Fooks, W. D. Schulze, S. Wu, and J. Yan. 2017. Nudging charitable giving: three field experiments. *Journal of Behavioral and Experimental Economics* 66: 137–149.

CHAPTER 11

Messer, K. D. 2006. The conservation benefits of cost-effective land acquisition: a case study in Maryland. *Journal of Environmental Management* 79: 305–315.

Messer, K. D. 2011. Maximizing conservation in Pangaea. *Problem Based Learning Clearinghouse.*

Messer, K. D., and J. R. Fooks. 2013. *ODSTweb Training Example: Maryland Highway 301 Step-by-Step Instructions and Results.* Baltimore: Maryland State Highway Administration.

APPENDIX A

Dujmović, J. J. 2007. Continuous preference logic for system evaluation. *IEEE Transactions on Fuzzy Systems* 15(6): 1082–1099.

Dujmović, J. J. 2014. An analysis of penalty and reward for partial absorption aggregators. In *Proceedings of the 2014 World Conference on Soft Computing*, Berkeley, CA.

Dujmović, J. J. 2018. *Soft Computing Evaluation Logic: The LSP Decision Method and Its Applications.* Hoboken, NJ: John Wiley.

Dujmović, J. J., and H. L. Larsen. 2007. Generalized conjunction/disjunction. *International Journal of Approximate Reasoning* 46: 423–446.

Dujmović, J. J., and H. Nagashima. 2006. LSP method and its use for evaluation of Java IDE's. *International Journal of Approximate Reasoning* 41(1): 3–22.

Miller, George A. 1956. The magical number seven, plus or minus two: some limits on our capacity for processing information. *Psychological Review* 63(2): 81.

Index